The Western Epistemic Tradition and the Scientific Study of Religion

The Western Epistemic Tradition and the Scientific Study of Religion

Donald Wiebe

SHEFFIELD UK   BRISTOL CT

Published by Equinox Publishing Ltd.

UK: Office 415, The Workstation, 15 Paternoster Row, Sheffield, South Yorkshire S1 2BX
USA: ISD, 70 Enterprise Drive, Bristol, CT 06010

www.equinoxpub.com

First published 2023.

© Donald Wiebe 2023

All rights reserved. No part of this publication may be reproduced or transmitted in any form or by any means, electronic or mechanical, including photocopying, recording or any information storage or retrieval system, without prior permission in writing from the publishers.

British Library Cataloguing-in-Publication Data

A catalogue record for this book is available from the British Library.

ISBN-13	978 1 80050 272 7	(hardback)
	978 1 80050 273 4	(paperback)
	978 1 80050 274 1	(ePDF)

Library of Congress Cataloging-in-Publication Data

Names: Wiebe, Donald, 1943– author.

Title: The western epistemic tradition and the scientific study of religion / Donald Wiebe.

Description: Sheffield, South Yorkshire; Bristol, CT : Equinox Publishing Ltd, 2023. | Includes bibliographical references and index.

Summary: "This book provides an account of how a science of religion was able to emerge from the devotional, catechetical, theological, and philosophical forms of 'religious studies' that have generally characterized this field of scholarship. This book is intended for students who are enrolled in religious studies programs, their teachers, university administrators, and others who are simply curious about the character of the study of religion." — Provided by publisher

Identifiers: LCCN 2022044363 (print) | LCCN 2022044364 (ebook) | ISBN 9781800502727 (hardback) | ISBN 9781800502734 (paperback) | ISBN 9781800502741 (epdf)

Subjects: LCSH: Religion—Study and teaching.

Classification: LCC BL41 .W56 2023 (print) | LCC BL41 (ebook) | DDC 200.71—dc23/eng20230414

LC record available at https://lccn.loc.gov/2022044363

LC ebook record available at https://lccn.loc.gov/2022044364

Indexing by Joel Ruimy, www.joelruimy.com

Typeset and edited by Queentson Publishing, Hamilton, Canada.

Contents

PREFACE	ix
1. Setting the Boundaries for the Scientific Study of Religious Phenomena	1
2. The Deep History of the Scientific Study of Religious Thought and Behaviour	25
3. From Myth to Proto-Science: A Transformational Turning Point in the History of Human Thought	45
4. The Rise and Decline of the Sciences in the Hellenistic Period	65
5. Latin Christendom and Scientific Thought in the Middle Ages	85
6. The Renaissance, Scientific Revolution, and Enlightenment	105
7. The Age of Discovery and the Protestant Reformation	125
8. Crossing a Threshold in the Scholarly Study of Religion	147
9. Modernity, Postmodernity, and the Study of Religion	167
10. Epilogue: A Scientific Revolution in Slow Motion	189
BIBLIOGRAPHY	193
INDEX	205

Dedicated to
Luther H. Martin
Colleague, Collaborator, Critic and Friend

— Preface —

The Western Epistemic Tradition and the Scientific Study of Religion

This book is primarily intended for students who are enrolled in a religious studies program of one sort or another, or readers who are simply curious about religion and the study of religion. My objective is to provide an account of how the scientific study of religion was able to emerge from the devotional, catechetical, theological, and philosophical forms of the study of religion that has characterized religious life in the West, and still dominates college and university campuses around the world. Although elements of the scientific study of religion can be found in intellectual engagements with religion throughout the Western epistemic tradition, a strictly scientific study is relatively new and radically distinctive in that it excludes any kind of theological engagement with religion and is best described as being a neutral, non-religious mode of inquiry. Knowledge of what the scientific study of religion amounts to clearly depends on understanding the nature of scientific thought itself, as well as when and how it came to ground and characterize what British philosopher Ernest Gellner called our modern Western epistemic tradition. That tradition has its origins in the cosmological thought of the ancient Milesians and their successors in the sixth century before the common era. In a sense, therefore, understanding the character of a scientific study of religion demands that I start my story with them. It is clear, however, that this introduction cannot provide a detailed history of the development of science and the sciences over a twenty-five hundred year period, or of the myriad of arguments for and against such an enterprise. Therefore, I will provide an "episodic history" of the emergence and development of the science of religion, in which I pick out the most significant historical achievements of human thought that have brought us to the threshold of that enterprise today. However, before going down that path some attention will have to be paid to the fact that the notions of both religion and science are problematic for scholars in this field.

Scholars in the field of religious studies today seemingly are unaware of the long-standing controversy over the very notion or definition of religion, even less those who study religion from related fields such as anthropology and sociology. Certainly those entering the field will likely not have engaged those terminological discussions, debates, and disputes in any depth. For that reason, I open the book with an overview of those debates and a proposal for setting the boundaries of this field of study. I show why the enterprise should not be dependent on finding a universally acceptable definition of the term. Rather, it is important to recognize that much of the confusion exists because we forget that the term religion is an abstract English noun that has no empirical reference. I argue that this discipline should be bounded not by definition but by a subject matter—human thoughts and behaviours framed by *beliefs in* culturally postulated supernatural agents and events. In chapter two, I show that comprehending the nature of science, and therefore of the scientific study of religion and its emergence as a cultural reality, requires some understanding of our cognitive psychology and its import for the development of science. This chapter does not provide a history of the emergence of the sciences, but it does provide an evolutionary account of the cognitive foundations underlying modern scientific modes of thought which are dedicated to achieving ("disinterested") knowledge for its own sake.

My episodic history of the emergence of the idea of a scientific study of religion proper then, begins with Chapter 3, in which I show that the early Greek philosophers and cosmologists from the Milesians to the Atomists challenged a mythopoetic form of thinking and advanced a new understanding of knowledge as rationally justifiable beliefs. This rejection of cultural mythologies in favour of critical inquiry has often been referred to as the first Enlightenment in the West, and I argue that it clearly constituted a kind of proto-science which formed the basis of the eventual development of the modern Western epistemic tradition. That development however does not always trace a smooth trajectory. Opposition to such proto-scientific thinking soon regained its former dominance in the religio-metaphysical thought of Socrates and Plato. The mythic mind of our ancient forebears, that is, did not disappear with the rise of critical thinking; it is still very much alive, and remains so, in all of us, today.

In Chapter 4, I show that there is a kind of back and forth between the growth of science-like disciplines and religious and metaphysical systems of thought in the Hellenistic period and during the time of the Roman

Empire. Although some historians of science believe that this period saw the emergence of a new type of what has been called "nature-knowledge," few argue that any of them amounted to a genuine scientific revolution. In Chapter 5, I show the early decline of interest in science-like thought under the cultural dominance of Christianity. As the cosmological thought of the Milesians declined under the dominance of Platonism, so interest in critical rational thought about nature declined under the spread of Christianity. Nevertheless, as the influence of Aristotle waxed during the Middle Ages, Christian thinkers began to draw on critical rational thought to defend Christian dogma, giving rise to a hybrid mode of thought that blended mythic and rational-critical modes of thought. Although reminiscent of Plato's earlier attempt to blend the proto-scientific thinking of the Milesians with the traditional religio-mythic thought of their forebears, this Aristotelian development made a positive contribution to the flowering of science in Europe.

There is general agreement among historians of science that a fully scientific revolution in thought did not occur until the sixteenth and seventeenth centuries. In Chapters 6 and 7, I show that social and political developments in the late Middle Ages and Early Modern Europe made possible the modes of analysis and argumentation that resulted in an expansion of intellectual life beyond the boundaries of the Church. I argue in these chapters that we see here in these socio-political developments the advancement of the modern Western epistemic tradition that first came into view with the ancient Greeks.

As some historians have put it, it is in the period between the Renaissance and Romanticism that we see the formation of the *modern*, rather than a scientific, study of religion, but in Chapter 8, I provide evidence to support the argument that it is not until the second half of the nineteenth century that Victorian developments in the field originated the very idea of a strictly scientific study of religions. However, as I point out in Chapter 9, the emergence of such an idea was no guarantee that such a study would be established in the curriculum of the modern research university.

As I have already intimated, this book intends to introduce students in religious studies courses and programs—and those who teach them—to the appropriateness of the idea of restructuring the study of religions and religion in our research universities as a scientific undertaking. Fully understanding what is meant by the notion of "a scientific study" of anything has required providing a historical account of what made possible the emergence of the notion of science itself, not only the historical emergence of such thought, but also the evolutionary development of human cognitive capacities necessary for scientific thought and the socio-cultural conditions necessary to support that thought. I have avoided documented references to issues in dispute discussed in the literature of the field. Because no author can hope to have the expertise to speak authoritatively on the whole range of topics touched on in this book, or an in-depth historical knowledge of the whole sweep of history covered in this book, I have chosen to introduce readers entering the field to the best authors with whom I am familiar to cover these bases, and I do so by permitting the authors to speak for themselves, citing their sources inline rather than referencing their works in endless footnotes. I trust this will make the argument of the book easier to grasp and the book an easier and more pleasant read.

The idea for this book came to mind when I delivered lectures on the history of the scholarly study of religion while I was visiting professor in the Department for the Study of Religion at Masaryk University in the Fall of 2014. I thought this history would benefit students in the Department but also provide the preliminary research necessary for a book on the emergence and development of the scientific study of religion in the West. The decision to reduce my teaching load by half and my confinement to home demanded by the COVID pandemic (2020–2021) finally made time available for me to return to my notes for this book. I am grateful to Professor Aleš Chalupa and his colleagues for the invitation to teach a course of my own choosing in the Department, and to the students who attended the lectures and engaged in critical discussions of the foundations for a scientific study of religion. I also wish to thank the teaching staff and graduate students in the Department for discussions, formal and informal, about the nature of this field during my time at Masaryk University and in subsequent visits.

As usual, I wish once again to thank Professor Luther Martin for the time and energy he has spent in discussing the views I present in this book, and for a careful and critical reading of the text. The red ink of his "track changes" and associated comments have strengthened the arguments offered in the text and made the story being told easier to follow. He is not responsible, however, for any errors of fact that might remain or for infelicities of expression that may still be found. I also wish to thank Janet Joyce for pointing out that I had cut the story short by making no mention of significant developments in the field, both positive and negative, in the twenty-first century. I wish to express my appreciation here for Anthony Palma's continuing critical interest in my work and for his careful reading of and remarks on an earlier draft of this book. I am also deeply grateful to Dr. Russell B. Adams for

Preface

his excellent editing, advice and meticulous work in preparing this manuscript for printing and publication. Finally, I want to thank Joel Ruimy for creating an index that will highlight for the reader the book's core issues and themes.

Portions of this book have previously been published. Chapter 2, "The Deep History of the Scientific Study of Religious Thought and Behaviour" first appeared in *e-Rhizome* 3(1): 1–20 (2021); Chapter 3 first appeared under the title "Philosophical Reflections on the Pre-Socratics: A Contribution to the Scientific Study of Religions," in *Theorizing "Religion" in Antiquity*, edited by Nicholas P. Roubekas, 81–102 (Equinox, 2019); Portions of the following essays appear in Chapter 9: (i) pp. 261–264 and 266 of "Dissolving Rationality: The Anti-Science Phenomenon and Its Implications for the Study of Religion," in *The Science of Religion: A Defence, Essays by Donald Wiebe*, edited by Anthony Palma (E. J. Brill, 2018); (ii) pp. 122–125 of "American Influence on the Shape of Things to Come: Religious Studies in the Twenty-First Century," in Donald Wiebe, *The Learned Practice of Religion* (Bloomsbury Academic, 2021); and (iii) pp. 187–191 of "Its Never Been Better: Comments on the Current State of the Science of Religion" in Donald Wiebe, *The Learned Practice of Religion in the Modern University* (Bloomsbury Academic, 2021).

— 1 —

Setting the Boundaries for the Scientific Study of Religious Phenomena

Introduction

In the late nineteenth century, an academic study of religion emerged as a somewhat independent enterprise in the modern universities of Europe, distinct from the ecclesiastical control that had characterized its earliest beginnings. By the mid-twentieth century, scholars in that field strove for greater clarity in distinguishing themselves from both religious and theological interests. Achieving that goal, it has often been argued, was predicated on clearly defining the nature of "religion," the subject of study by the new discipline. Without distinguishing religion from other purely psychological and social aspects of human existence, it was argued, it would be impossible to demarcate the boundaries for the new discipline and to be able to distinguish the specific methodological tools necessary for describing, understanding, and explaining its subject matter in a manner equivalent to those found in the natural and social sciences.

Given the desire since the 1950s to gain epistemic respectability as a bona fide discipline in the modern university, the quest for a definition of religion that could ground the new discipline was on. The voluminous literature on the topic that was, and still is, being generated, however, only reveals that no consensus on a definition of religion that could establish its study as an academic enterprise was ever found. In some quarters that quest for a proper definition of religion replaced the original intent and objective of the new discipline. For them, religion was a chimerical reality, socially constructed in an attempt to gain political power. For others, religion was the name designating a non-natural, supernatural, reality within which human existence was submerged, and demanded respect rather than scientific analysis and explanation if it was to be understood. Indeed, the new discipline was generally seen as a crypto-religious enterprise given over to the betterment of humankind.

The history of the search for a definition of religion that might ground a study of religion as a respectable field of teaching and research in the context of the modern university, then, has failed to achieve its objective. I suggest here that the search for a definition of religion was misguided from the beginning. The word "religion" is an abstract English noun that has no empirical reference range and could not, therefore, point to an intersubjectively observable subject for what the patrons of an academic study of religion sought, and any non-natural reality to which it might be thought to point would be beyond any explanatory framework. In contrast to this history of the search for epistemic credibility of what is presently sanctioned as a respectable discipline in the modern university, I will argue that the discipline needs to be regarded as a genuinely scientific enterprise which can only be achieved by recognizing its subject matter to be the thought and practice of individuals and groups generally referred to as religious, i.e., whose thoughts and practices are legitimated by their claims to the authority of superhuman agents.

Diversities in the study of religions and religion

Catechesis and, more formally, theology have been significant elements in the study of religion provided by universities in Europe, Britain, and North America. Since the middle of the twentieth century, however, departments offering such studies have gradually removed themselves from ecclesiastical control, although still, in some sense, being engaged in a similar, although perhaps more sophisticated, intellectual activity. In the literature in the field this is often described as a "reflective exercise" involving a "deeper conversation" with something called "religion itself." This something (or "religion itself") is considered to exist in a different ontological register from everyday phenomena and is, therefore, a metaphysical reality and therefore beyond simply the study of the thought and practice of individuals and communities. This metaphysical reality, it is argued, is, or should be, the true object of interest for the so-called study of religion. That this enterprise is carried out in Western colleges makes it reasonable to refer to it as the academic study of religion but does not by virtue of that fact necessarily make it a scientific enterprise which restricts its interests to problems and concerns in the natural rather than metaphysical realm of reality.

My primary objective here is to bring to light significant developments in early European thought that made possible the emergence of the scientific study of religion as one type of study of religion among many. A type of informal religious education, obviously, preceded the emergence of any critically self-conscious intellectual attention being paid to religion as a this-worldly phenomenon that is ultimately grounded in a transcendent ontological reality.

The earliest form of conscious intellectual attention to religion involved being able to provide some kind of spiritual account of the nature and meaning of the natural physical universe and human existence in it. The knowledge required for this came by way of divinely revealed Truth vouchsafed in sacred texts—a knowledge that was obtained not for its own sake, but for the devotee's edification and spiritual growth. It was, therefore, not simply an everyday epistemic achievement but rather a catechetical transmission of a kind of wisdom-knowledge through devotional attention. A more scholarly development of this kind of religious thinking later emerged by blending such catechetical and devotional thought with the quest for a more widely shareable systematic articulation of the faith—that is, a theology of the essentially mystical character of religion as other-worldly and beyond the understanding of human reason alone. Such a study of religion strove for the credibility of the science of the day and amounted to a natural theology—what might reasonably be called faith-imbued science.

The scientific study of religion, or Science of Religion, emerged only after the Scientific Revolution in sixteenth-century Europe. It is succinctly described as an empirical and theoretical study of religious phenomena for its own sake. Religion as some mysterious, non-natural reality is given no attention because it is not open to rational description or theoretical explanation. But the beliefs about the existence of such a transcendent ontological reality are available for scientific description and explanation, as also are the human behaviours associated with such beliefs. But such a study of religion came under strong criticism, not only from theologians and other religious devotees, but also, towards the end of the twentieth century, from scholars in the field influenced by postmodern and deconstructionist modes of thought. All thought, postmodernists maintain, is permeated with human interest that makes the creation of a neutral framework for an uncomplicated objective study of religion impossible. Thus, a study of religion, like any study, is necessarily reflective and requires the student of religion consciously to engage with the issues of religious truth, value, and meaning. A reductionistic explanation of religion—whatever that may turn out to be—is rationally questionable; study of religion will of necessity, postmodernists maintain, require engagement with it. Postmodernists, however, deny that their approach to the study of religion is merely a repetition of the devotional approach to the study of religion that reveals its essential character.

The brief sketch of the likely path by which religion became a subject matter for scientific analysis and explanation that I will provide here will also show how confusing the use of the word religion has become in the process. That confusion has generated a considerable literature on the value of the term itself; of determining its true referent (if any) and meaning, as well as how a study of it, whatever it is, can be undertaken. Nevertheless, I have no intention of engaging here in the debates over the definition of religion (or of science). In fact, as paradoxical as it may seem, I hope, for the most part, to avoid use of those two key terms. Michael Hobart captures, at least in part, the problem I will face in discussing the emergence of this new enterprise or would-be discipline of the science of religion in his *The Great Rift: Literacy, Numeracy, and the Religion-Science Divide* where he insists that "Each term has a long history of its own, and each historically has cast wide definitional nets around its catch. So much so that defining them in our own day has become quite problematic" (Hobart 2018, 2).

On not defining religion or science

In an essay on "The Very Idea of Religion" (2000), Paul J. Griffiths, a Christian philosopher and historian of religions, maintains—with special attention to the proposal put forward in my book *The Politics of Religious Studies: The Continuing Conflict with Theology in the Academy* (1999)—that creating or constructing a scientific study of religion is impossible. His claim, however, rests largely on the post-modern critique of the academic study of religion by historian Timothy Fitzgerald in his *The Ideology of Religious Studies*. According to Fitzgerald, the word "religion" as a non-theological concept does no genuine descriptive or analytical work. Understood as having reference to a supernatural or transcendental realm of reality, religion clearly delineates a field of (theological) study by differentiating religion—that is, what is religious—from the secular. But without that contrast, Fitzgerald maintains that students of religion have failed to come to a consensus about what distinguishes religion from non-religion. Rather, he insists, the word ends up as part of a western ideology that "has been exported to non-western countries in the context of colonialism" (Fitzgerald 2000, ix). As he puts it:

> Religion is really the basis of a modern form of theology, which I will call liberal-ecumenical theology, but some attempt has been made to disguise

this fact by claiming that religion is a natural and/or a supernatural reality in the nature of things that all human individuals have a capacity for, regardless of their cultural context. (Fitzgerald 2000, 4–5)

The disguises of this modern form of theology include comparative religion, phenomenology, and even, as he puts it, "the so-called science of religion," all of which still presume acceptance of the existence of some ahistorical or transhistorical reality that requires human subservience (Fitzgerald 2000, x). He concludes, therefore, that "Instead of studying religion as though it were some objective feature of societies, it should instead be studied as an ideological category, an aspect of modern western ideology, with a specific location in history, including the nineteenth-century period of European colonialization" (Fitzgerald 2000, 4).

I think it is widely acknowledged that the word religion is often used as though it names some ontological reality beyond the confines of the natural and social worlds of human existence. I agree with Fitzgerald that most of what is called the phenomenology of religion is largely a religious study of religion—that is, a liberal ecumenical form of theology—and therefore an ideology. I also have some sympathy for his suggestion that the word religion gained a certain plausibility in the academic world as a viable category, although I am not altogether sure as to what he means by calling it an analytical category. Nevertheless, I disagree with his claim that the word religion and its cognates should be entirely abandoned by scholars in this field of study.

Griffiths sees avant gardists like Fitzgerald as having shown that any attempt to use the word religion free from its traditional—explicit and implicit—theological assumptions is necessarily bound to end up simply creating "mystifying ideologies," and that the word should therefore be abandoned by scholars in this field of study. Griffiths, therefore, rejects my argument in support of establishing a science of religion by attempting to provide a scientifically constrained understanding of the word religion as "a coherent and useful (non-theological) concept" (Griffiths 2000, 34). His complaint is that I neither drop the use of the word nor respond to Fitzgerald's criticisms of it. As he puts it, I do not "show what can be done, intellectually speaking, with the scientific concept of religion" that I advocate (Griffiths 2000, 34). But his complaint is misdirected since I do not, in *The Politics of Religious Studies*, see definition of the word religion as an essential tool for the student of religion. I did in fact deal with the matter of the definition of religion in my earlier book *Religion and Truth: Towards an Alternative Paradigm for the Study of Religion* (1981) as describing a sphere of human behaviour by individuals and societies based on culturally postulated transcendental ontologies. I based my argument on the work of cultural anthropologist Melford Spiro to the effect that anthropologists focus attention on beliefs people have about gods or other supermundane realities and how particular human behaviours, at both the level of the individual and of society, are rooted in such beliefs (Spiro 1966). Anthropologists, Spiro argued, only deal with "talk about" such realities, not as actually existing in the world but only as presumed by devotees to exist. Spiro also maintained that the social scientist requires a word to designate the belief in the "culturally postulated existence" of such ontologically transcendent realms of reality that is empirically available in the thought and behaviour of the devotees and that religion is a word he finds adequate to that task. As I point out in *Religion and Truth*, it is to this end that Spiro talks about the definition of the term religion:

> In sum, any comparative study of religion requires as an operation antecedent to inquiry, an ostensive or substantive definition that stipulates unambiguously those phenomenal variables which are designated by the term. This ostensive definition will, at the same time, be a nominal definition in that some of its designate will, to other scholars, appear to be arbitrary. This, then, does not remove "religion" from the definitional controversy; but it does remove it from the context of fruitless controversy over what religion "really is" to the context of the formulation of the empirically testable hypotheses which, in anthropology, means hypotheses susceptible to crosscultural testing. (Spiro 1966, 91)

My aim in that discussion was to understand the methodological import for the scientific student of religion of the culturally postulated worlds for the devotees, which were not simply fictional objects but rather the truth about how that reality "beyond themselves" ultimately concerns them. But that is not a matter that needs to be taken up here. The point is that Griffiths' real concern with my *Politics of Religious Studies* is not with definition but with my adoption of naturalism in the study of religious phenomena.

In his criticism of what he calls my "faith in naturalism" Griffiths is aware that I do not argue for the truth of naturalism but rather espouse a methodological naturalism. That is, he acknowledges that I use naturalism as a tool "to rule out appeal to or use of God [or any other transcendental ontological realities] as an explanation of anything" (Griffiths 2000, 34). He therefore correctly notes that my "central claim is that the academic study of religion both can and ought to be understood as a science, which is to say that the only goals are understanding and explanation" (2000, 35).

Setting the Boundaries for the Scientific Study of Religious Phenomena

He ought therefore to have been aware that by use of the phrase "the academic study of religion" I mean only that study of religion that can be included as one among the many scientific research disciplines in the modern university where no scientist is formally required to adopt naturalism as metaphysically true but is, rather, only expected to work within the framework of its methodological implications. Therefore, Griffiths' hope that "Wiebe does not mean to imply that all those who take naturalism to be false should be purged from our public universities" (Griffiths 2000, 35) is nothing more than a mild form of argumentum ad hominem. Given that I consider academic freedom essential to the epistemic objectives of the modern research university, Griffiths can rest easy on that score. It needs pointing out, however, that the burden of proof for such a categorical claim about naturalism falls on Griffiths, and other like-minded scholars, as does the claim that religion is a sui generis transcendental reality that impinges on the natural world.

Settling the question as to the truth or falsity of naturalism, as with any other metaphysical claim, is not itself a scientific question, nor does that question need answering in order to judge the value of methodological naturalism for gaining consensual knowledge about the world and human existence in it. Therefore, trying to provide a definition of words that refer to objects, events, or behaviours in order either to describe or explain them is of little assistance. In this I follow the advice Karl Popper laid out succinctly in his *Unended Quest: An Intellectual Autobiography*: "...always remember the principle of never arguing about words and their meanings because such arguments are specious and insignificant" (Popper 1976, 17). It is interesting to note in this regard that in *Precept and Practice: Traditional Buddhism in the Rural Highlands of Ceylon* (1971), Richard F. Gombrich had already arrived at the conclusion that the search for a definition of religion in such a study is both trivial and futile, though he does not spell out in detail the basis for this view. He claims simply that everyone really knows what religion amounts to, or has in mind an hypothesis as to its nature.

Before moving on to a discussion of that unending quest for a definition of religion, however, it is essential to correct the claims Griffiths makes about the import of the contrasts he draws between Fitzgerald's view on the study of religion and mine. Both Fitzgerald and I, he asserts, argue that only a non-theological (non-religious) approach to studying what most professors in the field call religion—that is, understanding and explaining its influence on human behaviour—is possible, but that Fitzgerald shows will require rejection of the concept of religion. However, Griffiths—seemingly unaware that the discipline's subject-matter is simply a peculiar kind of human behaviour rather than some other-worldly something—claims that a science of religion is not possible because there is no intersubjectively available referent for the term religion. The problem, of course, is that the word religion has had an ambiguous reference range, including not only thought, practice, and behaviour of a peculiar sort, but that it also includes some transcendental reality that supposedly inspired such thought and behaviour. The solution to that problem, I will show, is to reject use of the noun religion as a designation of such a transcendental reality but to retain use of its cognates religiousness and religiosity, (as well as religious and religiously).

Types of non-theological understandings of religion

According to Griffiths, then, Fitzgerald has shown that a non-theological understanding of religion cannot ground a science of religion. I agree that Fitzgerald has shown that much academic study of religion since the middle to end of the nineteenth century and on, is based on the assumption of the existence of a transcendent realm of reality designated by the word religion. Theology, for example, is one such academic discipline. On this basis Fitzgerald argues—correctly—that much of what has been called religious studies and phenomenology of religion is also based on that assumption. But that is not news; that kind of study of religion has long been criticized as inappropriate in the context of the modern research university. This historical fact, that is, does not justify the claim that every possible use of the word religion and its cognates in talk about the study of religion must be abandoned on pain of incoherence or contradiction. This is not the only use of the notion (category) of religion. Neither Griffiths nor Fitzgerald provide reasons showing that those who argue for a scientific study of religion necessarily operate with the same or similar transcendental assumptions held by religious devotees simply by virtue of their use of the word religion, and therefore that they are engaged in a "crypto-Christian" intellectual enterprise. Furthermore, and contrary to Griffiths claim, Fitzgerald is not proposing a simple, non-theological approach to the study of religions; his so-called non-theological approach to understanding what religious studies or phenomenology of religion are all about is an anti-theological approach; its objective is to undermine the influence of religion, whether overt or covert, in shaping society. But Griffiths is blind to this anti-religious import of what he refers to as Fitzgerald's "occasional protestations that he is not against theology" (Griffiths 2000, 35).

Although wrong in characterizing Fitzgerald's approach to the study of religion as merely non-theological rather than anti-theological, Griffiths is

Setting the Boundaries for the Scientific Study of Religious Phenomena

correct in his claim that my proposed scientific approach to understanding and explaining religious thought and behaviour is non-theological. The use of the term religion in the scientific approach, that is, is not committed to the assumption of the existence of a transcendent world—a transcendental ontology, as Griffiths puts it—that grounds the concept of religion as used by theologians and phenomenologists. The scientific approach finds neither evidence nor argument to make a sound judgment about the truth or falsity of such metaphysical claims and therefore restricts itself to attempting to understand and explain the behaviour of those who believe such metaphysical claims. That is, the scientific student of religion recognizes that people now, and in the past, have shaped their thought and practice in relation to such diverse transcendental ontologies. The science of religion, therefore, concerns itself strictly with describing, understanding, and explaining the thought and behaviour of those persons who claim to live in both the natural world and a world beyond the natural world simultaneously, with the latter being an aspect of the natural world the scientists share with such devotees.

Whether Griffiths understands this analysis of the use of the word religion is unclear. But this is not his greatest problem with the proposal for a scientific study of religion. His primary complaints are focused rather on the notions of naturalism and the nature of the modern research university which are clearly elaborated, for example, in his treatise on *Religious Reading: The Place of Reading in the Practice of Religion* (1999). According to Griffiths, the naturalism that grounds a scientific approach to understanding and explaining religious phenomena involves a belief in the truth of naturalism which amounts to a commitment to a transcendental and, therefore, for him, a crypto-religious ontology. But the scientific study of religion does not rest on such a metaphysical epistemic truth claim. The scientific student takes on naturalism as a methodological tool, rather than a metaphysical doctrine, in the same sense that it is used by scientists in other fields of research in the modern research university. To explain religious beliefs and practices by reference to assumed realities beyond the natural world is a religious explanation which, for the scientific student of religion, also requires a naturalistic explanation.

To be clear, then, religion is not an empirical category; it does not point to some objective, that is, intersubjectively observable, reality in the everyday world of human existence. Insofar as the concept has been used in the singular to refer to some transcendent metaphysical reality that might be called religion itself it is a concept that has produced a peculiar kind of discourse which itself constitutes a culturally produced reality. As such, the concept makes sense but refers to something metaphysical and therefore not a possible object of scientific investigation. On the other hand, the concept in the plural, religions, points to a range of socially constructed realities that are available to scientific analysis, understanding, and explanation. Sociologist Christian Smith has put the matter succinctly in his book *Religion: What It Is, How It Works, and Why It Matters* as follows:

> When we use the analytical term "religion," we must not think that it refers to some specific, "least common denominator" super-religion or trans-religious entity, which can be partitioned into "denominations." No such thing exists. All that actually exists are particular religions. (C. Smith 2017, xx)

Aware of the multiple definitions of the word—substantive, functional, normative, or stipulative—Milton Yinger pointed out in his *The Scientific Study of Religion* that "[a] hundred or more [definitions of religion] can be gathered in the space of a few hours" (Yinger 1970, 4) which suggests that the word religion is simply an abstract English noun that is very much open to scholarly manipulation. So, to repeat myself, I think we are best advised once again to take Karl Popper's advice to

> [n]ever let [ourselves] be goaded into taking seriously problems about words and their meaning. What must be taken seriously are questions of fact, and assertions about facts: theories or hypotheses; the problems they solve; and the problems they raise. ... [Getting caught in the trap of determining the meanings of words, he exclaims] is the surest path to intellectual perdition: the abandonment of real problems for the sake of verbal problems.
> (Popper 1976, 19; emphasis in the original)

With this clarification of the notion religion we can transcend the divergent understandings of the meaning of the phrase the scientific student of religion. The scientific student's real or actual problem, that is, is not with the emergence of the concept of religion, or a critical understanding of its historical trajectory or its contemporary usage. Nor should such a study concern itself with the possibility of a metaphysical reality of some kind designated by the word/term religion. The real problem for the scientific student of religion, rather, is to explain what today is considered a peculiar type of human behaviour that can reasonably be described as religious in Melford Spiro's sense of "culturally patterned interaction with culturally postulated superhuman beings" (Spiro 1966, 97), but without epistemic commitment as to the ontological existence of those agents.

I understand Jonathan Z. Smith's argument in his essay "Religion, Religions, Religious" (1999) that the term religion can be used as a second-order category, but I think the term is so ontologically contaminated as to make it very difficult in trying to establish a clear disciplinary horizon for a distinctive kind of social-scientific discipline appropriate to the modern research university, since the conflict over the uses of religion in the singular has not yet abated. The discipline simply cannot do without at least oblique or indirect reference to the concept of religion which is so firmly fixed in the literature of the field. Scientific students of religion, however, have no interest in some metaphysical reality called religion itself although they readily acknowledge the widespread use of the term religion to refer to belief in such culturally posited metaphysical realities but restrict their scientific interests to describing, understanding, and explaining the broad range of human thought and practice inspired and influenced by such belief. The scientific student of religion, therefore, will be making liberal use of cognates of religion like religions, religious, religiosity, religiousness, religiously, to identify the intersubjectively available subject-matter of their scientific investigations and theorizing.

Defining religion: A never-ending quest

My encounter with the fractious history of the definition of religion problem came early in the happen-stance transition in my academic career from philosophy of religion to what was then widely referred to as "religious studies." In part, that transition occurred in the final year of my doctoral studies at the University of Lancaster when Professor Smart asked me to teach an undergraduate course on "Theories of Religion." It was suggested that in preparing for that task I might give some consideration to Wilfred Cantwell Smith's book *The Meaning and End of Religion* (1962). In that book, and elsewhere, Smith contends that the concept of religion has been seriously misunderstood. He argued that its depth of meaning had been occluded by the emergence of the importance of religious belief in Medieval Christian thought. He saw this emphasis on the role of belief as a great western heresy in the history of Christianity, and he maintained that abandoning use of the word religion was essential to understanding Christianity. That is, properly understanding the full meaning of Christianity as a religion in the early period of its formation—awkward as is this way of putting the matter—he argued, can only be achieved if the term religion is replaced with the terms faith (as *fiducia*/trust in God) and tradition (as *fides*/beliefs about God) as the full expression of the trust in God expressed in the historical tradition of the Church's life. A similar stance in this regard had already been taken by Cornelis Petrus Tiele in his two volume Gifford Lectures *Science of Religion* (1897). Tiele, that is, contrasted the psychological/spiritual reality of religion in the depth of the human soul with the (observable/material) tradition in which it finds expression, but he, unlike Wilfred Smith, did not counsel rejection of the word religion. Ninian Smart (1973), also without rejecting use of the word religion, argued that a full understanding of the import of that concept would require distinguishing the focus of religion—that transcendent ontological reality of religion as such to which it points—from its expression in the life and practice of the religious devotee. Most such views, I think, have been influenced to a significant extent by Gerardus Van der Leeuw's understanding of the concept in his *Religion in Essence and Manifestation* (1938).

A more recent—and less religion-friendly—intellectually serious recommendation for jettisoning the term religion is presented in anthropologist Maurice Bloch's essay "Why Religion is Nothing Special but is Central." According to Bloch, religion is an ethnocentric term and he argues that what corresponds to it in archaic cultures is what he calls "the transcendental social." That notion, not to put too fine a point on it, refers to the kind of broad imaginative world in which most archaic cultures are steeped that includes not only the gods but the living and the dead in an indissoluble system of interaction. He maintains that "[o]nce we realize this omnipresence of the imaginary in the everyday, nothing special is left to explain concerning religion" (Bloch 2008, 6). However, he is also aware that in certain historical circumstances "the kind of phenomena we call religious take on a separate appearance that seems to distinguish it from the more inclusive transcendental social" (Bloch 2008, 4).

In *Before Religion: A History of a Modern Concept*, Brent Nongbri also argues against the general use of the modern term religion because, he claims, it names something that persons in ancient and other non-western cultures would not recognize (Nongbri 2013, 153). Nongbri argues that using the term to account for some "timeless mysterious things that have always been present to some degree in all human cultures throughout history" (Nongbri 2013, 15) cannot, as modern scholars have maintained, be traced to ancient sources. Other ancient and modern cultures, he argues, did not and do not carve up their worlds with religion being an isolated sphere of life separate from other spheres such as economics or politics, for example, as wholly secular spheres of life. Nongbri therefore rejects use of that modern concept of religion, (although not use of the word religions), for example, in scholarly talk about "ancient Mesopotamian religions, ancient Greek religions, or any other ancient religions" (Nongbri 2013, 153) because all these traditions existed before religion in its modern form in Europe and Anglo-

American scholarship. Carlin A. Barton and Daniel Boyarin support such a deconstruction of the modern term as inadequate translations of the Latin term *religio* and the Greek term *thrēskeia*, or as useful for understanding ancient attitudes, beliefs, and practices. According to them the Latin and Greek terms "imagined more richly the ancient 'forms of life' that they evinced" (Barton and Boyarin 2016, 2). On the basis of analysis of these terms, beyond that presented in the brief studies offered by Nongbri and others, they claim to have "demonstrated conclusively what others have surmised: Translating *religio* and *thrēskeia* by religion obscures more than it reveals" (Barton and Boyarin 2016, 212).

Deconstructive lexical studies of this kind are helpful in understanding the real epistemic objectives of the field, still widely referred to as Religious Studies, namely arriving at a proper description and explanation of a distinctive range of human beliefs and behaviours. Unfortunately, however, such work is often invoked in support of a political deconstruction of the scientific enterprise itself, which is committed to seeking an explanation for why people believe in unobservable transcendental ontologies and live their lives constrained by the behavioural import of those beliefs. One sees this, for example, not only in Fitzgerald's work but also in works like Russell McCutcheon's *Manufacturing Religion: The Discourse on Sui Generis Religion and the Politics of Nostalgia* (1997), his and William F. Arnal's *The Sacred is the Profane: The Political Nature of Religion* (2013), in David Chidester's *Empire of Religion: Imperialism and Comparative Religion* (2014) and in Daniel Dubuisson's *The Western Construction of Religion: Myths, Knowledge, and Ideology* (2003) and his *The Invention of Religion* (2019). These scholars, among many others, all claim that the concept religion is steeped in Western ideology and therefore of no value in the study of cultural belief systems involving reference to a transcendent reality. Being fundamentally a Christian term, Dubuisson writes, it is unfit "for describing each of the configurations [of experiences of such realities] observed in the infinitely mottled ensemble of all human cultures" and its adoption has exerted an unwholesome "influence on the birth and development of the History of Religions as an academic discipline" (Dubuisson 2019, 15, 16).

There are many academics in this field of research and scholarship who have argued for the positive benefits of retaining use of the term religion for establishing the disciplinary boundaries of the field. Jonathan Z. Smith, for example, argued that the term is essential to establishing the horizons of the discipline. The term religion, as he put it in his article "Religion, Religions, Religious":

is a second-order, generic concept that plays the same role in establishing a disciplinary horizon that a concept such as "language" plays in linguistics or "culture" plays in anthropology. There can be no disciplined study of religion without such a horizon. (J. Smith 1999, 281–282)

Benson Saler, in his 1993 book *Conceptualizing Religion: Immanent Anthropologists, Transcendent Natives, and Unbounded Categories*, argues that what is needed is a definition that can identify phenomena as religious without reference, either implicit or explicit, to the notion of its essential nature or universal meaning, but which is able to appreciate the diversity of religious thought and expression around the world. He therefore proposes that the academic student of religion accepts the value of prototype theory on which to construct a family-resemblance approach to defining religion in a way that can provide a rich framework within which to describe and explain a wide range of distinctive human behaviours associated with culturally created transcendent realities beyond the natural world.

The authors of essays in *The Pragmatics of Defining Religion: Contexts, Concepts, and Contents* edited by Jan G. Platvoet and Arie L. Molendijk, published in 1999, also moved in a decidedly different direction with the problem of definition. The pragmatic approach they advocated argues for the use of definitions of religion that are anti-essentialist and anti-hegemonic, and therefore tailored to different types of enterprises. They were particularly concerned about definitions with reference to what they refer to as New Age religiosities and the deinstitutionalization of religions. They are convinced that there is no hope of, or need for, a universal "true definition of religion" that can form the basis for a common methodological and theoretical framework for the scientific study of religion, but they do not feel it necessary to jettison the term altogether.

Even this brief overview of the "definition of religion literature" dedicated to grounding an academic research discipline in the modern university, suggests, as Dubuisson puts it, that no "intellectually satisfying definition has [ever] been found for the word" (Dubuisson 2019, 15). I think it is very unlikely such a definition will suffice in the future and will argue that it is time that academia give up that quest. Although Saler's proposal, and that of many of the authors in the Platvoet/Molendijk edited volume, escape some of the problems of earlier substantive and functional definitions proposed, those proposals nevertheless suffer from the ambiguity generated by the multiplicity of the mutually exclusive definitions already in circulation, and from the negative moral implications of the political critiques linking this field of scientific analysis and theory to imperialism and colonialism.

Setting the Boundaries for the Scientific Study of Religious Phenomena

Although I agree with Jonathan Z. Smith's suggestion that students of religion can opt to ground a scientific study of religious thought and practice by way of a stipulative definition of the term, it has not garnered much support and I do not think that option would provide the discipline with much relief from the negative moral connotations attached to the word religion by postmodernists in the field.

Nevertheless, I understand the desire to make use of the word religion to name the discipline in which we are engaged. It would be cumbersome and tedious to have repeatedly to refer to the departments in which we work as, for example, the "Department for the Scientific Study of Human Thought and Behaviour Influenced by Belief in a Supernatural Realm of Existence Populated by Supernatural Beings Who are Interested in the Welfare of Human Beings." Following up on Nongbri's argument, I think Barton and Boyarin might be on the mark in claiming that using religion to translate *religio* or *Thrēskeia* "obscures more than it reveals" and therefore makes it impossible "to imagine more richly the ancient 'forms of life' that they evinced" (Barton and Boyarin 2016, 212, 2). Nevertheless, it is an historical fact that the English word religion—however it is used today—derives from the Latin word *religio* which is associated with beliefs in either superhuman or supernatural realms of existence—that is, with thought and behaviour that are widely understood to be religious.

The earliest use of the word *religio*, as Tom Holland points out in his book *Dominion: How the Christian Revolution Remade the World*, was connected with primordial rites and honours paid to the gods in the earliest days of an ancient city; rites that won divine favour, for example, for Rome. As in the Greek cities, the Romans feared what the gods might do to them if they neglected these rituals. As Holland puts it: "Any obligation owed the gods in exchange for their protection, any tradition or custom constituted a 'religio'" (Holland 2019, 118). All these practices were religiones that "bound the Roman people to the dimension of the supernatural" (Holland 2019, 118). Holland also points out that it is important to see that such practices involved beliefs in or about the gods but that such beliefs were not the essence of *religio*—rites and practices were the essence of *religio*. However, the meaning of the word changed with Constantine who, Holland argues, saw the "need for religiones that could join all the peoples of the world" (Holland 2019, 118). Constantine, Holland maintains, saw that acknowledging the primacy of Christ could achieve that end for the empire—it would define "for all Roman citizens a single, universally accepted due of religiones—and thereby to provide for the empire, amid all the many crises racking it, the favour of the heavens" (Holland 2019, 130). As Holland puts it: "True [r]eligio ... was a matter less of ritual, less of splashing altars with blood or fumigating them with incense, than of correct belief" (Holland 2019, 132). For Constantine, "the surest way to join a people as one was to unite them not in common rituals, but in common belief" (Holland 2019, 134). In this case, it appears, *religio* came to refer to some transcendental ontological/spiritual reality that was expressed in doctrine, in moral behaviour, and in ritual practice.

In late antiquity the word *religio* came to signify the life of a monk or nun whereas life outside the monasteries or convents took place in the order of the *saeculum* (the world) setting up the dichotomy between the sphere of religion over against the sphere of the secular realm so characteristic of the modern use of the word religion postmodernists decry. As Holland points out, Augustine was the first to use the word *secularia* for the things that are caught up in the flux of mortal existence—i.e., to refer to things in the natural rather than in a supernatural realm. But use of the word secular did not at the time have the meaning we attribute to it today—that is, as referring to a religiously neutral realm of existence. That, as many scholars argue, only comes after the Reformation in which *religio*, as Luther conceived it, is used to describe not the communal life of the Catholic *religio*, that is, life in a religious order, but a private relationship with God. As Holland describes it, this Protestant *religio* "lay in the inner relationship of a believer to the divine. Faith was a personal and private thing" (Holland 2019, 416). "As such," Holland continues, "it existed in a sphere distinct from the rest of society: from government, or trade, or law. There was the dimension of the religious, and then there was the dimension of everything else: the 'secular'" (Holland 2019, 416). This Protestant use of the word, therefore, further gave shape to the modern concept of religion deplored by the postmodernists. As Holland points out, this use of the term became widespread with the coining of the English term/word secularism by a British newspaper editor as a neutral term on the basis of the implicit two realms of Protestant theology—namely, the supernatural and the natural realms, with the former as the non-material realm of religion itself, and the latter the non-religious realm in which religion finds material expression or embodiment.

It is obvious that the English word religion—and its cognates—etymologically derives from the Latin word *religio* and is burdened with a multiplicity of meanings in the history of its usage in the West. Its original reference-range, it appears, covered a distinctive kind of human thought and behaviour that involved belief in and deference to superhuman or supernatural agents. In its historical development, however, it also came to include reference to an independent, metaphysical reality that it is assumed grounds human thought about, and is behaviourally deferential to, superhuman and supernatural agents. It is this dualistic understanding of religion that came to characterize much, if not most, of the academic study of religion in our modern western research universities. Criticism of that enterprise as itself a form of religious thought and life is not without justification given the failure of the nascent scientific enterprise to distinguish religion itself, a metaphysical reality, from religious thought and behaviour related to religion itself—the first being a culturally postulated supramundane world beyond explanation by reference to the mundane natural world of everyday existence, with the latter being intersubjectively observable behaviour as an object of scientific explanatory interest. The only way of avoiding this, I will argue, is to carefully restrict use of the noun religion in discussion of theoretical concerns and make liberal use of its cognates such as the adjective religious to describe intersubjectively observable human behaviour connected with belief in and commitment to culturally imagined transcendent realities and supernatural agents, and the plural noun religions to refer to observable social structures and institutions that embody such beliefs in practice.

A brief excursus on naturalism

Academics engaged in the scientific study of religion do not, contra Griffiths, have faith in naturalism. In making that claim Griffiths fails to understand that they are not engaged in some type of metaphysical discourse but rather adopt naturalism as a methodological tool. There is no question here of having faith in a methodological tool. In adopting methodological naturalism, the academic study of religion in the context of the modern research university, like the natural and social sciences, restricts its concerns to understanding and explaining intersubjectively observable physical, biological, or social phenomena. The scientific study of religion, therefore, eliminates from consideration what many scholars in the field have referred to as religion in itself—a metaphysical something which finds expression, so to speak, in religious thought and behaviour. This is not a form of eliminative reductionism of religion to something else; it is simply to remain agnostic with respect to metaphysical claims of any kind including religion itself. Consequently, the scientific student of religion refuses to define the noun religion in favour of the study of a range of human psychological and social behaviours that involve a commitment to the existence of metaphysical realities such as supernatural or superhuman agents. This, of course, precludes invoking supernatural beliefs to explain the existence of such cultural postulations. Such beliefs, that is, lack rational warrant and publicly available evidence in their support. Using the adjective religious to label such beliefs is appropriate, however, given their historical association with the metaphysical idea of religion itself.

The import of such epistemic agnosticism (which, in the case of the study of religion, amounts to methodological atheism) in a strictly scientific approach to the study of religious phenomena, however, is seen by many scholars in the field as pragmatically incoherent. Edward Slingerland, for example, argues that such a fully physicalist framework implies that understanding and explaining human thought and behaviour can be achieved without reference to the notion of meaning which appears to be essential to human existence. As he affirms, everyone wants "to live in an environment rich with human meaning" (Slingerland 2018, 179). Slingerland insists that such physicalism amounts to adopting a crude eliminative reductionism that can only be overcome by way of integrating the humanities into the sciences to produce what he calls a "productive explanatory reductionism." He spells out what he means by this notion under the rubric: "The Limits of Physicalism: Why We Will Always Be Humanists" (Slingerland 2018, 188f.). Drawing on the work of Canadian philosopher Charles Taylor, Slingerland argues that humans are a "peculiar type of animal" because they not only exist and function in a physical realm in the universe, but must also be able to function morally in a very different and complex sort of realm. As a social species, he maintains, humans simply "cannot avoid having to orient [themselves] with respect to it" (Slingerland 2018, 194). He is right, of course, to argue that at the present time we can provide more reasonable explanations of human behaviour in terms of the intentional character of human behaviour and by way of reference to an emergent moral level of reality. As Slingerland puts it: "For the peculiar type of animal that we are, moral space is as much a part of reality as physical space, in that we cannot avoid having to orient ourselves with respect to it" or evade "the strong pull of human-level truth" (Slingerland 2018, 194, 197). Slingerland therefore maintains that the existence of such a moral space shows "the limits of a thoroughly "scientific" approach to [the study] of human culture" and the need for the sciences to embody humanistic approaches in understanding and explaining human behaviour (Slingerland 2018, 171, 182, 200). Slingerland therefore concludes his analysis as follows:

> As humanists, we are not in fact faced by the stark choice of either a meaningless, mechanistic universe as an endless nightmarish maze of contingent

discourses. It is possible to be an empirically responsible intellectual, and embrace a thoroughly naturalistic approach to one's subject matter, without losing sight of the inescapable human reality of this emergent level of explanation. (Slingerland 2018, 200)

No one, I think, would disagree with Slingerland's claim that "agent-like intentionality and mental concepts emerge as useful ways to think about the world ..." (Slingerland 2018, 185). Few natural scientists, moreover, would agree that these emergent concepts point to an ontologically distinct realm beyond the physical world in which they are presently found to be useful. Even Slingerland acknowledges that there is no empirically defensible account of dualism and that Darwinism has clearly shown "that human beings are merely physical systems" (Slingerland 2018, 188, 198). But, speaking scientifically, Slingerland cannot in the same breath espouse a view of the universe as simultaneously mechanistic and meaningful. His advice therefore that we "embody" the humanities in the sciences appears to be motivated by a moral objective to place an epistemic limit on the sciences and not simply a rational response to reason and evidence that reveal the objective limits of the sciences. The feeling and desire humans generally have "to live and work in an environment rich with human meaning" (Slingerland 2018, 179) as Slingerland puts it, does not justify his claim that even scientific students, qua scientists, must also be, humanists. Methodologically speaking, this is a recipe for introducing moral, political, and even religio-theological agendas into the search for an explanatory understanding of religious thought and behaviour.

Dealing with science

The concept of science is very much a modern creation. It was never an ancient category, as G.E.R. Lloyd points out in his book on Greek Science After Aristotle (Lloyd 1973, 7). Lloyd acknowledges in his later work, *Demystifying Mentalities*, that there were, as he puts it, "analogous ambitions" but nevertheless insists that "there was no science as we know it today in ancient civilizations" (Lloyd 1990, 23). He reiterates the point in his *Ancient Worlds, Modern Reflections: Philosophical Perspectives on Greek and Chinese Science and Culture*, writing: "In no ancient language was there a term that exactly corresponds to 'science,' even though they have rich vocabularies to talk about knowledge, wisdom, and learning" (Lloyd 2004, 12). What is clear in Lloyd's work, however, is that modern science is not only one among the many claimants to knowledge but represents the ideal mode of knowledge production and therefore constitutes the benchmark for all knowledge claims. That claim, however, does not provide an answer to the question as to what science is "in itself," so to speak, or how it will be used in the present volume. But providing a quick and easy definition of it will not be possible. I am mindful on this score of John Ziman's caution in his *Public Knowledge: The Social Dimensions of Science* written nearly fifty years ago, that "[t]o answer the question 'What is Science?' is almost as presumptuous as to try to state the meaning of life itself" (Ziman 1967, 1). A little more than a decade later, in his *Reliable Knowledge: An Exploration of the Ground of Belief in Science*, Ziman advised his readers that "Science is such a complex human activity, so much part of our civilization, so rapidly changing in form and content, that it cannot be judged in a few simple sentences" (1978, 1). A matter he emphasized again in his *Real Science: What It Is and What It Means*, insisting that science "is too diverse, too protean, to be captured in full by a definition" (Ziman 2000, 12). Nevertheless, by the late 1970s he was ready to assert with confidence that science is more than simply personal knowledge; that "it can consist only of what can be communicated from person to person" (Ziman 1978, 1). He coined the word consensible in 1973 to indicate that scientific knowledge must be social in the sense of its claims being open to intersubjective testability. In summary, then, Ziman argues that science is a social pursuit of knowledge for its own sake, a notion that first emerged in ancient Greece. "My argument," he wrote in 2000, "is that this notion [of 'basic science'] is little more than an idealized image of 'academic science' [science as carried on in our modern research universities], a social institution whose features are taken to be characteristic of science in general" (Ziman 2000, 55); what he calls "our ideal of a 'mode of knowledge production'" (Ziman 2000, 58). This, as I have already noted, may only be one among the many claimants to knowledge, but I agree with the philosopher Alan Chalmers's insistence in his *Science and Its Fabrication* "that it is possible and important to distinguish the aim of producing scientific knowledge from other aims and that the distinction is essential for an adequate explanation and appraisal of science" (Chalmers 1990, 95).

Whatever concerns have been raised about defining science apply equally to the question of whether there is a scientific method. The philosopher John Arthur Passmore raised that concern in his *Science and Its Critics* by acknowledging that there is no such thing as the scientific method but nevertheless still recognizing that methods used by scientists are distinctive. He described his position as follows: "There is no established method, whether it be inductive or deductive, of getting things right. There are only methods which will make it less likely that scientists will commit certain kinds of errors" (Passmore 1978, xx). Lewis Wolpert raised the same concern twenty years later in his book *The Unnatural Nature of Science*, claiming that "defining the nature of science with rigor and consistency turns out to be extremely difficult. It is even doubtful that there is a scientific method except in very broad and general terms" (Wolpert 1992, 101).

I think, therefore, that the literature on science and scientific method provides sufficient ground on which to declare such a definitional project futile at best, and to reject the abstract word science as if it refers to some Platonic type of reality beyond the world we actually inhabit. I think philosopher Susan Haack, in her book *Putting Philosophy to Work*, provides a far more reasonable way of using the word science—if it is absolutely necessary to use it—as reference to "a federation of kinds of inquiry into material and social phenomena, differentiated from other kinds of inquiry such as history or literary scholarship by the questions within its scope (Haack 2013, 199). I shall justify my suggestion that we have no more need for the abstract English noun "science" than we do for the abstract English noun "religion" by way of Haack's account of how the sciences work presented in her *Defending Science Within Reason: Between Scientism and Cynicism* (2003).

The sciences, Haack argues, are thoroughly humanly created enterprises, continuous with the most ordinary of empirical enquiries involving a refinement of everyday thinking. They are attempts to give a true account of what the world is and how it operates. Scientific enquiry, therefore, is not categorically different from other kinds of enquiry, but it is distinguished from them by use of special devices and techniques by which the sciences amplify everyday empirical enquiry. She spells them out in more detail in an earlier essay entitled "Puzzling Out Science" in her book *Manifesto of a Passionate Moderate* as including:

> systematic effort to isolate one variable at a time; systematic commitment to criticism and testing; experimental contrivance of every kind; instruments of observation from the microscope to the questionnaire; all the complex apparatus[es] of statistical evaluation and mathematical modeling; [a constantly developing instrumentation], and the engagement, cooperative and competitive, of many persons, within and across generations.... [The sciences have] by all the means just listed, enormously deepened and extended the range of experience and the sophistication of reasoning of which [they] avail [themselves]. (Haack 1998, 96–97)

In *Defending Science Within Reason*, she lists their epistemic virtues as follows:

respect for evidence, care and persistence in seeking it out, good judgment in assessing its worth.... [It is] the method of experience and reasoning: making an informed conjecture, seeing how it stands up to available evidence and further evidence ... and then using [good] judgment whether to drop it, modify it, stick it out, or what? (Haack 2003, 167)

It is this sense of scientific that I have in mind when talking about the natural and social sciences and, in particular, what has been called the academic study of religion. I see them neither as the only sources of knowledge, nor as categorically different from everyday ordinary empirical enquiry. I do not, therefore, consider scientific claims, as Haack puts it, as "epistemologically privileged" but I do see them as "epistemologically distinguished." They are so distinguished because their objective is the advancement of knowledge for its own sake and not partial to any personal, social, cultural, or political interest. Were scientists perceived as partial to some personal or social interest—as either critics or caretakers of society, or aspects of it—this special epistemic status would be lost.

In conclusion: Focusing on the questions to be answered and the problems to be solved

At a couple of stages in this essay I suggested that students of religion would be wise to follow Karl Popper's advice against the search for absolute clarity in the concepts they use in responding to the questions and problems that emerge from their interest in religious thought and behaviour. In concluding this essay, I advert once again to this advice. He writes that:

> If because of lack of clarity a misunderstanding arises do not try to lay new and more solid foundations on which to build a more precise "conceptual framework," but reformulate your formulations ad hoc, with a view to avoiding those misunderstandings which have arisen or which you foresee. And always remember that it is impossible to speak in such a way that you cannot be misunderstood: there will always be some who misunderstand you. If greater precision is needed, it is needed because the problem to be solved demands it. Simply try your best to solve your problems and do not try in advance to make your concepts or formulations more precise...
> (Popper 1976, 30; emphasis in the original)

I think this advice is of special importance for those engaged in the scientific study of the thought and practice of individuals and groups generally referred to as religious. The word religious is invoked to label human thought and practice that is "framed" by beliefs in the existence of supernatural agents.

There is no need for the word or concept of "religion" which is an abstract noun and therefore irrelevant to the naturalistic study of a peculiar range of empirically observable human behaviours. Indeed, I have shown here that invoking religion to designate the subject matter of this scientific undertaking has been counter-productive in that it has generated fruitless deliberations on how to define the term rather than focusing on proper descriptions of and explanations for a specific range of human behaviours these academics are interested in understanding.

The enterprise often referred to as the scientific study of religion, is not an inquiry into the character of some non-natural or supernatural reality, as is often assumed, but only of a type of observable human behaviour flowing from belief in a culturally postulated super-natural world. The scientific study of religion, therefore, is neither a study of the metaphysical realities postulated by the devotee—although it will include inquiry into what the devotees believe about the imaginative realities their culture has brought into existence—nor of the terms themselves used by scientists in this enterprise. The devotee, psychologically, lives in both a natural and preternatural world simultaneously. But the scientist lives in a wholly natural world.

— 2 —

The Deep History of the Scientific Study of Religious Thought and Behaviour

Introduction

It is generally understood that the field of scholarship widely referred to in the modern university as "religious studies" was a late nineteenth- and early twentieth-century creation of intellectuals interested in seeking a non-theological understanding of religious thought and behaviour. It differed from theological understanding of such thought and practice in that it was free from direct ecclesiastical control. In that sense, it was secular but not scientific in the sense the concept "science" obtained with and after the Scientific Revolution in sixteenth- and seventeenth-century Europe. In today's world, the notion of "scientific knowledge"—including the processes required for producing it - sets the benchmark for all epistemic claims made about the world and its contents.

The most obvious fact about this achievement is its late arrival in the life of Homo sapiens; it did not arrive on the scene, so to speak, with the arrival of anatomically modern humans. This is not, however, to deny that our evolutionary and historical forebears carried on in the world without knowledge of it and about it. But the knowledge they possessed was both less than and more than scientific and without understanding this it will not be possible even to give a reasonable account of the nature of "scientific study" itself, which is foundational to explicating what we mean by talk of the "scientific study of religion." My objective in this chapter, therefore, is to provide an account of the evolution—the deep history—of the cognitive capacities of the human mind that ultimately led to the creation of scientific thought, and the interplay between those cognitive capacities and the cultural realities they made possible, including religious thought and practice. I hope to accomplish this by way of a curated overview of the relevant literature on these topics.

The cognitive capacities of our hominin ancestors overlap to a great degree with their evolutionary forebears, but their social and cultural development produced significant difference. Tracing those developments will require some awareness of the episodic cultures of early primate cognition, knowledge of the evolutionary transitions from the mind of our ape ancestors to species-specific modes of human thought, and knowledge of the pre-historical and historical transformations of those evolved human cognitive capacities that emerged under the pressure of cultural changes. On the one hand, our deep evolutionary history will be able to account for the cognitive foundations underlying the nature of scientific thought but not for its actual emergence in human culture. As cognitive archaeologist Steven Mithen points out

> [b]y the end of the last ice age the complete cognitive foundations for science appear to have been in place..., [but] the emergence of science as a discrete domain of behaviour is likely to have required a suite of social, historic, and economic circumstances that had not yet arisen in human history.
>
> (Mithen 2002, 40)

A scientific mode of thought would have been irrelevant for dealing with the everyday issues facing our evolutionary and historical forebears, and perhaps even dangerous, given that carefully "thinking through" matters in response to the normal everyday dangers facing them could have been positively dangerous. In examining the archaic pre-historical phase of human cognitive development, on the other hand, it will become clear that religious thought, for example, had a significant role for archaic human communities in "make[ing] sense" of their world…[by showing] how things in the universe cohere" (Cohen 1994, 506). This clearly suggests that the religious (mythopoetic) mode of thought long preceded the emergence of the science-like mode of thought that would require a peculiar set of social, political, and economic conditions for its establishment.

Some problematic views on the nature of scientific thought

There is some literature relevant to my concern in this chapter I think potentially misleading in understanding the history of scientific thinking. I have in mind here, for example, Robin Dunbar's use of the concept of "science" in accounting for transformations of thought processes in our primate forebears and the application of the concept to describe the thinking of infants and children by Alison Gopnik, Andrew Meltzoff, and Patricia Kuhl. These authors are reputable scientists and there is much to be learned from their experimental work, from the books to which I will refer, and from their other publications. Nevertheless, I find their use of the concept "science" to lack the nuance essential in accounting for the evolutionary and historical changes in human modes of thought that ultimately made possible the emergence of modern science.

In *The Trouble With Science*, Robin Dunbar, an anthropologist and evolutionary psychologist, maintains "that the scientific method is not merely typical of all humans, but is also a key feature in the lives of most birds and mammals" (Dunbar 1995, 58), and he therefore calls them "nature's own scientists" (Dunbar 1995, 59). Dunbar also maintains, as do some developmental psychologists, that "children are natural scientists" (Dunbar 1995, 79). This should be obvious, he maintains, because non-human animals, like humans, must be able to negotiate their way in their respective ecological niches or perish. Both humans and other animals, he insists, do so in a scientific way; that they have a method "for finding out about the world that combines empirical observation with causal inference" (Dunbar 1995, 55). Insofar as they are able to do this, he argues, they are engaged in "low-level empirical [cook book] science" (Dunbar 1995, 56) that permits them to learn about the regularities of their worlds which is essential to their wellbeing. Dunbar is well aware that science "does not consist simply of inductive generalizations"; that it "also consists of explanations for those empirical generalizations," and because of that awareness he claims that animals can "store information about the world in the form of hypotheses" and that they are able, therefore, to "use the rules of logic to make a 'leap of inference'" in responding to their changing environments (Dunbar 1995, 63). Drawing on the work of Claude Lévi-Strauss, Dunbar also claims that our hominin ancestors operated in a fashion beyond a mere "cookbook" type of science, often making "attempts at explanatory science as well" (Dunbar 1995, 56). Dunbar, therefore, concludes that "science is a genuine universal characteristic of all advanced life forms"; it "is something intrinsic to life itself...[and] really is just plain simple learning of the kind with which we are all familiar" (Dunbar 1995, 75).

There can be no doubt that there is some continuity in the cognitive capacities of our primate forebears and those that ground the thought processes of modern human persons, but to claim that there is no significant difference between what Dan Dennett calls the "uncomprehending" thought processes of our primate forebears (which will receive attention below) and those that characterize modern scientific thought is not persuasive and can only hinder a proper understanding of the nature of the modern sciences. The claim of Alison Gopnik and Andrew N. Meltzoff in their book *Words, Thoughts,*

Theories "that the processes of cognitive development in children are similar to, indeed perhaps even identical with, the processes of cognitive development in scientists" (Gopnik and Meltzoff 1997, 3) is similarly problematic for an adequate understanding of the origin and nature of the modern sciences. For them, children have the same theorizing abilities which continue into adulthood (Gopnik and Meltzoff 1997, 20). Their argument that central elements of the scientific mode of thought are "a basic part of our evolutionary endowment" (Gopnik and Meltzoff 1997, 21) is beyond objection, as I will show below, but their further claim that "we can think of organized science as taking natural mechanisms of conceptual change, designed to facilitate learning in childhood, and putting them to use in a culturally organized way" fails to see how critically important cultural organization of those cognitive capacities are to the emergence of the modern sciences. The same criticism applies to the thesis in *The Scientist in the Crib: What Early Learning Tells Us About the Mind* by Alison Gopnik, Andrew N. Meltzoff, and Patricia K. Kuhl. They write: "We think that children learn about the mind by being psychologists. They make predictions, they do experiments, they try to explain what they see, and they formulate new theories based on what they already know" (Gopnik, Meltzoff, and Kuhl 1999, 55–56). These authors may be correct in pointing out "that babies and scientists share the same cognitive machinery" (Gopnik, Metlzoff, and Kuhl 1999, 161) but they are not correct in suggesting, as I think they do, that babies and young children consciously "think, observe, and reason…[as well as] consider evidence, draw conclusions, do experiments, solve problems, and search for truth" in the way that modern scientists do (Gopnik, Meltzoff, and Kuhl 1999, 13). They acknowledge that babies and young children "don't do this in the self-conscious way that scientists do" but they do not seem to recognize the "gap" that scientific self-consciousness creates between the knowledge of the child and that found in the modern sciences.

Cognitive transformation in the evolutionary emergence of the human mind

In *The Prehistory of the Mind: The Cognitive Origins of Art and Science*, Steven Mithen provides an overview of the emergence of the modern human mind by suggesting the evolutionary changes in brain structure and cognitive capacities of the many ancestors of Homo sapiens sapiens since its common ancestor, the chimpanzees, six million years ago. In undertaking this task Mithen depends heavily upon the work of evolutionary psychologists such as Leda Cosmides and John Tooby, rejecting the notion that the human mind acquires its contents entirely from its cultural environment. According to evolutionary psychologists, understanding the history of the evolution of the human mind can only be achieved in recognizing that the mind is not simply a blank slate and a general-purpose learning machine but rather that at birth it possesses a multiplicity of specialized mechanisms and cognitive processes that contain knowledge about the world hardwired in the brain's adaptation to its environment. Mithen, however, modifies the massive modularity thesis, found in many evolutionary psychologists, in his account of the emergence of the modern mind through the various evolutionary transformations of brain and mind in our ancestors, from the Pleistocene and Palaeolithic to the Holocene.

Mithen looks at three phases in the emergence of the modern mind. The first is dominated by a domain of general intelligence of which little is known, the second phase is one in which that general intelligence is supplemented with specialized intelligences, each isolated in its own domain, and the third period is one in which the specialized intelligences—cognitive capacities—work together with a flow of knowledge and ideas between and among them. The intelligences, or cognitive capacities, of the second phase include a natural history intelligence, a technical intelligence, and a social intelligence concerned with understanding the natural world, the physical world, and their social interactions. These cognitive capacities arise from an intuitive knowledge of the natural world essential to life as hunter-gatherers, an intuitive physics necessary in making tools and other artifacts essential to their existence, and an intuitive biology essential in understanding and interacting with conspecifics, all of which are hardwired in their adaptation to a constantly changing environment. There was a continuous growth in these intelligences or cognitive capacities in humans from nearly two million to 100,000 years ago, but their isolation was overcome some 30,000 years ago, producing what Mithen calls a "cognitive fluidity" that allowed these different behavioural domains to influence each other. This in turn, as Mithen puts it, made possible new reflective ways of thinking and subjects to think about, which in turn made possible new and different ways of behaving. He writes, for example, that

> as soon as a language started acting as the vehicle for delivering non-social information and ideas into the domain of social intelligence, reflexive consciousness could also get to grips with the non-social world. Individuals could now become introspective about their non-social thought processes and knowledge. As a result, the whole of human behaviour was pervaded with the flexibility that is characteristic of Modern Humans. (Mithen 1999, 192)

Indeed, it "is the defining property of the modern mind" (Mithen 1999, 210). He writes in conclusion,

> The human mind is a product of evolution, not supernatural creation...[and] I have explained how the potential arose in the mind to undertake science, create art, and believe in religious ideologies, even though there were no specific selection pressures for such abstract abilities at any point during our past. (Mithen, 1999, 215).

This cognitive potential is the natural origin of both religious and scientific thought.

Merlin Donald also traces the evolution of the cognitive capacities of Homo sapiens in his book *Origins of the Modern Mind: Three Stages in the Evolution of Culture and Cognition* announcing in the Prologue to the book that the human mind is "a mosaic structure of cognitive vestiges from earlier stages of human emergence" and that its "cognitive architecture is highly differentiated and specialized" and not, therefore, a tabula rasa (Donald 1991, 2–3, 5). Donald argues that there are three major evolutionary transitions from the minds of ape to that of modern humans, involving a complete redesign in the form of human thought and culture. Primate cognition, he points out, produces an episodic culture which he describes as lives "lived entirely in the present, as a series of concrete episodes, and the highest element of their system of memory representations seems to be at the level of event representation" (Donald 1991, 159). Apes therefore have a great deal of situational knowledge but cannot represent those situations in order to reflect on them. Thus, even though apes have a degree of conscious awareness, Donald argues that "[t]he pinnacles of episodic [ape] culture [only mark] the starting point of the human journey" (Donald 1991, 152). The first step towards the modern human mode of thought is from the episodic to a mimetic form of culture that gave rise to what Donald calls the archaic form of human culture of Homo erectus. The tool-making abilities of H. erectus, he claims, would have placed "demands on the intellect that go beyond the concrete, time-bound episodic mentality" of the apes (Donald 1991, 164) and created a culture "intermediate between the episodic mind and the symbolic representational systems of modern Homo sapiens (Donald 1991, 161). Homo erectus, therefore, would have been capable of representing many aspects of its physical and social environment relevant to its survival and expression of its intentions, although it would not have had the capacity for language. Donald maintains that this mimetic level of representation is foundational to modern human culture. The next major step towards that modern human culture for Donald involves the cognitive capacities that made possible the transition in cultures from mimetic to a mythic culture that begins with the emergence of our immediate human ancestor—archaic H. sapiens—about 200,000 years ago. Although little information about the earliest stages of this development is available, Donald points out that there is evidence of an important cognitive breakthrough about 50,000 years ago with the development of cognitive innovations leading to the development of new tools and technologies that made possible cultural advantages for this species over other species. Most significant in this transition was the development of the capacity for speech, a "tool" that increased our species capacity for cooperative behaviour and made possible an integrative mode of thought allowing the mind, as Donald puts it, to go "beyond the episodic perception of events, beyond the mimetic reconstruction of episodes, to a comprehensive modeling of the entire universe" (Donald 1991, 214). It is a narrative mode of thought, then, that constructs myths to orient its place in the world—to 'make sense' of the world—that dominates the intellectual life of our hunter-gatherer forebears from about 40,000 to 10,000 years ago. In his *A Mind So Rare: The Evolution of Human Consciousness* Donald emphasizes how important this leap to language for creating a shared, collective account of reality was in the development of anatomically and behaviourally modern humans:

> Once we have leaped into a narrative mind-set, our worlds become virtual ones.... Stories can become so influential and so deeply rooted in the daily operation of the culture that they assume a special cognitive status, that of myth.... This is an awesome power, unequaled in the history of cognition.
> (Donald 2001, 295)

A third major cognitive transition in human thought, Donald argues, marks a significant break from the earlier cultural patterns found in the evolution of our species which, he maintains, constitutes a significant "break with the dominances of spoken language and narrative styles of thought" (Donald 2001, 269). Donald writes: "Three crucial cognitive phenomena appear to have been underdeveloped, or virtually absent, in oral-mythic culture. These phenomena are graphic invention, external memory, and theory construction" (Donald 2001, 272, emphasis in the original), which make possible "formal arguments, systematic taxonomies, deduction, verification, differentiation, quantification, formal methods of measurement, etc." (Donald 2001, 274) that, ultimately, leads to the disenchantment of mythic thought, though not necessarily to its total abandonment. As the narrative/mythic mode of thought/mind gave rise to religious thought, even though it also "signalled the first attempts at symbolic models of the human universe"

(Donald 2001, 267), so the new theoretic mode of thought ultimately made possible modern scientific thought. Before leaving discussion of Donald's account of the emergence of the modern mind it must, however, be pointed out that his theory reveals that the modern human mind is the product of multiple levels of awareness—a cascade of stages in the evolution of Homo sapiens. He asserts that each successive stage in that evolution has magnified the previous stage and significantly changed the culture associated with each. It is clear, therefore, that human cognitive capacities are not simply biological phenomena but also, in some sense, socio-cultural forces. It is also the case that, under a specific set of psychological or socio-political conditions, either one or the other of these modes of thought, or a hybrid mode of the two, may play a dominant role in response to a new set of economic, social, or political conditions in society.

It is important in discussing the development of human modes of thought to recognize that there is no radical discontinuity with that of H. sapiens' forebears. As Michael Tomasello insists, in order to understand the uniquely human mode of thought it must be situated in its evolutionary context. We need to keep in mind that human thought processes depend upon the mental predispositions we have by way of natural selection in our ancestors' interaction with the physical world, including such basic cognitive capacities as perception, memory, and the capacity to conceptualize and categorize. These predispositions can be thought of as hardwired templates in the mind in terms of which we automatically respond to events in our environment. As Mithen pointed out, these predispositions, as specialized types of intuitive knowledge, were gained not by individual experience but rather, were hardwired into the brain in our evolutionary development, and such intuitive "knowledges" constitute what we now generally refer to as "folk knowledge." Cognitive scientists generally posit four such types of folk knowledge: (i) Folk Physics which includes "understanding" physical and mechanical causal connection, clearly important with respect to natural hazards; (ii) Folk Biology which includes knowledge of biological phenomena of growth and decay and makes possible differentiating animacy and agency from physical objects and artifacts; (iii) Folk Psychology which makes possible distinguishing intentionality from mere agency; and (iv) Folk Sociology or social intelligences and the capacity for cooperative and social existence. Such hardwired knowledges were essential in our evolution in making possible rapid responses to dangers in our evolutionary environment of adaptation and ensuring appropriate social interaction with each other. However, as Merlin Donald points out, our forebears also moved beyond these shared cognitive capacities with the emergence of language and with it the transition from mimetic to a mythic mode of cultural development and, finally, to a transition to a complex symbolic culture which, ultimately, was conducive to scientific thought. It is the unique, species-specific, character of these later developments in modes of human thought that Tomasello sets out in a series of studies as discontinuous, "[t]o an unprecedented degree," with what preceded it: See *The Cultural Origins of Human Cognition* (1999), *Origins of Human Communication* (2008), *Why We Cooperate* (2009), *A Natural History of Human Thinking* (2014), *A Natural History of Human Morality* (2016) and, *Becoming Human: A History of Ontology* (2019). Tomasello argues that

> the changes we see in human societies beginning with the advent of agriculture and cities are not due, on anyone's account, to any kind of biological adaptation. The changes would seem to be sociological only.... [They] are built primarily on cooperative skills and motivations biologically evolved for small-group interaction. (Tomasello 2009, 104)

According to Tomasello, it is the social dimensions of human thinking, involving joint and collective intentionality that created "an identifiably different type of thinking" in H. sapiens, from that of their primate forebears living in competitive societies (Tomasello 2014, 4). Such shared intentionalities, that is, make possible processes of social coordination—a kind of cultural cognition. Without awareness of the critical nature of these kinds of social interaction, he argues, there would be no possibility of becoming "objective"—in the sense of overcoming our multiple individualistic perspectives—or accounting for science. In this regard, Tomasello rejects Gopnik's views that children behave like scientists because it is "insufficiently social" (Tomasello 2019, 85).

In *A Natural History of Human Thinking* Tomasello writes:

> In order to survive and thrive, humans were forced, twice, to find new ways to coordinate their behavior with others in collaborative (and then cultural) activities and to coordinate their intentional states with others in cooperative (and then conventional) communication. And this transformed, twice, the way that humans think. (Tomasello 2014, x)

The first transition involved the "creation of a novel type of small-scale collaboration in human foraging" including pointing, gesturing, and pantomiming, and the second emerged because of inter-group competition wherein "group life as a whole became one big collaborative activity, creating a much larger cultural ground via collectively known cultural conventions, norms and institutions" (Tomasello 2014, 5). It was a change of ecology about 400,000 years ago that effectively brought about the first transition. The radical changes in the environment, Tomasello argues, required greater interdependence among hominins in that period than ever before in procuring their daily sustenance which forced them to develop new forms of cooperative communication in foraging and scavenging activities. This clearly involved greater social coordination among members of the band that exceeds the intentionality of what he calls the cognition for competition that characterized great ape social activity (Tomasello 2014, 26–27). The need for early humans to be able to make judgments about potential collaborative partners, he argues, brought about "a uniquely human form of [what Tomasello calls] second-personal joint engagement requiring species-specific cognitive skills and motivational propensities" (Tomasello 2014, 43). Thus, whereas the great apes make individual decisions with respect to obtaining food, members of the genus homo make joint decisions with others "in which two individuals engage with the intentional states of one another both jointly and recursively" (Tomasello 2014, 47). Thinking here was not, however, fully socially normative because the partners in such a "we-intentional" act "were concerned [only] with how their partner evaluated their cooperative behavior and comprehended their communicative acts, not with the group's normative standards" (Tomasello 2014, 79).

The second transition occurred about 200,000 years ago with the emergence of a collective intentionality which amounts to creating cultural conventions in which the group, as Tomasello describes, "became more than a loosely structured pool of collaborators ..., [becoming instead] self-identified cultures with their own 'histories'" (Tomasello 2014, 84). Humans now thought in terms of cultural conventions, norms, and institutions that involved "effacing of one's own perspective in deference to the more 'objective' perspective of others in the group" (Tomasello 2014, 122). The objectivity here is not that of the modern sciences but refers rather to the existence of social and institutional facts which are objective facts about the world in which modern humans function even though, as Tomasello puts it, they are "observer relative" facts, "created by individuals in social groups," and can, unlike physical facts, be dissolved by individuals in social groups (Tomasello 2014, 91). Tomasello therefore concludes that "[h]uman thinking has [at this stage] become collective, objective, reflective, and normative; that is to say, it has now become full-blown human reasoning" (Tomasello 2014, 123). Humans, Tomasello argues in his *Becoming Human*, unlike apes, do not use one another as social tools. Rather, through joint and collective intentional activities they have become "cooperatively dependent" on one another which has created uniquely human "supraindividual social structures" (Tomasello 2019, 318).

The prehistory of science

In "Human Evolution and the Cognitive Basis of Science," Steven Mithen, somewhat like Robin Dunbar, maintains that we must recognize that the foundations of science go back at least as far as our common ancestor, the great apes. He maintains, for example, that they "most likely already engaged in hypothesis testing and made acute observations about the natural and social worlds" (Mithen 2002, 40). Unlike Dunbar, however, he does not credit our non-human ancestors with science, even of the empirical cookbook variety. Rather, he maintains that the "capacity for science [cannot] be entirely reserved for modern humans [because] several of our ancestors employed, and were perhaps reliant on, *key elements of scientific thinking* for their survival" (Mithen 2002, 24, emphasis added). Some of those "key elements" match those referred to by Dunbar, such as making extensive and detailed observations of the natural world, using tools to extend human perception, showing concern for causation, generating and testing hypotheses, and accumulating knowledge over time. Mithen recognizes that such capacities have been employed at various stages of hominid and early human development (Mithen 2002, 24). However, whether societies that made use of these various capacities in one way or another in that evolutionary development should be described as possessing science Mithen writes: "It is a moot point, one that depends upon how the term is defined" (Mithen 2002, 37). He sees the evolutionary development of such capacities in the eventual emergence of H. sapiens more cautiously as transitions in modes of thought. Early hominids, for example, show continuity with the great apes in their possession of a detailed knowledge of their natural environments involving drawing generalizations and the making of tools. But none of this for him really amounts to scientific knowledge. He acknowledges that early humans, even though still pre-linguistic, possessed an understanding of causation but notes that this kind of knowledge was generally restricted to their social world. Extension of such causal thinking to the natural world, he admits, would have constituted scientific thought, but this, he insists, was not present in their thinking. Mithen notes that in their daily lives, Neanderthals, for example, were engaged in "planning, hypothesis testing, and meticulous observation of the natural world" but that this did not amount to an accumulation of knowledge over time. Mithen also points out that H. sapiens emerging in Africa about 130,000 years ago displayed a very different type of mentality—yet another transition in thought that can reasonably be seen as the emergence of a new mode of thought. Anatomically modern humans, according to him, that is, possessed a more complex language than their forebears, which made possible the emergence of a symbolic culture with a greater ability to invent and make use of technology. Nevertheless, not even in this context, according to Mithen, does one find the emergence of a scientific mode of thought but only the development of further foundations necessary for the emergence of science.

It is clear, therefore, that even if, as Mithen claims, all of the cognitive developments essential to the emergence of scientific thinking were in place by the end of the last Ice Age, that would not constitute evidence that scientific thinking actually existed in those societies. The new cognitive capacities that developed over time from the early hominids to anatomically modern human beings made possible significant technological advances, but they did not give birth to scientific thinking. As Mithen explains: "While the mixing of pigments, construction of dwellings, planning of foraging activities and the reading of tracks may have involved scientific modes of thought, these were most likely also intimately tied into religious beliefs which many would consider the precise opposite of scientific thinking" (Mithen 2002, 37). Despite the ambiguity in his reference here to "scientific modes of thought" rather than simply "elements" of a scientific mode of thought, Mithen concludes by acknowledging that "the emergence of science as a discrete domain of behaviour is likely to have required a suite of social, historic and economic circumstances that had not yet arisen in human history" (Mithen 2002, 40); a suite of behaviours involving "a very particular set of social and economic circumstances leading to an isolation of…[the religious and scientific] modes of thought from one another" (Mithen 2002, 37).

Interestingly, Tomasello denies that there is a radical discontinuity between our thought and that of our evolutionary forebears and yet also maintains that the human form of thinking is unique. For him,

> With modern humans and their skills of conventional linguistic communication, we get to full-blooded reasoning, where "reasoning" means not just to think about something but to explicate in conventional form—for others and oneself—the reasons why one is thinking what one is thinking.
> (Tomasello 2014, 110)

In his *Becoming Human* Tomasello draws on work by Hugo Mercier and Dan Sperber showing that this emerges from the perceived need of "epistemic vigilance" where one does not know everyone in the group of which they are members. "In this kind of social context," he writes:

> one could not expect others to accept a perspective or argument on trust. Individuals therefore started giving others reasons for why they should believe what they were telling them, typically pointing out facts that supported their view. Giving reasons in this way is a normative enterprise because it does not involve one individual attempting to overpower or coerce another into believing something, but rather it involves a third element—an impartial fact that does not depend on one's point of view—to adjudicate: "you do not have to take my word for it, just consider for yourself this reason." (Tomasello 2019, 171)

Thus, although claiming that this does not amount to a radical discontinuity of human thought from that of their evolutionary forebears, Tomasello nevertheless insists that human thought is "much more complex than the cognition and thinking of other primates" (Tomasello 2014, 124) and is therefore uniquely human. Although he points out that the processes of joint and collective intentionality that characterizes human thought at this stage "are universal in the human species," he also notes that they were expressed differently in different groups of humans because of "culturally specific cognitive skills and ways of thinking for their own local purposes" (Tomasello 2014, 141). Tomasello, no more than Mithen, then, believes that prehistoric human thought is a form of scientific thinking because it is not a mode of thought dedicated simply to achieving disinterested knowledge about the physical world but was selected for its role in supporting cooperative human behaviour of which little is seen in our evolutionary ancestors. However, like Mithen, Tomasello makes clear that the forms of "Western science and mathematics," as he puts it, would simply not have been possible without these earlier evolutionary cognitive developments (Tomasello 2014, 141, 142).

In *The Enigma of Reason*, Hugo Mercier and Dan Sperber, like Tomasello, recognize the need to provide an evolutionary explanation for reason and reasoning as peculiar human cognitive mechanisms. "While reason has obviously benefited from various cultural enhancements," they write, "the very ability of a species to produce, evaluate, and use reasons cries out for an evolutionary explanation" (Mercier and Sperber 2017, 3). Reason, they argue, is not synonymous with logic; it is rather a special form of inference which is the basic avenue to obtaining knowledge that goes beyond the power of the senses. They maintain therefore that an intellectualist approach that understands reason as a kind of "cognitive add-on" is simply unable to overcome the failure of past "sophisticated reasoning on reasoning ... [in] providing a consensual understanding of reasoning itself" (Mercier and Sperber 2017, 21).

Mercier and Sperber therefore reject the common sense picture of reason as providing the foundation for our beliefs and actions which, they point out, is not supported by the evidence. It is modules in the human brain that produce unconscious inferences that generate many of our beliefs and motivate human action. These modules have no need of reason in performing these functions and reason's role in human thought, therefore, must be sought elsewhere. Reason comes into the picture only after beliefs are formed—its true role being to justify the epistemic claims, and actions based on them. As Mercier and Sperber write, "reasons are for social consumption" (Mercier and Sperber 2017, 123); they are of great importance as aids to cooperative social interaction:

> Reason, we argue, is a mechanism of intuitive inferences about reasons to justify themselves and to convince others, two activities that play an essential role in their cooperation and communication …. [R]eason evolved as an adaptation to a very special ecological niche, a niche that humans built and maintain for themselves with their intense social relationships, powerful languages, and rich culture. (Mercier and Sperber 2017, 107)

Cooperative social interaction is essential in every society and its members will be called upon to justify the claims they make about the world and the behaviors in which they engage. So, "reason didn't evolve to enhance thinking on one's own but as a tool for social interaction" (Mercier and Sperber 2017, 333); it evolved for providing good reasons for a reticent audience for one's beliefs and actions. Reason, therefore, is a 'reputation management mechanism' to protect one's reputation as a solid citizen. According to Mercier and Sperber,

> By giving reasons to explain and justify yourself, you do several things. You influence the way people read your mind, judge your behavior, and speak of you. You commit yourself by implicitly acknowledging the normative force of the reasons you invoke. You encourage others to expect your future behavior to be guided by similar reasons (and to hold you accountable if it is not). You also indicate that you are likely to evaluate the behavior of others for reasons similar to those you invoke to justify yourself. Finally, you engage in a conversation where others may accept your justifications, question them, and invoke reasons of their own, a conversation that should help you coordinate with them and from which shared norms actually progressively emerge.
> (Mercier and Sperber 2017, 185–186)

Given this account then, reason is not itself a module in the brain. What has evolved, rather, is a more modest module—an intuitive inference module that produces intuitions about reasons (Mercier and Sperber 2017,

200–201). Reason, that is, did not evolve to be used by philosophers and metaphysicians, or in courts of law; rather, it evolved to be used in the informal contexts of people exchanging many short arguments in support of particular beliefs and actions.

Having provided a scientific account of reason and reasons, Mercier and Sperber nevertheless speak "in praise of reason" in their conclusion. They claim to have put reason back where it belongs, level with other cognitive mechanisms." But they acknowledge as well that, like other evolved cognitive mechanisms, reason is not only as complex, subtle, and powerful as are they, but that it "may well be the most original and characteristic feature of the human mind" (Mercier and Sperber 2017, 91).

In addition to its social function, they point out that "reasons" can "produce reflective conclusions about the things reasons are themselves about" (Mercier and Sperber, 329). In this respect reason can "exploit properties of reason in general [like] relevance, clarity, or strength" as well as specific types of reasons [such as] the force of precedent in reasons concerning coordination, from parent-children relationships to legal matters" (Mercier and Sperber 2017, 329). This makes reason useful not only for justifying oneself but also for "evaluating the arguments others produce to convince us." (Mercier and Sperber 2017, 332), and they admit that this kind of back-and-forth argumentation is something scientists can make use of in distinguishing good from bad argumentation in justifying knowledge claims about the world and its contents. In fact, philosophers of science like Karl Popper, for example, see scientific knowledge as the product of just such a back-and-forth process, a process Popper refers to as conjectural-refutational thinking.

Contrasting the scientific thought style to pre-scientific thought

This brief overview of the various transitions in the modes of thought in the evolutionary development of our non-human and pre-historic human forebears provides no evidence that any of them possessed something like our modern mode of scientific thought. There is simply no indication in that deep or proximate history of H. sapiens of the existence of a mode of thought that characterizes the modern sciences as they emerged in Europe in the sixteenth and seventeenth centuries. Even though all the cognitive capacities necessary for genuine scientific thought are there, it is clear that what Claude Lévi-Strauss and others have referred to as the "science of the concrete" or "archaic science" is essentially a matter of a new technology and not science. Lewis Wolpert, for example, writes in his *The Unnatural Nature of Science: Why Science Does Not Make (Common) Sense* that:

> The technological achievement of the ancient cultures was enormous, and Lévi-Strauss is right to pose the question of how it was achieved. But whatever process was involved, it was not based on science. There is no evidence of any theorizing about the processes involved in the technology nor about the reasons why it worked: for example, it was enough to know that adding charcoal to the molten mixture would accelerate the smelting of iron. Metalworking was an essentially practical craft based on common sense. The goals of the ordinary person in ancient times were practical ends such as sowing and hunting, and that practical orientation does not serve pure knowledge. Our brains, that is, were selected to help us survive in a complex environment; the generation of scientific ideas play no role in this process. (Wolpert 1993, 27)

Wolpert acknowledges that the centuries of learning through methodical observation and testing of hypotheses in archaic technological creations "makes it seem that primitive technology involved processes very similar to those of science," but, like Mithen and Tomasello, he points out that the learning process did not require theorizing of the kind found in the modern sciences (Wolpert 1993, 26). Wolpert, that is, rightly recognizes that our cognitive capacities were selected for dealing with our immediate environment and that the slow processes of critical reflection and scientific theorizing would have been useless in responding to the immediate needs of our forebears and dangerously slow in responding to the immediate dangers in their environment. In that context, he insists, seeking scientific understanding of the physical world would have been unnatural (Wolpert 1993, 11).

Historian Richard W. Bulliet also provides a particularly cogent and insightful critique of this notion of archaic science in his *Hunters, Herders, and Hamburgers: The Past and Future Human-Animal Relationships* where he shows why Lévi-Strauss's account of the domestication of animals was not the achievement, as Lévi-Stauss puts it, of a "genuinely scientific attitude, sustained and watchful interest and a desire for knowledge for its own sake" (quoted by Bulliet 2005, 102). Bulliet remarks:

> What prompts Lévi-Strauss to postulate early man engaging in a special type of long-term scientific thinking and experimentations is, in the specific case of animal domestication, his assumption that humans desired to derive material uses, "nutritious or technologically useful properties," in his words, from captive wild stock and could only be achieved through prolonged experimentation and observation, an application of "scientific thinking" and a quest for "knowledge for its own sake" seems to be the only answer. But would this assumption of a brief but amazingly productive spurt of scientific thought in Neolithic time have been required if affective uses had been taken into account? (Bulliet 2005, 103)

Bulliet says no. As he puts it:

> A cardinal difference between affective uses and material uses is immediate gratification. The warm feeling we get from playing with baby animals requires no time lapse and no quest for knowledge for its own sake. Nor does it require domestication. A baby wild animal is just as cuddly as a baby domestic animal...Historically, therefore, if immediately gratifying some sensibility played a significant role in prompting people to keep some specimens of a particular species captive over many generations, it might be possible to explain the eventual emergence of the genetic tameness in that species without recourse to theories of prehistoric scientific thought and a quest for knowledge for its own sake. In this scenario, the exploitation of products, talents, and labor would constitute subsequent discoveries arising well after the species had become genetically tractable. (Bulliet 2005, 105)

Understanding the deep history of the human mind as a cascade of cognitive capacities, with each successive stage in the evolution of H. sapiens increasing the range of knowledge available to the species, will make it possible for us to account for what anthropologist and philosopher Ernest Gellner calls the great gap between the primitive and the modern mind. Gellner describes this development in his essay "An Ethic of Cognition" as "the biggest, most conspicuous simple fact about the human world" (Gellner 1979, 175). Without recognizing that fact, the different cognitive capacities employed in primitive/archaic and modern communities, he argues, it will be impossible to understand the emergence and persistence of "religion" (religiosity and religions) or a scientific study of religion. In Gellner's essay "The Savage and the Modern Mind," he clearly spells out four distinctions between contemporary "primitive" and modern modes of thought. The first is the use of idiosyncratic norms in primitive thought in which norms are espoused that have both epistemic and moral import simultaneously. The scientific outlook of modern western societies is mechanistic, rather than "agentic" or "enchanted," and therefore is in conflict with traditional societies' provisions of a meaningful world-picture framed by their use of idiosyncratic norms—its "bending of the regularity expectations in the interest of the local status system," as Gellner phrases it (Gellner 1973, 172).

A second crucial distinction, Gellner argues, is found in the low cognitive division of labour found in primitive societies, which is accompanied by a proliferation of roles for individuals in such societies. The agentic or enchanted vision works, he argues,

> through the systematic conflation of descriptive, evaluative, identificatory, status-conferring, etc. role of language [and that] a sense of the separability

and fundamental distinctness of the various functions [originally and innocently introduced as a neutral analytical device], is the surest way to the disenchantment of the world. (Gellner 1973, 174)

In the modern context, once concepts become tools for explanation they cannot be allowed, on pain of the loss of coherence and efficiency, to be tools for other purposes. Gellner illustrates this point by showing how empiricist thought, for example, has discouraged what he calls "boundary-hopping" in the use of the same concept with respect to matters in the physical and transcendent worlds. "Orderly and regular conduct," he writes, "is exacted from concepts, as it is from people" (Gellner 1973, 176).

A third crucial area of distinction between the primitive and modern modes of thought Gellner maintains is the diffused and persuasive quality of what he calls the entrenched clauses of the intellectual constitution of the primitive mind. Gellner is fully aware that all societies have such entrenched clauses, ("sacred," that is, untouchable and unquestionable claims), but are much more numerous and extensive in primitive societies. In modern societies, he writes, "much less of the fabric of life and society benefits from reinforcement from the sacred or entrenched convictions" (Gellner 1973, 178).

"Diplomatic immunity of cognition" is Gellner's rubric for a fourth significant distinction between the primitive and modern modes of thought. By "cognitive immunity" Gellner means that in modern societies ever greater areas of knowledge acquire autonomy from "the social, moral, and political obligations and decencies of society" (Gellner 1973, 176). In primitive societies, as he points out, knowledge claims are subject to the same kinds of obligations and sanctions as are other kinds of conduct, whereas in modern societies this is not so—knowledge claims are not controlled according to the effects they may have, for example, on faith claims. This is especially important since such epistemic autonomy does not mean that epistemically justified knowledge claims are not necessarily philosophically (or religiously) neutral and can, therefore, and often do, come into conflict with the entrenched clauses of older traditional belief-systems. That is precisely why knowledge claims require autonomy relative to the social, political, moral, and religious orders of society. Thus, as Gellner writes in his "Pragmatism and the Importance of Being Earnest," "what distinguishes the scientific thought style from pre-scientific ones is notably the fact that instead of satisfying many criteria—including social cohesion, authority-maintenance, morale, etc.—it sheds all but one, i.e., explanatory power and congruence with the facts" (Gellner 1981, 55).

It is clear from Gellner's analysis of primitive/archaic thought that there exists a great gulf between it and the scientific mode of thought found in modern human society. He argues that an explanation for the steps in our evolution that ultimately made possible the emergence of our modern sciences is necessary. As noted above, Tomasello has pointed out that we see in the flourishing human cultures found in Europe 40,000 years ago a full-blooded mode of thinking that rested on modern human skills and capacities for linguistic communication which provides the potential for the emergence of a science-like mode of thinking but does not itself amount to scientific thinking. It appears, moreover, that it is precisely the narrative mode of human thinking that made possible that full-blooded mode of thinking that also constituted a road-block of sorts to moving from a mythic to a theoretic/scientific stage of human thought. The transition from mimetic to mythological thinking, Donald points out, created "a predominantly narrative mode of thinking" (Donald 1991, 257): "Group narrative skills," he writes, "leads to a collective version of reality; the narrative is almost always public" (Donald 1991, 257). This is a type of knowledge very different from the natural history knowledge and technical knowledge essential to the welfare of hunter-gatherer societies, and it is as differently motivated from the objectives underlying archaic technology and natural history knowledge as it is from the modern objective of seeking knowledge for its own sake. It amounts to the social construction of reality. As historian of science, H. Floris Cohen argued in his *The Scientific Revolution: An Historical Inquiry*, our archaic forebears encased their knowledge of the physical, biological, and social realms in the "framework of a larger conception of how things in the universe cohere," expressed in stories projecting purpose and meaning into both the animate and inanimate world around them (Cohen 1994, 506). They made sense of their world in terms of the intentions of human and non-human agents. The naturalness of this agent-oriented mode of thought, as Donald has pointed out, dominated Upper Palaeolithic, Mesolithic, and Neolithic societies and still persists in some fashion today. As Donald states: "[i]t continues today in many traditions, and its vestiges are still highly visible in some sectors of postindustrial civilization. Its exact outer boundary cannot easily be drawn" (Donald 1991, 275). A causality-oriented mode of thought, claims Donald, has, clearly, "become the dominant thought form of postindustrial society" and although it has not wholly displaced religio-mythic thought socially, it undermines its epistemic credibility, a project that required "a wrenching cultural transformation" (Donald 1991, 275) often referred to as a process of demythologization, or disenchantment, of the world.

Conclusion

The evidence provided by evolutionary cognitive science and the 'pre-history' of H. sapiens clearly supports Mithen's view that "the emergence of science as a discrete domain of behaviour is likely to have required a suite of social, historical and economic circumstances that had not yet arisen in human history [with our archaic forebears]" (Mithen 2002, 40). I am persuaded by Donald's claim that the cultural transformation of the human mind, which he refers to broadly as the emergence of the theoretic attitude, occurred in ancient Greece (Donald 1991,340). Lewis Wolpert also presents a formidable argument in support of the claim that this transformation occurred in ancient Greece. However, unlike Wolpert, I do not believe that what emerged in ancient Greece amounted to what we today think of as science. Wolpert is certainly correct in his claim that "unlike technology or religion," a transition away from and toward a science-like mode of thought originated "only once in history in Greece" (Wolpert 1993, 35). Following Karl Popper, I believe the evidence will show that the mode of thought developed by the Milesian philosopher-cosmologists amounted to an enlightenment of sorts that ultimately made possible the emergence of a genuinely scientific mode of thought in sixteenth- and seventeenth-century Europe. Proving that matter, however, will be the burden of the remaining chapters of the book.

— 3 —

From Myth to Proto-Science: A Transformational Turning Point in the History of Human Thought

Introduction

In this chapter I will trace the cultural transformation of the human mind that cognitive scientists have argued was essential for the emergence of a science-like mode of thought as a discrete domain of human behaviour. Such a transformation, that is, would have required significant changes in the social, political, economic, and cultural conditions of human existence. Given the significant agreement among scientists and historians that such favourable conditions conducive to the birth of new intellectual pursuits first occurred in Ancient Greece, I will focus attention here on what can best be described as the demythologization of ancient thought, a necessary preliminary development making possible the eventual emergence of scientific thinking.

The revolutionary character of pre-Socratic thought

Implicit in the thought of the pre-Socratic cosmologists from the Milesians to the Atomists lies a new understanding of "knowledge" in which beliefs are open to rational criticism and assessment. This kind of knowledge about the world and states of affairs in the world simply amounts to the espousal of beliefs about an objectively existing reality that has found rational and evidential support. This "knowledge as rationally justifiable beliefs" stands in radical contrast to knowledge as metaphysical "Truths" regarding indisputable realities such as the gods and the meaning of life vouchsafed to people either by way of revelation, intuition, or imagination. Such "Truths" are, in effect, local world views—that is, products of the human mind—rather than accounts of a purely rationally established reality. The transition from knowledge as "Truth" to knowledge as comprising beliefs that under rational criticism are potentially either true or false amounts to the creation of a new cultural value of "knowledge as rationally justified belief for the sake of that knowledge alone." It is the emergence of this new conception of knowledge as entirely reliant on autonomous reason that constitutes a "critical episode" in the development of human thought essential to the eventual emergence of science (and of the scientific study of religion) as we understand it today.

Half a century ago, Jan de Vries gave serious attention to the importance of intellectual developments in ancient Greece for the field of Religious Studies as an academic discipline. Most important for de Vries, was the work of the Ionian (Milesian) natural philosophers which, he maintains, "wiped out the whole system of solid and simple belief in the Olympic gods" among the intellectuals of Athens, many of whom ultimately produced reductionist theoretical explanations of religion and the gods (de Vries 1967, 5–6). "In company with the speculations of the philosophers," de Vries noted in his comments on Herodotus, "mention should be made of the germ of a science of religion, which one is almost inclined to call 'ethnological'" (de Vries 1967, 11).

I am not persuaded by de Vries's suggestion that we can see the germ of a science of religion in the thought of the Ionian natural philosophers and other pre-Socratic intellectuals. Nor am I persuaded by others who see the Ionians as having created science or a "truly scientific outlook." I am convinced, however, that this period in the history of human thought constitutes a "critical episode" in the ultimate emergence and development of a scientific study of religion that, at times, has flourished in some of our research universities. Ionian cosmological thought seems, in fact, not only to have undermined naive belief in the Olympian gods, but nurtured various forms of atheism, and fostered reductionist explanations for belief in gods and 'the divine.' Pre-Socratic thought, however, is not uniform in this regard. Other pre-Socratics provided alternative accounts of the gods, including the construction of what we would today refer to as natural theologies, as well as sophisticated conceptions of "the divine" that seem indistinguishable from the elemental substance or substances of their explanatory accounts of the cosmos. Although the emergence and development of atheism in this period —as a more radical form of criticism of religion than that contained in the sophisticated forms of religious thought just mentioned—was a significant factor in making a scientific study of religion possible, the very possibility of such criticism is itself the result of a more general revolutionary development in human thought. The attempt to explain the world without reference to myth and religion, that is, involves a "transitional mode of thought" that unconsciously amounted to a disenchantment of the world in favour of knowledge of the world that ultimately provided the foundation for a genuinely scientific study not only of the natural world but of the social world as well. That is, knowledge for the sake of knowledge alone, as well as the emergence of a form of critical reason (reasoning) as a non-moral instrument of inquiry necessary for obtaining such knowledge, emerged unintentionally as new cultural values from the "religiously disinterested this-worldliness" of pre-Socratic thought (Guthrie 1950, 92).

In this chapter I set out the import of the two hundred or so years of pre-Socratic thought for the emergence and development of a scientific study of religion and religions in our modern research universities. My objective here is not that of trying to make a new and original contribution to "pre-Socratic studies," or to interpretive studies of the fragments of any or several of the major pre-Socratic philosophers. There is more than one mountain of critical analyses and philosophical interpretations by experts in this field and I hope here to take the measure of those studies insofar as they relate to their relevance for scientific study of religion and religions. I will focus attention, for the most part, on the Milesian/Ionian cosmologists who were the first thinkers who attempted to provide a wholly rational account of the nature of the world in terms of a primary material substrate and natural processes of its transformation, and their successors, that found its culmination in the atomism of Leucippus of Miletus and Democritus of Abdera. As G. S. Kirk, J. E. Raven, and M. Schofield put it: "Atomism is in many ways the crown of Greek philosophical achievement before Plato. It fulfilled the Ultimate aim of Ionian material monism..." (Kirk, Raven, and Schofield 1983, 433). I agree here with Kirk, et al. that it is important "not to exaggerate the sheer irrationality" of the pre-Milesian thinkers (Kirk, Raven, and Schofield 1983, 72) and to recognize that Hesiod, for example, exercised "a useful kind of reasonableness in grading and synthesizing tales from different regions and with different emphases" (Kirk, Raven, and Schofield 1983,73). However, Kirk et al. also recognize that while many early Greek philosophers were slow in rejecting a mythic mode of thought, the Milesian revolution ultimately resulted in the substitution of logical and critical rational thought for myth in accounting for the world. The Milesians must in hindsight, then, be seen as having crossed a threshold in human modes of thought made possible not in terms of new cognitive capacities of the human brain but by significant changes in Greek society and culture.

It must be acknowledged that there are significant difficulties for scholars to have total confidence in understanding and in justifying their claims regarding the pre-Socratics. Some may think, therefore, that this uncertainty will cast doubt on my claims about the import of pre-Socratic thought for the study of religion. I recognize that judgments reached on the basis of this scholarship will be less than conclusive but I believe it will provide a reasonable (i.e. a non-arbitrary and plausible) basis for my claims about the revolutionary character of early pre-Socratic thought.

Recognizing ambiguity of the evidence

Daniel Graham—editor of *The Texts of Early Greek Philosophy: The Complete Fragments and Selected Testimonies of the Major Presocratics* (2010)—rightly points out that what we know of pre-Socratic thought is only available in fragments and from reports on their thought by other philosophers, doxographers, and biographers who have made use of their work to support their own interests. This, clearly, is a serious handicap. As G.E.R. Lloyd warns: "We should never underestimate how difficult it is to recover ancient aims, goals, preoccupations, and expectations" (Lloyd 2004, 188). Even though Graham insists that no one is in a position "to offer any final readings" of the pre-Socratic fragments, he acknowledges that contemporary philosophers have been able to "offer increasingly sophisticated interpretations" of them (Graham 2010, 13). It is on the basis of such modern and contemporary interpretations of pre-Socratic thought that I will rely in arguing that the Milesians created a new, transitional, mode of thought that was not wholly under the constraints of myth and religion. I agree, for example, with J.-P Vernant's assessment that this Milesian mode of thought grew out of the past as well as away from it, and it is this growth away from the mythic past that crosses the threshold separating mythopetic and religious modes of thought from a new critically rational mode of thought (Vernant 1983, 365). Nevertheless, I remain aware that this assessment may be tagged as the product of "retrospective history," as historian of philosophy Michael Frede labels it. He writes: "it is very much in hindsight that we can see that Thales [of Miletus] started a tradition that contributed to the formation of the discipline that came to be known as philosophy" (Frede 1996, 6). Frede further claims that there "is no reason to suppose that Thales conceived of the wisdom he aspired to as entirely a matter of theoretical insight" (Frede, 1996, 8). However, this does not constitute evidence in support of Frede's claim that Thales' cosmological speculation was wholly constrained by his pursuit of a "broader wisdom." Indeed, Frede admits that "we have to acknowledge that the Presocratics from Thales to Democritus, as part of the general concern for wisdom, tried to provide an account of reality as a theory of nature" (Frede, 1996, 8). It is precisely that interest in a theory of nature that constitutes a revolutionary development in the long history of human thought, whether or not Thales intended to create that new tradition.

I am somewhat uncomfortable in trying to make a case that pre-Socratic philosophy as a whole constituted a significant "episode" in ultimately making possible the scientific study of religion and religions. My anxiety is of a similar nature to that of Francis M. Cornford who wrote that any student in any branch of knowledge knows

> the expert will frown upon some of his statements as questionable in content and dogmatic in tone, and will mark the omission of many things for which no room could be found. But it will do him good to sit back in his chair and look for the main outline, so often obscured by detail. (Cornford 1965, ix)

Like Cornford, I think it possible for us to discern ways in which the early Greek philosophers contributed to the emergence and development of what we today recognize as science.

The centrality of Socrates to clarifying the evidence

I shall begin my examination of the contribution of pre-Socratic philosophy to modern life by drawing on Cornford's claim that Socrates must be seen as a central figure in assessing that influence because of Socrates' "conversion of philosophy from the study of Nature to the study of human life" (Cornford 1965, ix). Cornford's account of that conversion of philosophy brilliantly, but inadvertently, captures the significance of the Milesians' transitional mode of thought that breaks free of what Gilbert Murray (1946) called the "inherited conglomerate" of ancient Greek culture even though Conford overstates its accomplishment as science.

Cornford's aim in his *Before and After Socrates* is "so to describe the early Ionian science as to show why it failed to satisfy Socrates" (Cornford 1965, ix), and to present Socrates' thought as "revolutionary" (Cornford 1965, 1). I will show, however, that a critical analysis of Cornford's argument will reveal the thought of the Milesian/Ionian cosmologists to be a genuinely revolutionary development in the history of human thought and Socrates' "philosophy" to be counter-revolutionary. That Ionian transitional thought, however, is best understood as an "extended patchy revolution," (Wooton 20015) starting with the Milesians and culminating in the thought of the Atomists roughly two hundred years later. The new, non-mythic, mode of thought of the atomists, described by Benjamin Farrington as "an admirable introduction to scientific culture [and] an admirable training in rational thought," was achieved in a step-wise fashion, as he explains, "marked by the names of Thales, Anaximander, Anaximenes, Pythagoras, Parmenides,

Zeno, Melissus, Empedocles, Anaxagoras, Leucippus and Democritus... These names mark an epoch in the history of humanity" (Farrington 1965, 60). Thales, as Farrington claims in his *Science in Antiquity*, is the first person "known to history to have offered a general explanation of nature without invoking the aid of any power outside history" (Farrington 1936, 40). In his later *Greek Science* Farrington points to the significant difference in the Babylonian account of the appearance of the world as involving the god Marduk fashioning a rush mat piled high with dirt that rests upon the sea from that of Thales' account of the world as also resting on water by pointing out that "[w]hat Thales did was to leave Marduk out" (Farrington 1944, 30). Even though this development did not create science as we understand it today, with the Milesian cosmologists, as I have intimated above, an "incipient new mode of thought" appeared, not wholly distinct from what preceded it, yet a new, religiously and mythically disinterested way of thinking about the world that played a significant role in the eventual emergence of modern Western science and, therefore, the possibility of a scientific study of religions.

Socrates turned his back on this "science-like" tradition of thought which sought to provide a theoretical account of the world, and nearly brought that tradition of rational cosmological thinking to an end. As Kirk, et al. put it:

> [U]nder the mature Socrates and the Sophists, the old cosmological approach—by which the primary aim was to explain the outside world as a whole, man being considered only incidentally—was gradually replaced by a humanistic approach to philosophy, by which the study of man became no longer subsidiary but the starting-point of all inquiry.
> (Kirk, Raven, and Schofield 1983, 452; emphasis added)

Although one must also agree with Kirk, et al. that this "reorientation" of philosophy was in some sense a natural product of the pre-Socratic movement itself, (even though also determined in part by social factors), this does not undermine the counter-revolutionary character of Socratic thought; Socrates' "humanistic" approach to understanding "man," that is, amounted to a return to a modified form of mythopoetic thought. Cornford, I think, captured that difference perfectly in the following passage:

> The Socratic philosophy is a reaction against this [Ionian] materialistic drift of physical science. In order to rediscover the spiritual world, philosophy had to give up, for the moment, the search after material substance in external Nature, and turn its eyes inwards to the nature of the human soul. This was the revolution accomplished by Socrates, with his Delphic injunction "Know thyself." (Cornford 1965, 27–28; emphasis added)

It is clear, then, that Socrates represents not a revolutionary development in human thought but a reactionary and counter-revolutionary development because Socrates saw religiously disinterested Ionian cosmological thinking as a crisis for society that can only be resolved by a return to a religiously interested, self-involving mode of thought.

Even though the Ionian development is not the birth of what we understand as modern science, it does amount to a new mode of thought both continuous and discontinuous with that which precedes it, and Cornford is fully aware of this. "All the histories of Greek philosophy from Aristotle's time to this day," he writes,

> begin with Thales of Miletus. It is generally agreed, [he continues], that with him something new, that we call Western science, appeared in the world—science as commonly defined: the pursuit of knowledge for its own sake, not for any practical use it can be made to serve.
> (Cornford 1965, 5; emphasis added)

Although disagreeing with Cornford's definition of science here, he rightly recognizes that what has emerged with the Milesians is the new cultural value of seeking knowledge for the sake of knowledge alone that is so characteristic of modern science. As Cornford puts it, Milesian thought

> is marked by the tacit denial of this distinction between two orders of knowledge, experience and revelation, and between the two corresponding orders of existence, the natural and the supernatural. The Ionian cosmogonists assume (without even feeling the need to make the assertion) that the whole universe is natural, and potentially within the reach of knowledge as ordinary and rational as our knowledge that fire burns and water drowns.
> (Cornford 1965, 14–15)

As I have intimated above, I am in agreement with Lloyd that the Ionian mode of thought is not a simple and "sudden breakthrough" to "truly modern science" (Lloyd 2004, 13). There was no quantum leap here, no absolute discontinuity from all that preceded it. The pre-Socratics as a whole only slowly rejected—overcame—what Gilbert Murray described as "the thick atmosphere of tradition and convention" (Murray 1946, 66) that defined their society. In *Demystifying Mentalities* Lloyd points out that science emerges, at least in part, due to "a rhetoric of legitimation," (Lloyd 1990, 43) but he also insists that Greek science is not either just a myth or magic (Lloyd 1990, 70). I find his earlier discussion of Greek science in his *Magic, Reason, and Experience* to the effect that there is general agreement that between the sixth and fourth centuries BCE a new mode of thought emerged that has some appearance of being scientific even though it is also continuous with myth and magic, reasonable in light of his insistence that the new mode of thought has "some features of a paradigm switch" (Lloyd, 1979, 26-27). Without having to assume that there was a uniform set of beliefs among pre-Socratic thinkers as to the ideas (concepts) of cause and effect, and without drawing conclusions about the nature of ancient Greek speculative thought as a whole (Lloyd 1979, 233), Lloyd arrives at a conclusion that I find reasonably encapsulates the achievements of the Milesian cosmologists and many of their successors. As he sees it:

> The development of philosophy and science in ancient Greece is a unique turning-point in the history of thought. So far as the Western world goes, our science is continuous with, and may be said to originate in, that of ancient Greece. (Lloyd 1979, 264)

In the following section I will lay out briefly what that unique turning-point amounts to.

Transcending myth: Not a miracle, just an extended patchy revolution

In his "Prolegommena to the Study of Ancient Philosophy" Gilbert Murray describes "inherited conglomerates" as "the thick atmosphere of tradition and convention" found in almost all thought in ancient human societies within which thought is "stifled and imprisoned." "One of the great lessons which anthropology has taught us," he continues, "is the overpowering influence on mankind of tradition and tribal custom, of inherited taboos and superstitions" (Murray 1946, 66). Murray rightly notes that even though "these inherited conglomerates have practically no chance of being true or even sensible," it seems that "no society can exist without them or even submit to any drastic correction of them without social danger (Murray 1946, 67). Despite these claims, however, Murray also points out that the early Greek philosophers paid little or no regard to the Olympian gods and that "as soon as philosophy began [they] rose above their traditions and conventions" (Murray, 1946, 69, 71).

Karl Popper's essay "Back to the Presocratics" provides a brilliant analysis of the Milesian cosmologists that supports Murray's claim about philosophy transcending the "inherited conglomerate" as well as Lloyd's claim about philosophical thought in ancient Greece constituting a unique turning-point in the development of human thought. Like Murray, Popper is aware of how early Greek thought had been stifled and imprisoned in tradition. According to Popper, the Milesian cosmologists freed themselves from the "inherited conglomerate" by limiting their interests to seeking knowledge of how the world came to be what it is, and by creating a new way of achieving such knowledge by substituting critical debate and rational discussion for myth and religious revelation as legitimate sources of knowledge. Thales, Popper maintains, actively encouraged criticism of his views rather than encasing them in unchallengeable narratives (myths). This, Popper argues, was a "momentous innovation" because it led

> to the realization that our attempts to see and to find the truth are not final, but open to improvement; that our knowledge, our doctrine, is conjectural; that it consists of guesses, of hypotheses, rather than final and certain truths; and that criticism and critical discussion are our only means of getting nearer to the truth. (Popper 1965, 151)

Popper arrived at this conclusion by way of a close examination of the structure of Anaximander's theory of the architecture of the cosmos which, he argues, could only have been derived by way of criticising Thales' theory. Thales, according to Popper, was the first thinker to try to understand the structure of the cosmos and to determine the material of which it is made. Anaximander, likely a student of Thales, sought the same kind of knowledge but was not persuaded by Thales' account of the cosmos. For Thales, the stable position of the earth was predicated on the assumption that it was supported by water. Anaximander, it appears, was clearly aware that if such a theory were developed consistently it would lead to an infinite regress, requiring a similar hypothesis to account for the stability of the ocean upon which the earth floats. Anaximander's theory avoids this problem by hypothesizing that the earth is a globe situated at the centre of the universe and encircled by spheres on which the planets and stars were fixed. Anaximander, that is, attempts to account for the stability of the earth by appealing to its structural symmetry and the equality of its distance from all other bodies in the universe.

Popper sees Anaximenes as the least productive of the Milesian cosmologists but recognizes that, although he misunderstood Anaximander's theory, he did not shrink from criticizing it. Heraclitus and Parmenides, among other pre-Socratic philosophers, Popper argues, also adopted this mode of thought in trying to understand the nature of the cosmos, leading ultimately to Leucippus and Democritus. Following these debates and discussions, he writes, amounts to a "splendid story" that is "almost too good to be true" (Popper 1965, 148). "In every generation" of the pre-Socratics, he continues, "we find at least one new philosophy, one new cosmology of staggering originality and depth" made possible by the development of a tradition of critical thought that contributed not only to an escape from the "inherited conglomerate" of ancient Greece, but to laying the groundwork for the ultimate emergence of modern science. As Popper writes:

> I assert that there is the most perfect possible continuity of thought between...[the theories of the Presocratics] and the later development of physics. Whether they are called philosophers, pre-scientists, or scientists matters very little, I think. But I do assert that Anaximander's theory cleared the way for the theories of Aristarchus, Copernicus, Kepler, and Galileo.
> (Popper 1965, 141)

According to Popper, then, the hypotheses/theories of the Milesians clearly indicate that they were not interested either in reforming religion or in attempting to replace it. With respect to the objective of explaining the cosmos, they simply ignored it. This does not mean, however, that there is absolutely no continuity of thought from the pre-Milesians to the early Milesian and other pre-Socratic philosophers. W.K.C. Guthrie, for example, has rightly reminded those interested in the earliest Greek philosophers to remember "how close were the Greeks in early times, and many of the common people throughout the classical period, to the magical stage of thought" (Guthrie 1950, 12). E. R. Dodds was entirely right to criticise as "naive and historically inaccurate" those who see "rationality bursting miraculously and full-blown onto the scene of human history at the time of the Milesians, totally distinct from the form of thought that precedes it" (Dodds 1951, 108). More recently Richard McKirahan has also pointed out that the Milesians took over much from Homer and Hesiod including "a belief in the divine governance of the world" (McKirahan 1994, 71).

Despite these reminders of continuity between ancient Greek myth and Milesian/Ionian philosophy, however, it is neither naive nor historically inaccurate to investigate the question as to whether there exists a significant difference between the mythic and Milesian modes of thought that follows on the heels of leaving the gods out of consideration in the search for an understanding of the cosmos. The question of continuity and discontinuity between the old and the new in the historical development of societies and cultures, that is, is not much different from the same issue in biology which recognizes that continuity in the evolution of species does not exclude development; that is, discontinuity. One need not, therefore, ignore the effect of the "inherited conglomerate" in the thought of the early Greek philosophers in order to recognize the genuinely new contributions made by them. This is clearly demonstrated by Robert Hahn in his account of how Anaximander's work builds on that of Hesiod. Anaximander's work, as he characterizes it, is a "rationalized version of Hesiod's Theogony [and] an Hellenized version of the Babylonian creation story, the Enuma elish" and not a mythological account (Hahn 2010, 11). Anaximander's account of the cosmos, that is, makes no reference to divine beings in order to determine the substance of which the world is made or to explain its structure.

I am not suggesting here that the "shelving of the Olympian gods" by the early Ionian thinkers amounted to an espousal of atheism tout court. However, their attempt to understand the world independent of religious thought and public cult amounts to a form of methodological atheism. Whether they were religious or not, that is, it is clear that their intellectual interests were simply to gain knowledge about the world—its primary substance, the principles of transformation of that substance, and the architecture of the universe and all that is in it—supported by reason and rational speculation and therefore open to criticism. Such a rational approach to understanding the world is, so to speak, methodologically incommensurable with mythic or religious accounts that invoke divine agents who capriciously intervene not only in human social events in the world but also in its natural processes. Their thinking, therefore, amounts to the crossing of an epistemic threshold that ultimately made possible a disenchantment of the world (by displacing agentic explanations in favour of natural/mechanical explanations) and the production of criticisable knowledge claims. They displaced narrative with argument in their accounts of the world. It is in this sense that one can speak of a Milesian/Ionian/pre-Socratic revolution in human thought—referring to the development from the Milesians to the Atomists—despite the fact there is a degree of continuity between it and the mythic and quasi-rational modes of thought from which it emerged.

In formulating this argument, however, it should nevertheless be borne in mind that it is not the case that archaic societies antedating these philosophical developments did not investigate natural phenomena. It is obvious that our brains evolved for understanding and dealing with the immediate, everyday-ordinary world around us. Had our archaic forebears not been able to grasp/understand the external world for what it is, they would not have survived. However, as historian of science H. Floris Cohen, among other historians and paleoanthropologists, has argued, such knowledge was not carried out in a systematic and socially and culturally disinterested fashion. It was, rather, generally pursued within the framework of what he calls "a larger conception of how things in the universe cohere"—that is, within a narrative (mythic and metaphysical) framework of meaning. Moreover, I think Cohen is entirely right to argue that even if it had been "pursued as an activity in its own right [as with the Milesians], it is most unlikely to have survived at all" (Cohen 1994, 506). Anthropologist and philosopher Ernest Gellner in his account of the radical difference between "The Savage and the Modern Mind" (1973) also captures the essence of this development from traditional pragmatic societal interests in the natural world to a more focused and neutral interest in knowledge of the natural world for its own sake. In his analysis of the "gap" between archaic (mythopoetic) and modern modes of thought, he points out, for example, that the mythopoetic mode of thought in traditional societies provides a general vision of what is normal for society—its social and moral order—which grounds a framework of meaning within which its members function and constitutes its cognitive baseline for understanding the world. In such traditional societies, that is, there is a systematic conflation of the descriptive, evaluative, and status-conferring role of language that produces an enchanted framework of existence. What the early Greek philosophers achieved, to use Gellner's language, was to provide autonomy to knowledge from "the social, moral and political obligations and decencies of society." The pre-Socratic philosophers, therefore, even if not with conscious intent, in effect created a new cultural value of "knowledge for the sake of knowledge alone" that gave it what Gellner calls "diplomatic immunity" from all other cultural values and catapulted the Greeks beyond their "inherited (mythic) conglomerate." This intellectual achievement, as I note above, amounted to the crossing of a threshold in human modes of thought which can only be attributed to significant changes in the structure of Greek society, a matter that does not need elaboration here.

Religion, criticism, and the disenchantment of the world

A summary of the intellectual achievements of the "Milesian revolution" that have contributed to making a scientific study of religion possible include both those developments that have, in the long run, contributed to the emergence of modern Western science two millennia later, and those that opened contemporary religion and religious thought to criticism. It is somewhat artificial to see these developments as independent from each other, but it will be helpful to look at them separately.

What is clear from the history of scholarship on the pre-Socratic achievement—viewed as a cumulative development from the Milesians to the Atomists—is that even though this revolution cannot be accredited with the creation of a fully scientific mode of thought, it provided the foundation for its future development. It did so, one might say, in its inadvertent disenchantment of the world by way of its focused interest in explaining the physical/natural world. In seeking an explanation for the world in terms of a primal substance and transformations of that substance via physical/mechanical causes rather than by way divine agency, the Milesians "discovered nature," which, in a sense, involved displacing the gods. The Milesians, that is, depended upon the creation of criticisable conjectures as to the "nature" of the physical/natural world and, with respect to their primary intellectual objectives, they ignored the mythic narratives about the inscrutable (uncriticisable) will of the gods. They depended instead on the unaided use of reason—autonomous reason as a kind of non-moral instrument of inquiry—in an intellectual atmosphere of critical discussion of one anothers' hypotheses. Maria Michela Sassi describes this transition in thought as follows in her book on *The Beginnings of Philosophy in Greece* (2018 [2009]):

> By setting aside the idea of the gods as authors of the cosmic order, the Ionian cosmologies open an entirely new horizon; new manufacturers of knowledge independent of ritual are reclaiming ownership of a concept of the cosmos that is quite free from mythical representation. (Sassi 2018, 60)

In proceeding as they did, therefore, the pre-Socratics created several elements essential to the eventual development of scientific thought, namely, the liberation of reason from the constraints of a narrative (mythic—intuitive or revelational) mode of thinking and the creation of a new cultural value of "knowledge for the sake of knowledge alone." Furthermore, by not paying attention to the stories of the gods in Homer and Hesiod in their accounts of the cosmos, the Milesians not only undermined the myths as sources of knowledge—rather than as mere beliefs—about the world, they opened up the possibility of making the gods themselves objects of religiously disinterested (that is, a Popperian conjectural-refutational type of) explanation. Belief in the gods was subjected to reforming criticism and even given up entirely. The gods were often seen as mere human contrivances and, therefore, metaphysically non-existent. Consequently we see in the pre-Socratics, and in the atheism and atheist theories of religion they spawned, "the germ of a science of religion" (de Vries 1967, 11).

The disbelief in the old mythological conceptions of the gods (and other forms of atheism) does not comprise the whole of the pre-Socratic tradition. Xenophanes' reforming criticism of Olympian religion is a well-known example of this. Although Xenophanes had acquired an Ionian scientific outlook he did not reject belief in, or simply ignore, the gods. He was clearly aware of how the conception and descriptions of the gods varied from one culture to another. His interest appears to have been spurred by the potential for the harmful influence of beliefs in the gods on human behaviour. He rejected the widespread belief that Homer and Hesiod possessed superhuman or special mental abilities that permitted them to see the gods, and denounced the way they depicted the gods. Nevertheless, he still held a belief in the gods. Although his conception of the gods was still anthropomorphic in character, it was a moral improvement on the Olympian theology of Homer and Hesiod that held sway among the general populace in ancient Greece. Moreover, his argument for a morally more acceptable belief about the gods was presented not on the basis of a revelation but as rationally justifiable.

Xenophanes' explicit concern with transforming the widespread Homeric perception of the gods disseminated through the general populace is but one type of argument in support of belief in the existence of the divine in ancient Greek society. Belief in the divine, even if only implicit, persisted even among the intelligentsia despite the fact that although the "philosophers threw off the artificial creations of 'Homer and Hesiod,' [they] could not get rid of the more primitive and instinctive religion"—what Gilbert Murray called the "inherited conglomerate" (Murray 1946, 71). Jan Bremmer (2007) similarly points out that the atheism of the ancient Greeks was not a genuine rejection of belief in the gods but was rather a "soft atheism" involving the mere rejection of the gods as expressed in popular belief. Philosopher James Thrower put forward a similar view writing: "What is certainly true [about the pre-Socratics] is that they laid the foundations for the decline of the old mythological conception of the gods and of traditional religion—though this, of course, only at the intellectual level" (Thrower 2000, 17). Thrower further maintains that one can discern in the pre-Socratic period "the beginnings of a more sophisticated conception of the divine which will in Plato and Aristotle to a large extent displace the traditional religion and in its later developments became a genuine alternative to it" (Thrower 2000, 33). Richard McKirahan, in summarizing the results of his examination of the pre-Socratics, also maintains that although they did "away with gods governed by human passions, emotions, and caprices" in accounting for the world purely in terms of natural processes (McKirahan 1994, 70-71), he nevertheless insists that the Milesians were "unanimous in recognizing the divine nature of their primary substances ..." (McKirahan 1994, 60), a theme already presented by Werner Jaeger in his *The Theology of the Early Greek Philosophers* (1947). David Sedley in his *Creationism and Its Critics in Antiquity*, moreover, maintains that in pre-Socratics like Anaxagoras and

Empedocles we find the assumption that the world is governed by a divine power and that it is therefore not possible to assume that the naturalistic thinking of the pre-Socratics and religion are "mutually exclusive modes of thought" (Sedley 2007, 31)—a somewhat odd conclusion given that the Phaedo presents Socrates as questioning the coherence of Anaxagoras' philosophy which ultimately was the reason for Socrates' rejection of the entire tradition of cosmological speculation in the philosophical thought that preceded him.

There should be no surprise that belief in the Olympian gods was widespread among the general population of ancient Greece. Nor should we be surprised to find that some pre-Socratic thinkers rejected the notion that any and every belief in a "divine" reality of some kind amounted to the espousal of an irrational belief. It is clear that some attempted to "purify" traditional anthropomorphic religious beliefs by supplanting them with belief in a kind of non-anthropomorphic religionism that they considered to be complementary to the kind of knowledge of the natural world that interested the ancient Greek cosmologists. Such beliefs persist even today in a world that most scholars and intellectuals think of as scientific. As physicist Richard Feynman has claimed, scientists have perpetually made discoveries about our world for the past few hundred years, but not in the sense that science has played a large part in art, literature, or in the general population's attitudes to and understandings of the world (Feynman 1998, 62-63). The epistemic value of religious belief, however, is ambiguous at best when compared with the kind of belief claims about the nature of the world and its contents that were open to critical discussion and possible rejection (an early form of falsification) that characterized the "epistemic results" of the new Milesian-to-Atomist methodology. The problem is particularly obvious with the application of this "new methodology" to the gods and religion as part of the "contents" of the world. It is unclear, that is, whether such religious belief—belief in the reality of divinity—actually transcends the boundaries of myth. It does not appear that it can. Paul Veyne, in his *Did the Greeks Believe in their Myths: An Essay on the Constitutive Imagination*, maintains, that myth and reason are not opposites since "[n]o positivist criticism can adequately deal with mythology and the supernatural" (Veyne 1988, 2) and that historians of religion, therefore, will have much to gain in recognizing the reality of a discourse of "truth" in the plural rather than the singular. In effect, therefore, Veyne is denying that the Milesian-to-Atomist development of pre-Socratic thought constitutes a revolutionary achievement in which reason, so to speak, gained its independence from myth and can therefore subject myth to critical reflection. His argument, however, is flawed and it is the revolution in thought created by the pre-Socratics that will stand as the real contribution of ancient Greek philosophy to the historical and scientific study of religion.

Can believing re-enchant the universe?

Veyne is aware that there may have been many in ancient Greece who believed in the gods in a superstitious manner, but he points out that there was also an educated public who understood that they could no longer believe in the "supernatural" (his term) "in the old way." Consequently, he claims, they created a "new type" of supernaturalism that would not conflict with the rational thought that had emerged with the Milesians. Veyne sees such intellectuals as being in a "complicated state of mind" in that they rejected "the marvelous" and at the same time were convinced "that legends had a true basis" (Veyne 1988, 56-57). According to Veyne: "Among the learned, critical credulity, as it were, alternated with a global skepticism and rubbed shoulders with the unreflecting credulity of the less educated." He maintains that in ancient Greece these

> attitudes tolerated one another, and popular credulity was not culturally devalued. This peaceful coexistence of contradictory beliefs had a sociologically peculiar result. Each individual internalized the contradiction and thought things about myth that, in the eyes of the logician at least, were irreconcilable. The individual himself did not suffer from these contradictions; quite the contrary. Each one served a different end. (Veyne 1988, 54)

"The truth,"—that is, the truth of the mythic tradition—is the world of values (the world view) forged by a people (group, state, nation) in response to the plurality of forces it faced, reflected in the "marvelous" world of its myths. What the truth is for any particular group or person, then, is simply the value system within which each functions, which implies the existence of a plurality of truths and world views. As Veyne puts it:

> This [kind of] truth is the child of the imagination. The authenticity of our belief is not measured according to the truth of their object. Again we must understand the reason, which is a simple one: it is we who fabricate our truths, and it is not 'reality' that makes us believe. For 'reality' is the child of the constitutive imagination of our tribe. (Veyne 1988, 113)

I agree with much of Veyne's analysis here: the plurality of truths in effect amounts to comprehensive world views that embody the aims, objectives, goals, values of society/ tribe/culture, and as such are subjective, imaginative constructs rather than discoveries of worlds of value existing independent of human thought. From the perspective of Ionian-type thinkers, of course, these truths do not amount to knowledge, although they are believed by the unsophisticated members of these societies, and in their framework such beliefs constitute knowledge—for them. But those beliefs do not amount to knowledge for the sophisticated members of society for, as Veyne notes, "[t]ruth is the name we give to choices to which we cling" (Veyne 1988, 127); these are commitments to live by—as if these affirmations (beliefs) reflected the world as it is in itself. The notions of "true" or "false" do not apply to them.

Where I disagree with Veyne over this matter is that he refers to "scientific truth" as indistinguishable from the "imaginative" Truths of myth and religion, maintaining that science itself is a myth (a Truth). As he puts it:

> Science finds no truths, either mathematicized or formalized; it discovers unknown facts that can be interpreted in a thousand ways .... Sciences are no more serious than the humanities, and since, in history, facts are not separable from interpretation and one can imagine all the interpretations one wishes, the same must be true in the exact sciences. (Veyne 1988, 115)

Veyne, therefore, is unaware that science-like thinking—and the proto-scientific thinking of the Milesians—is not concerned with moral value and meaning. He fails to see that such thinking values only knowledge for the sake of knowledge alone, which engages one only in making justified empirical or theoretic propositional claims about the world or states of affairs in the natural and social worlds—that is, epistemic claims open to debate and criticism—and not with value or meaning (though knowledge for its own sake is a value). There is, moreover, a clear distinction between "scientific knowing" and "mythic belief" in that only the former is committed to the discovery of, and ongoing accumulation of, intersubjective knowledge about the world and events in it, while the latter is a (subjective) product of the collective imagination of the community that "discovers" (that is, creates) values that make possible a cooperative and meaningful existence for its members and ensures society's continued existence.

Contra Veyne, then, what is new in the "Milesian revolution" or the "Ionian Enlightenment" as many have referred to the philosophy of the pre-Socratics, is the implicit distinction between belief and knowledge which is ultimately responsible for the (likely unintended) creation of the new cultural value of knowledge for the sake of knowledge alone. Veyne's account of the existence of an intellectual elite in ancient Greece, too sophisticated to take the stories of the gods in Homer and Hesiod at face value yet convinced of the existence of a divine, supernatural reality and of its value to society, is beyond question. However, that sophisticated belief in the supernatural is no more open to critical discussion and debate characteristic of the work of the Milesian and other Ionian cosmologists than are the mythic beliefs of the ordinary ancient Greek citizen because, as Veyne argues, those beliefs were not mere propositional claims (knowledge) about the world or states of affairs in the world that could be either true or false. They were instead moral Truths about the meaning of human existence intuited (created) by the human imagination that reason cannot adequately explain or understand. But in being beyond critical rational examination and analysis these Truths, like the mythic accounts of the gods in Homer and Hesiod, would eventually be ignored by those thinkers seeking a naturalistic explanation of the world.

The transition in understanding of "knowledge" as beliefs that are open to rational criticism and assessment—and therefore potentially either true or false—that lay implicit in the thought of the pre-Socratic cosmologists, therefore, amounts to possession of what classicist Henk S. Versnel (2011) refers to as "low intensity" beliefs (*assensus, fides*), that is, belief simply as holding a thing to be true even if it has not been fully demonstrated and is not therefore beyond falsification at some point in the future. Versnel contrasts that sort of belief with what he calls "high intensity" belief (*fiducia*), that is, belief that involves not only a cognitive conviction (certitude without certainty) but also commitment or trust. The rationally supported low-intensity beliefs of the pre-Socratic cosmologists, therefore, stand in radical contrast with the indisputably high-intensity beliefs ("Truths") about the gods and the meaning of life vouchsafed to people either by way of revelation or intuition. It is the emergence of this new conception of knowledge as justified belief, obtained by way of reliance on unaided (autonomous) reason, that constitutes a "critical episode" in the development of human thought essential to the eventual emergence of science as we understand it today.

Ancient Greek philosophy and the historians

Just as the cosmologists were interested in the subject of change in the natural world, the early Greek historians were interested in accounting for changes that occur in the activities of human communities. T. J. Luce, Professor of Classics at Princeton, points to the influence of the work of the Ionian cosmologists—although not in any immediate or direct way—as a particularly important influence on the rise of history as a new genre of literature capable of "standing on its own and with a character and premises special to it" (Luce 1997, 2). He writes:

> Another important influence on the birth of history, in addition to Homer, was philosophy. The first philosophers, known as Pre-Socratics...most of whom are preserved in fragments quoted in later writers, began to look at the world in a new spirit, rejecting simple acceptance of traditional beliefs (the 'inherited conglomerate') in favor of critical inquiry and creative explanations. (Luce 1997, 7)

A number of histories of the origin and development of the study of religion suggest that we might find its origin in Herodotus (480–430 BCE). In some sense that is true—Herodotus took interest in a wide range of habits, customs, and religions of a number of the dozens of nations he visited in his travels, including, for example, those of the Assyrians, Babylonians, Egyptians, and various Greek city-states. In looking at the Babylonians, for example, he describes their religious practice of requiring every woman in the country having "once in her lifetime [to] go to the temple of Aphrodite and sit there and be lain with by a strange man" as one of the ugliest and most shameful among nations (Histories, 1.199). In discussing the customs of the Egyptians he claims that they are the exact opposite of that of other nations noting, for example, their reverence for the gods is excessive but that women are not dedicated to any god, male or female, while men are dedicated to all gods and goddesses. Of particular interest for Herodotus is the Egyptian acknowledgement of Heracles "as one of the twelve gods," as well as their lack of knowledge of the Heracles that the Greeks knew. These few instances, of course, do not make Herodotus a comparative religionist or historian of religion, but they do show that he is not so deeply entrenched in Greek life that he is simply taking the stories at face value. His *Histories*, that is, constitute a radically different genre of literature that, as historian M. I. Finley asserts, systematically questioned "the supposedly known facts ...in rational, human form" (Finley 1959, 2). He, like the Ionian cosmologists before him, had an open mindedness about the gods and was willing to examine and debate their nature and history. In a sense, therefore, it is not inappropriate to suggest that just as the cosmologists engaged in a kind of proto-scientific work—as did the authors of the Hippocratic Corpus—Herodotus is also a kind of proto-historian of religions.

—4—

The Rise and Decline of the Sciences in the Hellenistic Period

Introduction

My aim in this chapter is to provide a brief account of the advancement of the "science-like" thinking of the Pre-Socratics in the Hellenistic period which, in cultural rather than political terms, as Luther H. Martin has suggested, stretches from the death of Alexander the Great to the decrees of Theodosius in the last decade of fourth century of the Common Era (Martin, 1987, 4–6). This overview will show why the argument that Aristotle and his successors, or the Pre-Socratics before them, gave birth to science, is misleading. There is no evidence that either group of philosophers adumbrated what is understood today as a scientific methodology in the study of the natural world. Their philosophical interest in the nature of the physical world, however, produced a kind of "proto-science"; natural philosophies that, while exhibiting some continuity with the mythic mode of thought from which it emerged, demythologized nature, substituting causal for agentic explanations of it. There is general agreement, however, that Aristotle and his successors advanced the "natural philosophy" of the Pre-Socratics, and there is some evidence to suggest that it is not altogether inappropriate to speak of the emergence of "Hellenistic sciences" during this period. Nevertheless, for reasons I shall spell out, I think that evidence does not justify the claim made by some that these developments amounted to a scientific revolution.

Pre-Socratic philosophy-science

It has often been argued that the historical-cultural developments of the period in ancient Greek thought, sometimes referred to as the Pre-Socratic Enlightenment, gave birth to a new, scientific mode of thinking. William Arthur Heidel, for example, in his *Heroic Age of Science*, wrote: "That the

Greeks developed science can be denied only if one defines the name in terms which are applicable to nothing but the most recent formulas" (Heidel 1933, 1). Samuel Sambursky maintained that the intellectual developments that followed on the transcendence of logos over mythos in the thought of the Milesian cosmologists in the sixth century BCE is "similar to the birth of modern science," as he claims in his *The Physical World of the Greeks* (Sambursky 1962 [1956], 18). "Greek science appears to us," he wrote, "as a continuous effort to rationalize nature, resulting in the gradual extension of the concept of law to every observed sphere of the physical universe" (Sambursky 1962, 213). In *The Origin of Scientific Thought*, Georgio de Santillana describes those ancient Greeks as the progenitors of "abstract reason" which has since been called "scientific rationalism" (de Santillana 1970 [1961], 40). Daniel E. Gershanson and Daniel A. Greenberg, in their *Anaxagoras and the Birth of Physics*, argue that although the origins of science reach back into pre-historic time,

> the emergence of natural philosophy as an experimental and theoretical pursuit in a form fundamentally the same as its present one can be said to have occurred in the Hellenic world at about the same time that the last prophets were preaching in Israel and the first consuls were ruling in Rome.
> (Gershanson and Greenberg 1964, 3)

In the previous chapter I argued that the socio-cultural and political ethos of Miletus in the sixth century BCE made possible the emergence of a new set of intellectual interests limited to seeking knowledge about the origin and operation of the physical cosmos. Indeed, I have argued, with Francis Cornford, that the break with the mythic mode of thought that dominated Greek society constitutes a major revolution in human thought, as significant as any of the major developments in the cognitive capacities in the evolution of the human mind described in Chapter 2. However, even though the project of the Milesian cosmologists culminated in the brilliantly imaginative atomic theories of Leucippus and Democritus, I also argued that this Milesian revolution in thought did not give birth to science as we know it today. I described their achievement rather as a science-like mode of thought. In this I agree with G.E.R. Lloyd's claim that "the idea of a sudden breakthrough [in ancient Greek thought] by which truly modern science can be recognized is chimerical" (Lloyd 2004, 13). But this does not mean that there was not a revolutionary development of human thought with the Pre-Socratics. I agree with Lloyd's claim that we must see more than simply the discontinuities in Greek thought when dealing with the question of the emergence of science. For the most part, I agree with him that the evidence suggests "there was no science as we know it today in ancient civilizations. Yet there were analogous ambitions …" (Lloyd 2004, 23) which are those in which we ourselves are engaged (Lloyd 2004, 188). The analogous ambition is implicit in the unconscious creation of the revolutionary and radically new value of "knowledge for the sake of knowledge alone." This, however, does not amount to the emergence of science, although it is an important aspect of science. Rather "the analogous ambition" amounted to an implicit critique, but not necessarily to a wholesale abandonment of, the mythic thinking of their forebears.

I note here that G.E.R. Lloyd came to a similar conclusion in his *Magic, Reason, and Experience* the subtitle of which is *Studies in the Origin and Development of Greek Science*. As he puts it, a new mode of thinking emerged between the sixth and fourth centuries BCE (Lloyd 1979, 26–27). The distinction early Greek philosophers drew between natural phenomena and supernatural intervention in the natural world, Lloyd maintains, was exceptional (Lloyd 1979, 27 and 234). He eschews, however, any suggestion that his account of this development describes the birth of a radically distinct, Lévy-Bruhlian mode of strictly logical thought. Application of Lévy-Bruhl's hypothesis of a logical distinction between primitive and modern modes of thought to ancient Greek philosophy, he insists, fails because the new inquiries did not drive out the old (Lloyd 1979, 142). His argument in this regard, however, is problematic. The critical issue is not one of the dominance or demise of either mode of thought but rather whether or not the different modes of thought are compatible; or even commensurable. That problem shows up in the conclusion he draws from his analysis: "The development of philosophy and science in ancient Greece," he writes, "is a unique turning-point in the history of thought. So far as the Western world goes, our science is continuous with, and may be said to originate in, that of ancient Greece" (Lloyd 1979, 262, my emphases). The question is: is modern scientific thought continuous with the thought of the Greek philosophers before or after the Milesian turning-point in Greek philosophy? Without clarifying this issue, Lloyd reasserts his rejection of a Lévy-Bruhlian account of this Milesian transition in thought. In concluding his book *Demystifying Mentalities*, he writes: "As a reaction to the apparently irrational in beliefs and practices, the appeal to a distinct mentality appears excessive, and it diverts attention away from what seem more promising avenues of investigation" (Lloyd 1990, 141). This is an odd response to his claim that exploring the consequences of distinguishing the literal from the metaphorical, and of clarifying the meanings of myth and magic, "played an important role in ancient Greek polemic during which science and philosophy defined and legitimated themselves in contrast to the existing more traditional repositories of knowledge" (Lloyd 1990, 73).

The revolutionary development of human thought with the Milesians came to a rather abrupt end with Socrates and Plato. It is not that Socrates provided an alternative spiritual or metaphysical account of the cosmos in opposition to the philosophical naturalism of the Ionian philosophers. But he opted instead to consider more important issues than determining the fundamental substance (or substances) of which the cosmos is made, the mechanisms of transformation of that substance (or substances) producing the cosmos, and the multiplicity of things to be found in the world. That is, Socrates triggered a counter-revolution in the history of ancient Greek thought. He rejected as ephemeral the new interests of the Milesian cosmologists in understanding and explaining the character of the physical universe and redirected intellectual attention to what we today would call the search for meaning. In turning his back on what was an incipient naturalist tradition, Socrates—as described by Plato in the *Phaedo*—was also rejecting the new cultural value of "knowledge for the sake of knowledge alone" that had been created by the cosmologists. This also involved a rejection of reliance on reason as an autonomous cognitive capacity—as a non-moral, non-religious, and non-political instrument of inquiry. For Socrates, reason was to be focused on achieving a meaningful moral existence. Plato provided a kind of rational justification for this counter-revolution in the intellectual development of the Greek mind by way of a hybrid mode of thought that combined myth laced with elements of Pre-Socratic thinking in a complex rationalist, metaphysical, and idealist system of thought in which he argued that the things that actually exist physically can only be understood in terms of the concepts—Forms—we have of them. Although some might consider Plato as having created a new mode of thought, neither he, nor Socrates before him, added anything new to the naturalist tradition of the Pre-Socratic period. But they did not entirely bring that tradition to an end. Aristotle, as Glanville Downey notes in his textbook, *Aristotle: Dean of Early Science*, turned Plato's thinking upside down and inside out and prevented that from happening (Downey, 1962). I will show, however, that Christianity's adoption of Aristotelian natural philosophy had the same effect on it that Plato had on the natural philosophy of the Pre-Socratics; it created a new hybrid mode of thought—theology—that was not destined to endure very long.

Aristotle and the birth of Hellenistic science

It is generally agreed that Aristotle not only worked within the framework of the Milesian revolution in Greek thinking but also improved on it in his own work. Indeed, for many scholars and commentators, Aristotle ultimately developed a scientific approach to understanding and explaining the world. In his book on *The Development of Physical Theory in the Middle Ages*, James A. Weisheipl, for example, contrasts Plato's notion of wisdom which, he writes, "could not be found in the study of transitory shadows [of the physical world], but only in the contemplation of ideas," with Aristotle's defence of the autonomy of the natural sciences (Weisheipl 1971 [1959], 16 and 87). In a more popular and wide-ranging work, *The Cave and the Light*, Arthur Herman spells out the same contrast, giving his book the sub-title *Plato Versus Aristotle and the Struggle for the Soul of Western Civilization*. On Aristotle he writes: "Aristotle is the true father of science and scientific method, by which we still mean a methodical process of observation, classification, and discovery.... He is also the inventor of the language of science" (Herman 2013, 45). Plato, on the other hand, is described as a sage concerned with wisdom rather than with knowledge. As David Newsome points out in his 1972 publication, *Two Classes of Men: Platonism and English Romantic Thought*, Coleridge insisted that people are either Platonists or Aristotelians, noting that throughout history Plato has been seen as concerned with "poetic truth" whereas Aristotle has been seen as having a scientific mind (Newsome 1972, 4). More recently, Armand Marie Leroi in his book *The Lagoon: How Aristotle Invented Science*, also contrasts the two modes of thought represented by Plato and Aristotle, referring to Aristotle's undertaking as a "scientific enterprise" (Leroi 2014, 78). He does this even though acknowledging that Aristotle's system of science "is riddled with religion," amounting to the invention of "a new theology that seamlessly interweaves prehistoric superstition with cutting-edge science" (Leroi 2014, 337). Nevertheless, he insists that Aristotle's thought "contained the elements of natural science" in a way that Plato's system did not (Leroi 2014, 346).

Given the complex developments in Greek thought in the Hellenic period as described in Chapter 3, I affirm the following comment set out by G.E.R. Lloyd in his book *Ancient World, Modern Reflections: Philosophical Perspectives on Greek and Chinese Science and Culture*, which provides an appropriate assessment of the progression of thought from the Milesians to Aristotle: "Evidently there was no science as we have it today in ancient civilizations. Yet there were analogous ambitions..." (Lloyd 2004, 23).

Lloyd writes,

> We should never underestimate how difficult it is to recover ancient aims, goals, preoccupations, and expectations, [but] there is still a sense in which [ancient scholarly] ambitions to understand and their endeavours to carry their contemporaries with them, are analogous to those we engage in ourselves. (Lloyd 2004, 188)

Nevertheless, as he had noted earlier, there was no "sudden breakthrough by which truly modern science can be recognized" (Lloyd 2004, 15)—not even in Aristotle, who did a great deal to recover the Pre-Socratic science-like tradition of thought.

In his *Demystifying Mentalities*, Lloyd describes the development of early Greek thought as constituting a rivalry among various claimants to knowledge (Lloyd 1990, 15). This was also his view of developments in Greek natural philosophy after Aristotle. Lloyd's attention in *Greek Science after Aristotle* is largely focused on "the history of differing conceptions of aims and justifications of different modes of inquiry concerning nature..." (Lloyd 1973, 7). Greek thought in the Hellenistic period, he argues, was eclectic, involving "no new rationale or justification for scientific research" (Lloyd 1973, 7). Instead, this was a period in which a range of special "sciences" were cultivated, with ethical and practical philosophic interests becoming dominant in the Roman period. According to Lloyd, therefore, there was still no breakthrough to something like modern science in this period. As he puts the matter: "anxiety about the uncertainties of human life [after the death of Alexander and the reshaping of the Mediterranean political landscape] is a prominent feature of the main philosophies of the time" (Lloyd 1973, 2).

Given the nature of modern science—science after the Scientific Revolution in Europe—Lloyd cautiously pointed out in his Preface to *Greek Science after Aristotle*, that what is known as Greek science is really embedded in philosophy which, however, was itself considered science in the period after Aristotle (Lloyd 1973, xii). But he also argues that the Hellenistic period produced more science-like thought in the cultivation of special fields of interest, like physics and biology for example, that are clearly distinguishable from broader philosophical frameworks. But he maintains that these developments do not constitute a "scientific revolution." As he acknowledges: "no new rationale or justification for scientific research was developed after Aristotle" (Lloyd 1973, 7).

Lucio Russo, Professor of Mathematics at the University of Rome, came to a radically different conclusion on this matter in his 1996 study, *The*

The Rise and Decline of the "Sciences" in the Hellenistic Period

Forgotten Revolution: How Science Was Born in 300 BC and Why It had to be Born Again (translated into English in 2004). According to Russo there was "an explosion of knowledge about the external world" in the Hellenistic period following the death of Aristotle; "Hellenistic science boomed in the third century BC" (Russo 2004, 10). As Russo argues, in this period

> for the first time, anywhere in the world... [we see] the appearance of *science* as we understand it now: not an accumulation of facts or philosophically based speculation, but organized effort to model nature and apply such models, or scientific theories... (Russo 2004, 1, my emphasis)

What Russo means by science here is "exact science" which is characterized by methodological unity and an "extreme flexibility in considering new objects of study" (Russo 2004, 18–19). He acknowledges that many characteristics of this exact science appeared in thinkers of the Hellenic period, and that the empirical work, such as Aristotle's botanical and zoological studies, is distinct from various types of pre-scientific knowledge and therefore also, to a certain extent, similar to his understanding of what science is. But finally, the scientific revolution "is a product of Hellenistic civilization" (Russo 2004, 21). That is, the result made clear that science is more than a matter of acquiring knowledge of specific fields of interest; rather, it involved the development of a hypothetico-deductive method applicable to a wide range of epistemic spheres (Russo 2004, 19 and 350). For Russo, the three "beacons" of the revolution are Euclid of Alexandria, Archimedes of Syracuse, and Herophilus of Chalcedon (Russo 2004, 6). Russo argues that the work of these three created and applied genuine scientific method.

Russo provides a fascinating account of developments in several areas of epistemic interest early in what is reasonably called Hellenistic sciences. Whether or not these interests and the methods applied in that work constitute a genuine scientific revolution in thought comparable to that in early modern European thought is clearly a matter of dispute. It is a fact, however, that a scientific revolution would involve a great deal more than simply recapturing the insights of Euclid, Archimedes, or Herophilus.

The death of Hellenistic science was very much a result of the resurgence of a religious mentality with the end of the existence of independent city-states in the reign of Alexander the Great and the concomitant radical social change that produced pervasive psychological and social upheaval in the various populations of his new empire. In his book, *The Greeks and the Irrational* (1951), E. R. Dodds, for example, refers to this period of history in the Mediterranean world as "an age of anxiety" in considerable need of religious solace. G.E.R. Lloyd as well sees this period as one of widening intellectual boundaries due to the contacts that military conquest permitted between Greeks and Barbarians, and that produced "anxiety about the uncertainties of human life" (Lloyd 1973, 2). Frederick Copleston captures well the effects of this cosmopolitanism and individualism in the Hellenistic period in the following passage of his *A History of Philosophy*:

> [T]he individual was inevitably cast adrift by himself, loosed from his moorings in the City-State. It was but to be expected, then that in a cosmopolitan society philosophy should centre its interest in the individual, endeavouring to meet his demand for guidance in life, which he had to live out in a great society and no longer in a comparatively small City-family, and so displaying a predominantly ethical and practical trend as Stoicism and Epicureanism.
> (Copleston vol. I, part II, 1962, 124)

Hellenistic philosophy, that is, while originating in individual plight, became an avenue for satisfying the religious needs and aspirations of the masses. This is what Gilbert Murray in his *Five Stages of Greek Religion* described as a "failure of nerve" which regarded the human capacity to deal with the vicissitudes of life as "a despair of patient inquiry, a cry for infallible revelation; an indifference to the welfare of the state, a conversion of the soul to God (Murray 1955 [1925], 119). This vacillation between knowledge and solace will become clearer as one understands fully what science really amounted to in the Hellenistic Period.

A resurgence of religion

In his book on *The Scientist in the Early Roman Empire* Richard Carrier maintains that the natural philosopher is an "ancient analogue to the modern notion of a scientist" (Carrier 2017, 7) and uses that term to denote all those intellectuals of the period who theorized about nature; but he reserves the word scientist for those who were also concerned with methodological issues (Carrier 2017, 26). Although Carrier claims that "scientific knowledge and methodology continuously improved between 400 BC and 200 AD," he allows that there were no significant advances between 300 and 1200 AD (Carrier 2017, 11 and 16). Somewhat like Russo, whose work was familiar to him, Carrier thinks that the difference between early Hellenistic and modern science is only a matter of degree (Carrier 2017, 22). He is not wholly consistent in this assessment, however, writing that

> "[t]hough not completely 'scientific' in the modern sense, the physicus was still often expected to actually go and look at the facts rather than merely

speculate or pass on a tradition..., and this could involve the physicus in science-like activities, sometimes in a nearly modern sense."

(Carrier 2017, 38 and 40)

He associates such science-like activities with the idea of the scientist as interested in obtaining knowledge for its own sake. Unlike Russo, Carrier sees Aristotle as having put natural philosophy/science on a formal footing and therefore sees him as the "grandfather" of these Hellenistic developments (Carrier 2017, 100). Of this period of time, he writes: "The Greeks and Romans generated more scientific advances, and a far wider array of hypotheses in natural philosophy for a broader range of subjects, than any other civilization before the 'scientific revolution'" (Carrier 2017, 97). In his estimation, this ancient intellectual activity represented the brink of a scientific revolution, but he also says that potential revolution was interrupted by the resurgence of mysticism and supernaturalism in the fourth century CE. In that period of the Roman Empire, he adds, one finds

"markers" of a pattern of overall decline such as "an increasing tendency toward preservation of an existent body of knowledge instead of its ongoing expansion" or even improvement coupled with a pervading "scepticism" ... [and] an actual loss of what we would call the "scientific spirit"...

(Carrier 2017, 302)

Russo, moreover, documents a decline in scientific studies as early as the second century BCE with some resumption of scientific research in the first and second centuries CE. He writes, "The level of science in the first two centuries of our era, though low if compared with the early Hellenistic period, is still high relative to later centuries ..., [but] the work is not original" (Russo 2004, 240). He continues "[a]s time went by the climate of what had once been the great Hellenistic centers got overrun by irrational winds" of religion and magic, after which, he claims, the decline of science was unstoppable (Russo 2004, 240). Indeed, he likens the latter to pseudoscience, which he describes as "the combination of irrational beliefs with a language borrowed from science but devoid of scientific methodology" (Russo 2004, 240). After the fourth century CE, he writes, "scientific activity" is found only in the writing of commentaries on and compilations of the work of earlier natural philosophers/scientists—"rehashings of older works" as he puts it (Russo 2004, 14). Moreover, the definitive end of interest in such scientific work, he suggests, is reasonably marked by the murder of the Greek mathematician Hypatia (Russo 2004, 14–15). For Russo, there is no interesting development until the early Renaissance, specifically when it is spurred by

Galileo at the end of the sixteenth century (Russo 2004, 305). He concludes that: "After the turnaround that occurred under the Enlightenment, ancient culture continued to be an essential influence on European science, but an unconscious one, like so many repressed memories" (Russo 2004, 391).

Carrier also acknowledges that science was not considered very important in early Roman education and in his *Science Education in the Early Roman Empire* he shows that the Greco-Roman elite made no serious effort to provide education to the populace in scientific fact or theory (Carrier 2016, 23–24). He writes that one would "look in vain for any supposed heyday of widespread science education in the ancient world" (Carrier 2016, 92); but he also allows that studying philosophy at all in the first two centuries of the Roman period "meant to some extent studying the sciences sufficiently for a reasonable lay understanding" (Carrier 2016, 101). He goes on to mention in his later book, *The Scientist in the Early Roman Period* that the Roman scientists and the elite in general "believed there had been and would continue to be progress in scientific knowledge, and that this was a valuable, useful, and desirable thing" (Carrier 2017 339). Thus, unlike Russo, he claims that "the amount and quality of scientific knowledge that entered general public consciousness would at least have been greater than any other culture—or indeed the Middle Ages" (Carrier 2016, 54), although there was little or no original scientific research after the third century CE, and only the writing of reference books and commentaries (Carrier 2016, 164).

Despite the support of scientists and science by the elite Christians of this period, Carrier argues, the latter rejected the scientific approach to obtaining knowledge, bypassing "nature, formal logic, and empirical observation, while their proper objective was not to understand the operation of nature but to know the will of God" (Carrier 2017, 520). Carrier continues,

> The Christian…did not believe in the empirical or rational methods that prevailed among natural philosophers, but instead belittled those methods as either useless or all but certain to lead to strife, folly, or even damnation.
> (Carrier 2017, 528)

They instead adopted what Carrier calls "an epistemology of the Holy Spirit" (Carrier 2017, 528). He found no evidence

> that any Christians valued observing, investigating, and explaining the natural world, or embraced curiosity about natural causes as a moral or valuable concern or believed in the value (or in some cases even the possibility) of what we (or even they) would call scientific progress. (Carrier 2017, 544)

According to Carrier, then, Christians were hostile and unsupportive of any such work and thus contributed to the ultimate rejection of scientific thought (Carrier 2017, 471). Nevertheless, Carrier also points out a most interesting fact—namely, that "[t]his did not prevent Christians from using the work of natural philosophers to support their own argument—as for example, in their many treatises on the value and possibility of resurrection" (Carrier 2017, 471). There is no inconsistency in Carrier's argument, however, because he clearly distinguishes the work of natural philosophers from that of the scientists in the Hellenistic and imperial Roman periods. John Herman Randall Jr. explores this matter further in his book, *Hellenistic Ways of Deliverance and the Making of the Christian Synthesis* (1970), bringing into focus important methodological implications regarding the relationship of science and faith in later Christian thought.

Rome's control of the Mediterranean world in the Hellenistic period, as Randall affirms, "made possible the development of the richest, the most enduring, the most enlightened and humane civilization the Western world has ever enjoyed." (Randall 1970, 82). But society in the early days of the Roman empire experienced a significant degree of social disintegration with the dissolution of political boundaries and the migration of populations throughout the Empire. The first century of the common era, as Randall describes it, saw

> a rise of asceticism, of mysticism, in a sense, of pessimism; a loss of self-confidence, of hope in this life and of faith in normal human effort; a despair of patient inquiry, a cry for infallibility; an indifference to the welfare of the state, a conversion of the soul to God…, an intensifying of certain spiritual emotions; an increase of sensitiveness, a failure of nerve.
>
> (Randall 1970, 104)

The social malaise clearly gave rise to a general anxiety about the uncertainties of life, which not only generated a resurgence of religion—a rebirth of pagan polytheism and the spread of Near Eastern salvation religions, with Christianity as one incarnation—but also came to dominate the intellectual interests of the philosophers from the fourth century CE onward. These and subsequent intellectual developments produced philosophers who functioned primarily as religio-ethical teachers and prophetic figures concerned with understanding the dangers inherent in the ambiguities of life and providing ways of deliverance from those dangers, rather than with understanding the physical world around them. "Under these conditions," Randall argues, "philosophy became the intellectual justification and interpretation of such a religious atmosphere" (Randall 1970, 106). Christian thinkers found in the views of those philosophers much that was consistent with their own understanding of the world and humanity's place in it, and incorporated this with great benefit into the formulation of their own beliefs. As Randall describes it, Christianity, only a minor sect in the Roman Empire to begin with, became the dominant institution in Roman society by building—"one assimilation after another of all the strands of Hellenistic experience"—a persuasive catch-all religio-philosophical system of thought. In this they drew heavily on the speculative thought of Neo-Platonism which provided an account of the world that "made sense" of human existence. As Randall explains, "[w]ith Augustine, the intellectual development of the ancient world ended in a completely worked-out and inclusive philosophy..." (Randall 1970, 137 and 232), and made available to Christian thinkers in the early Medieval period Plato's hybrid mode of thought—that combination of traditional Greek mythic with Pre-Socratic traditional thinking. This dominated early European thought, virtually unchallenged until the twelfth century CE and the recovery of Aristotle's work preserved by and commented on by Muslim scholars.

It is quite clear, then, that the political and social conditions that fueled the resurgence of religion and the flourishing of what can reasonably be described as pastoral philosophy, coupled with the loss of most of Aristotle's writings in the West, stymied further development of scientific interests. Epistemic examination of the natural world had reached its lowest point of development in the fifth century CE and remained there for the next five hundred years. Nevertheless, as many scholars have pointed out, the Hellenistic and early Roman periods were not altogether devoid of epistemic, practical, and technological interest about the natural world. One still sees cultivation in this period of what one would today refer to as particular types of scientific interest such as physics, biology, and medicine. "By A.D. 500," Edward Grant argues in his *The Foundations of Modern Science in the Middle Ages*, "knowledge of Greek had become rare and knowledges of the exact sciences even rarer" (Grant 1996, 18). Knowledge of Greek science during that time could only be found in what is referred to as the Latin Encyclopedic tradition of handbooks and manuals on the sciences and commentaries on ancient scientific authors. "Without access to the hard core of Greek science," he wrote in his earlier book *Physical Science in the Middle Ages*, "the Western world could not rise above the level of the Latin Encyclopedists" (Grant 1971, 13). But as George Saliba argues in his *Islamic Science and the Making of the European Renaissance*, that could not have occurred without the Islamic discovery of Aristotle's works and the development of Islamic Science based on them. However, even though the Islamic scientific tradition owed much "to the acquisition of the Greek scientific legacy," the Islamic contribution to the history of the development of modern science included much more than simply the preservation and transmission of Aristotle's texts to the West (Saliba 2011, 9).

According to Saliba, modern scholarship reveals a critical and creative contribution by Islamic philosophers to the Greek scientific tradition by way of reassessing and correcting errors in Aristotle's work, and that of his successors, as well as in creating whole new disciplines such as algebra and trigonometry (Saliba 2011, 69). He points out, for example, that there is historical evidence to indicate that "as soon as the Greek scientific texts were being translated they were also being immediately updated by the currently known material and put to use in new compositions, all in order to improve the kind of science that was then provided" (Saliba 2011, 89). Such intellectual sophistication is seen in the mathematical reconstruction of Ptolemy's Almagest which, Saliba maintains, was based on a "comprehensive understanding of the Greek philosophical tradition, where cosmology was read together with observational science, a reading that was nowhere to be found in any other civilization up till that time" (Saliba 2011, 93). In fundamentally correcting the mistakes in the Greek scientific tradition, and in creatively reforming, for example, Ptolemaic astronomy with improved techniques and methods of observation, Saliba shows that an Arabic/Islamic astronomy emerged that had "a catalytic role in producing other astronomical innovations, and became part of the universal legacy of astronomy" (Saliba 2011, 150). There is historical evidence, that is, to show that Arabic/Islamic astronomy attracted the attention of astronomers from outside the Islamic domain, including Copernicus' reliance on it. Saliba writes that Copernicus is not "a completely disconnected figure who was forging a new astronomy completely based on new grounds of his own construction" (Saliba 2011, 209). Saliba concludes by saying:

> it looks like the Renaissance men of science were apparently looking to the world of Islam for the latest scientific activities rather than looking to the Greek classical sources…[so that by] the time of the Renaissance…Arabic science was by then a competitive science that stood at least on equal footing as the science of the Greeks… (Saliba 2011, 230 and 232)

Saliba's final comment about Arabic scientific culture describes Luccio Russo's Hellenistic scientists as much as it does Arabic/Islamic scientists:

> They could produce brilliant scientists…ever so briefly, but they could not guarantee the continuous production of the scientists themselves through

the security of their income and position. As a result, the scientific production of the Islamic world was mainly driven by individual genius but only when those geniuses could by accident encounter the right patron who would offer support." (Saliba 2011, 254–255)

In passing, Saliba also points to religion's negative influence on the development of science in the Islamic world. Although the social, economic, and political conditions made possible—and sustained these scientific interests, it was nevertheless essential, according to Saliba, for Arabic/Islamic scientists to set limits to Aristotle's influence in order to prevent it from undermining the revealed truth of Islam. This was less of a problem for Christian scholars who espoused Aristotle's understanding of reason to justify their religious beliefs, although their adoption of Aristotelianism was ultimately to be as detrimental to the Faith as it was a barrier to the growth of science. Christian theology was predicated as much on Aristotelian philosophical commitments as on faith in a mythic revelation which, like Augustine's use of Plato, formed a hybrid mode of thought that would ultimately subordinate Christian faith to autonomous reason. At the risk of some duplication of argument, I spell out this parallelism on which I will elaborate in chapter 5.

Hybrid modes of thought, old and new

As I have indicated, the lesson Christians learned from Socrates (as described by Plato in the Phaedo) was not to focus their attention on simply seeking knowledge about the physical world but rather to turn to the question of the purpose of human action and the meaning of human existence. Francis Cornford, as I mentioned in chapter three, described this as Socrates's "discovery of the soul and of a morality of spiritual aspiration" requiring knowledge of a different kind from that sought by the Milesians (Cornford 1932, 37). In seeking knowledge of the world, the Milesians, along with other Pre-Socratic philosophers had brought about an intellectual revolution; they had brought about a mode of thought and knowledge acquisition involving reliance on observation and reason (logos) alone rather than on myth (mythos). Although not wholly rejecting traditional sources of knowledge, Plato nevertheless created a metaphysical framework to justify Socrates's "discovery," and drew on the work of Pre-Socratic philosophers to do so. In the process he "created" what is appropriately called a "hybrid mode of thought" combining logos with mythos.

As nineteenth-century British theologian Edwin Hatch puts it in his Hibbert Lectures of 1888—published in 1890 as *The Influence of Greek Ideas and Usages Upon the Christian Church*—this "philosophy of assertion, the philosophy of denial, and the philosophy of research were all outside the earliest forms of Christianity"; yet

> within a century and a half after Christianity and philosophy first came into close contact, the ideas and methods of philosophy had flowed in such mass into Christianity, filled so large a place in it, as to have made it no less a philosophy than a religion. (Hatch 1890, 124 and 125)

Although John Herman Randall Jr. provides historical evidence that shows how Augustine's use of Platonic and Neo-Platonic philosophy came to dominate the cultural, political and religious life in early medieval Europe, his claim that "[l]ike Socrates Augustine turned his back on trees and stones and sought man" seems to suggest the opposite (Randall 1970, 191). There is no evidence, however, to show that to be the case. As Richard Carrier, among other scholars, argues, the reliance on religious experience and revelation for their knowledge of God "did not prevent Christians from using the work of natural philosophers to support their own argument[s]…" for their religious beliefs (Carrier 2017, 471).

Early Christian apologists seem to have distinguished philosophical dialectic from the "science-like," rational accounts of the world provided by the scientists in the Hellenistic and imperial Roman periods. Keeping this in mind, it becomes clear that early Christian thinkers also learned a lesson from Plato—who had provided a metaphysical framework for Socrates's spiritual discovery—by creating a Platonic hybrid combination of traditional mythic and Pre-Socratic philosophical thought to provide rational justification for peculiar Christian doctrines they believed were divinely revealed. Cornford provided a helpful description of this mental maneuver:

> True, the central germ of Platonism, from first to last, is the new Socratic morality of spiritual aspiration; but under Plato's hands this germ has grown into a tree whose branches cover the heavens. Platonism is what the doctrine of Socrates never was, a system of the world, embracing that whole province of external Nature from which Socrates had turned away to study the nature and end of man. (Cornford 1932, 55–56)

Edwin Hatch made a similar claim regarding the influence of Greek philosophy on Christian thought in the Middle Ages, arguing that it "helped the Christian communities to believe as an intellectual conviction that which they had first accepted as a spiritual revelation," extending even to their knowledge of the natural world, although he did not wish to entertain the thought "that the dominance of the metaphysical element in it will be perpetual" (Hatch 1890, 207 and 349).

Edward Grant attempts to account for the foundations of modern science on these intellectual developments in the Middle Ages. He claims that

> [b]etween the fourth and eighth centuries of the common era, encyclopedic authors produced a series of Latin works that were to have significant influence throughout the Middle Ages, especially prior to 1200. (Grant 1996. 18)

His account, however, provides no indication of actual science-like developments during this period. It is true, as he points out, that translations of Aristotle's works also entered Europe during this period. It is also true that Aristotle's thought determined cultural developments in Europe "for centuries to come," just as Plato had before him. This was no doubt aided by the uptick in education from the tenth century and on because of the cash economy that transformed Europe between the ninth and thirteenth centuries. However, I do not think he has made the case that Aristotle, so to speak, "revolutionized Western scientific thought" (Grant 1996, 3). There is no denying that Aristotle had a major impact on medieval European thought, but there is wide scholarly agreement that it did not produce a major scientific advancement in the natural philosophy of the period, let alone constitute revolutionizing scientific thought—even though, in its corrected and transformed Arabic/Islamic mode, it made an indirect contribution to the Scientific Revolution in Europe. Grant is right to claim that "the way in which medieval scholars understood the structure and operation of the cosmos" was grounded in Aristotle's (empirical) scientific books, and that these works formed the basis for a natural philosophy more akin to the science-like work of the Pre-Socratics. Unlike Plato, that is, Aristotle championed the autonomy of rational thought free from religious, political, and other ideological constraints; and in this sense, it was more hospitable to scientific reasoning than was Plato's metaphysics. Grant is also right in his claim that "it would be a serious error to suppose that theologians opposed Aristotelian natural philosophy...," because, in fact, they all recognized the enormous utility of his thought in the service of their religion and theology (Grant 1996, 83–84). This is reminiscent of Augustine's view of the value of Plato.

Aristotle's work, as Grant claims, was largely praised for its apologetic support. "Western Christianity," he writes,

> had a long standing tradition of using pagan thought for its own benefit. As supporters of that tradition, medieval theologians treated the new Greco-Arabic learning in the same manner ... [as] a useful tool for the elucidation of theology...; an attitude that was developed and nurtured during the first four or five centuries of Christianity. (Grant 1996, 84)

However, as an apologetic tool, Aristotelian rationality was essentially subordinated to a religious agenda and became the basis for the core curriculum for all students in the emerging universities in Europe. In that religiously manipulated form, Christian theologians effectively promulgated a hybrid mode of thought in the same way Plato did in constructing his metaphysical understanding of the world by curtailing the full impact of the science-like thinking of the Pre-Socratics. That new hybrid mode of thought, incorporating rationality within an essentially mythic frame, became authoritative in medieval Europe—a situation that ultimately had to be transcended for genuinely scientific thinking to flourish. Interestingly, by incorporating a Pre-Socratic-cum-Aristotelian form of rationality for apologetic purposes, medieval scholasticism essentially "scientized" Christian thought by bringing theology into existence as an academic discipline and in the process leaving the Faith open to rational criticism. In attempting to extend the prestige and intellectual respectability to the Faith, Aristotelian Christianity initiated what became a fractious struggle for preeminence between faith and reason.

Early on in the history of this relationship Faith almost always "trumped" reason, as is clear in the case of Abelard's attempt to show the reasonableness of talk about God, but in doing so, as Richard Rubenstein put it in his book on *Aristotle's Children: How Christians, Muslims, and Jews Rediscovered Ancient Wisdom and Illuminated the Dark Ages*, faith placed "limiting effects on scientific inquiry" (Rubenstein 2003, 194). In that respect, the autonomy of reason in epistemic matters that emerged with the Pre-Socratics made no significant advance relevant to a scientific study of religious phenomena. But this fusion of faith and reason pushed the latter more deeply into the Christian faith, to use Rubenstein's terminology, than did Augustine's use of Plato's hybrid of Socratic faith and Pre-Socratic proto-scientific thought (Rubenstein 2003, 198). This development, I will show, supplanted the Platonized mode of Christianity preached by Augustine that had dominated Christendom since the fifth century, and has in the final analysis functioned as the benchmark for epistemic claims about the world and its contents. Both Plato and Aristotle invoked reason in defence of the Faith by fusing natural philosophy and ancient science on the one hand with faith in revelatory knowledge on the other. Aristotle, however, provided a more accurate and persuasive account of the natural world that gave his philosophy greater epistemic (scientific) credibility. Despite the similarity of intention of both Platonist and Aristotelian Christians to provide intellectual justification for the Christian Faith, Aristotle's work was much more powerful, exemplifying the ultimate import of the Milesian rejection of myth and espousal of the autonomy of reason in epistemic matters.

In Chapter 5 I will show how a set of social transformations of Medieval European society made possible the emancipation of reason from religious constraint and Aristotelian metaphysics. In part, those developments rest on what Guy Stroumsa refers to in *The End of Sacrifice: Religious Transformation in Late Antiquity* as "the most profound cultural but also religious transformations between Antiquity and the Middle Ages" (Stroumsa 2009, 54). The growth of Christianity in the third century and its dominance in the fourth, he argues, contributed to the "crumbling" of the "ancient religious framework" of the Greek and Roman world. The conversion of Constantine and the Christianization of the Empire, he writes, transformed society in bringing an end to sacrifice and, as Stroumsa describes it, "modernizing" religion by placing the accent in religion on belief rather than sacrifice, and therefore "on the interiorization and privatization of worship" (Stroumsa 2009, 62). The emphasis on belief—on myth and story—involving a profound psychological transformation of the individual (that is, on care for the Self) requires seeing them as "a new sort of people, unknown until then" (Stroumsa 2009, 30). It also gave rise to what Stroumsa calls "book (sacred scriptural) religions" that, he writes: "permitted the development of perhaps the most remarkable difference between the religions of the Book and ancient religions: the place reserved for theology at the very heart of religion" (Stroumsa 2009, 54).

Stroumsa elaborates on the import of this "axial shift"—as he refers to it in his *The End of Sacrifice and The Scriptural Universe of Ancient Christianity* (2016)—on understanding the historical character of religions. He claims that along with the disappearance of blood sacrifices and a collective identity rooted in an interiority that is expressed in terms of belief (Stroumsa 2016, 75) came the distinction between "true" and "false" religions. Implicit in that contrast is an incipient distinction of religious thought and behaviour from other spheres of life, which ultimately gave rise to distinguishing the sacred from the profane and, with that, the emergence of the notion of secularity. As I will point out in chapter 5, there is an almost inseparable connection, but intense relationship, between "religion" and knowledge in Late Antiquity and the early Medieval periods.

Conclusion

There is overwhelming agreement among historians of science that a fully Scientific Revolution in human thought did not occur until the sixteenth and seventeenth centuries of the Common Era. In H. Floris Cohen's comparative historical analysis of three types of nature-knowledge in his *The Rise of Modern Science Explained* —which includes Athenian, Alexandrian, and an enriched Alexandrian mode of nature-knowledge created by Renaissance humanists— he shows that none of them actually amounted to a genuine revolution in thought. He argues that it was not until around 1600 that "the scientific revolution broke out." As he puts it, that revolution came by way of a "[more limited] revolution [that] occurred within each of the three modes of nature-knowledge that had flowered during the previous one and a half centuries" (Cohen 2015, 102). Michael Hobart mounts a similar argument in *The Great Rift: Literacy, Numeracy, and Religion* showing Galileo (among others) to be the progenitor of modern science. He writes that the Scientific Revolution was created by "circumscribing an arena of knowledge in which the truths of nature would be sought and captured through analysis, through abstraction of relation-mathematics, and corroborated by means of experiment," not by philosophy (Hobart 2018, 287).

In chapters 5 and 6 I will show how a set of social transformations in Medieval European society emerging from the "religious revolution" in Late Antiquity made possible the emancipation of reason from religious constraint, and how Aristotelian thought made possible Galileo's introduction of mathematics into the study of the natural world.

— 5 —

Latin Christendom and Scientific Thought in the Middle Ages

Introduction

A science-like interest in the natural world declined as Christianity grew in strength, becoming the official religion of the Empire under the rule of Flavius Theodosius in the late-fourth century of the Common Era. As we have seen, the reaction of Socrates and Plato to the philosophical interests of their Milesian predecessors gave early notice of the fragility of the new science-like mode of thought the Milesians had created. Even though Aristotle breathed new life into natural philosophy, the intellectual environment needed for its flourishing failed to materialize. Geoffrey Lloyd, Lucio Russo, and other scholars of what has been called "Hellenistic science" correctly point out, as I argued in Chapter 4, that a "science-like" intellectual activity did not entirely disappear from the post-Alexandrian Mediterranean world. But by the fifth and sixth centuries of the Common Era, that mode of thought reached its lowest ebb. Between 500 and 1000 CE, as Edward Grant shows in his *Physical Sciences in the Middle Ages*, there was no longer a community of thinkers who could both comprehend and promote this kind of high-level philosophical thought about the natural world. There had been considerable economic deterioration and cultural stagnation since the fall of the Western Roman Empire in 476 with little or no improvement until the crowning of Charlemagne in 800 and the flowering of the Carolingian Renaissance. This period of history, once called the "dark ages," Grant asserts, reveals "the gradual disintegration and transformation of the Roman Empire and the triumph of Christianity as a state religion [that] almost inevitably serves as the larger historical background against which the decline of science must be viewed" (Grant 1971, 1).

There can be no doubt that this period of history is one that sees a steep decline of interest in the kind of proto-scientific and science-like enterprises that preceded it in ancient Greece and the Hellenistic era. Nevertheless, this subsequent period of history also harboured a number of significant ecclesiastical, political, legal, and social transformations, and intellectual developments, that contributed to a renewed scientific interest in the natural world that anticipated the sixteenth-century scientific revolution. My objective in this chapter is simply to provide some insight into this axial shift in thought, as one historian described it, that made possible a revaluation of the traditional relationship between reason and revelation (science and religion) that ultimately made possible the emergence of modern science.

Early educational and ecclesiastical developments

A new cultural climate emerged early in the ninth century CE with the crowning of Charlemagne who was committed to ending the cultural stagnation that had dominated early Medieval society and to reviving Classical learning. Inviting the greatest scholars of the age to his court, he created a system of education based on the liberal arts concerned primarily with imparting general knowledge, rather than professional, vocational, or technical training, and with developing intellectual capacities and abilities. His interests also extended to more advanced education for clergy and some laypersons in grammar, logic, and dialectical reasoning (the trivium). Some monasteries of the period became significant centres of new scholarship. Although these developments did not rise to the level of the cultural advances of the eleventh and twelfth centuries, the social, political, and cultural achievements of the Carolingian Renaissance, as some have argued, laid the foundation for the rise of Western civilization, including the groundwork for advances on the scientific achievements of the Hellenistic period.

The Investiture Controversy of the late eleventh and early twelfth centuries is of special interest regarding its import for the widespread acceptance of Aristotelian rationality in the twelfth and thirteenth centuries. Politically, this controversy was the most important conflict between secular and religious authorities of the Middle Ages. It began in 1076 as a dispute between the Holy Roman Emperor, King Henry IV, and Pope Gregory, over the issue of who had the authority to choose and install bishops (including the Pope) and abbots of monasteries, and was ultimately resolved by Emperor Henry V and Pope Callixtus with the Concordat of Worms in 1122. The Concordat makes a clear distinction between the spiritual authority of the Pope's Office and his position as a landed magnate. A person who was invested with the powers, privileges, and lands was subordinate to the Emperor, and a person who was invested with sacred or ecclesiastical authority was subordinate to the Pope. Ultimately, however, the Emperor renounced all authority to choose the Pope. Nevertheless, here, for the first time, we have the implicit adoption by the Church of a "doctrine" of the separation of Church and State. In his *Intellectual Curiosity and the Scientific Revolution: A Global Perspective*, Toby Huff—a sociologist with a deep interest in the history and philosophy of science—claims this created "breakthrough conditions" for many modern developments "ever after," including the sixteenth-century Scientific Revolution (Huff 2011, 147).

The legal revolution in medieval Europe and its import for the scientific revolution

Between the ninth and thirteenth centuries Europe was transformed from a land-based farming society to a money economy based on trade and industry. As trade became more important, towns and cities grew both in size and number of inhabitants, and with that the need for new legal arrangements to maintain good governance over the increasing number of economic and social institutions that emerged along with these economic changes. The secular world simply became too complex for the instruments of governance in play in feudal times and this gave rise to a legal revolution in late medieval Europe.

In his book, *The Rise of Early Modern Science: Islam, China, and the West*, Huff argues that the Investiture Controversy was essential to that revolution. As he puts it, that clash between King Henry IV and Pope Gregory VII was a major "intellectual and legal contest that produced the first modern system of law assumed to be of universal scope" (Huff 1993, 121). Huff points out that the legal supremacy of the clergy under the Pope effectively "created a new and autonomous legal order" with the rights of jurisdiction and thereby "established a model by which secular states could order their affairs" (Huff 1993, 127). The sacred/secular distinction, that is, "established the principle of the authority and legitimacy of reason over discordant authorities" (Huff 1993, 129). It also created new legal concepts, entities, procedures, and agencies that transformed society and put European life "on a new footing" (Huff 1993, 25 and 27).

The most important element of the legal revolution was its dependence on the theory of corporate existence, which Huff describes as "the fictive idea of a corporate legal personality." The concept of the corporation, as Edward Grant explains, was derived from Roman law, in which imperial authority could confer the privileges of a corporation on a public entity, though "it was only in the twelfth century that it began to receive full and systematic development" (Grant 2001, 98). "The objectives of corporations," Grant continues,

> was to protect the interests of its constituent members. To achieve this, corporations had to promulgate laws and statutes, which members were legally required to obey... The members gave up certain rights in order to acquire the protection of their respective corporations. (Grant 2001, 99)

This development, obviously, drastically altered the nature of social relationships in medieval society which was now comprised of numerous legally autonomous entities like towns, cities, commercial enterprises (including guilds of millers, weavers, bakers, and masons, for example), and professional guilds (of surgeons and physicians among others). As Huff notes, these legal developments created a new social and political dynamic by separating the religious and secular domains as separate and autonomous legal jurisdictions that was unique to the West (Huff 1993, 120, 126). This development, Huff claims, laid "the foundations for the rise and autonomous development of modern science" (Huff 1993, 119).

From cathedral schools to universities: A uniquely European development

In *A History of Science: From the Ancient Greeks to the Scientific Revolution*, Andrew Ede and Lesley Cormack show how "[s]uccessive waves of invasions following the fall of Rome disrupted all aspects of life in Europe," including its intellectual life. They write: "The physical destruction of war and economic collapse destroyed many collections of texts, educational institutions fell into ruin, and society turned from the pursuit of knowledge and empire to basic survival." But they also point out that "[d]espite the dire conditions, not all ancient knowledge was lost" (Ede and Cormack 2012, 65). The educational task in a crumbling Roman society, however, was largely relegated to the Church. For hundreds of years, therefore, the intellectual life in early medieval Europe was largely carried on in Cathedral and Monastic Schools.

In taking over that task, as Émile Durkheim argued in his *The Evolution of Educational Thought*, the Church unwittingly "impregnated itself with a civilization that was at odds with its own nature—introducing into itself that of which it would not be able to rid itself later." As Durkheim concluded:

> [I]f the Church really did play this role it was at the cost of a contradiction against which it fought for centuries without ever achieving a resolution. For the fact was that in the literary and artistic monuments of antiquity there

lived and breathed the very same pagan spirit which the Church had set itself the task of destroying, to say nothing of the more general fact that art, literature, and science cannot but inspire profane ideas in the minds of the faithful and distract them from the only thought to which they should be giving their entire attention; the thought of their salvation. (Durkheim 1977, 22)

General education in that period was limited to the seven liberal arts, with emphasis on the Trivium, although Quadrivium subjects were not wholly ignored.

In *The Rise of the Universities*, Charles Homer Haskin claims that there were no universities in the early Middle Ages because "there was nothing to teach beyond the bare elements of grammar, rhetoric, logic, [the Trivium] and the still barer notions of arithmetic, geometry, astronomy, and music" [the Quadrivium] (Haskins, 1959 [1923]). But, as Haskins also claims, there was a sudden influx of new knowledge from the Arab scholars of Spain, and their translations of the long-lost work of Aristotle, from the eleventh to the thirteenth centuries, that is, in the "Age of Translation." That new knowledge was heavily oriented toward logic and the natural sciences such as physics, mathematics, astronomy, and cosmology. In Edward Grant's view, this new knowledge "rendered obsolete the meager traditional curriculum of the cathedral schools" (Grant 1971, 21), and as Haskins intimated, it was the impetus to the emergence, almost spontaneously, of the medieval university. Although many universities grew out of cathedral schools and religious orders, Haskins adds that this "new knowledge burst the bonds of the cathedral and monastery schools and created the learned professions..." (Haskins 1959, 5). There was, for example, a significant demand for the training of secular clergy which was carried out in the Cathedral schools.

Whatever the full legacy of the Cathedral school, I think Grant is correct to claim that it was an important "step in the path to the formation of the university, which was a wholly new institution that not only transformed the curriculum but also the faculty and its relationship to state and church" (Grant 2001, 29). But in "the earliest phase of their existence," as A. B. Cobban has pointed out in his *The Medieval Universities: Their Development and Organization*, "the universities were guild organizations without permanent buildings" and many other elements that characterize the modern university (Cobban 1975, 35). More important, however, is the fact that it was an autonomous, self-governing, legal entity with its own statutes and privileges. It was a "corporation," a collective body of people with a common purpose treated as an individual or agent, like a business enterprise, or a religious order, and, writes Huff,

> [f]rom the point of view of the rise of early modern science, the most significant event was the legal breakthrough that allowed the formation of autonomous institutions of higher learning, namely the *studium generale* and the university" as corporations. (Huff 1993, 335)

Because the development of science depends on the existence of social, political, and cultural conditions, for Huff, there must be "multiple spheres of freedom" or "neutral zones" "within which large groups of people can pursue their geniuses free from censure of political and religious authorities"; the unique value of the universities was that they provided "public spaces within which the free flow of critical thought could flourish" (Huff 2011, 212, 166). It is not that the denizens of the early medieval universities objected to or ignored the precepts of Christianity, but these "mental neutral zones" prevented the courses of study (and research) from being "dictated by religious scruples or theological aversions, though religious purists and fundamentalists did attempt to impose such restrictions" (Huff 1993, 162). As Grant argues:

> To a remarkable extent, church and state granted to the universities corporate powers to regulate themselves, thus enabling universities to determine their own curricula, to establish criteria for the degrees of their students, and to determine the teaching fitness of their faculty members.
> (Grant 2001, 173)

Moreover, their corporate structure, Grant explains,

> provided [them] substantial stability… [that] allowed the teaching of natural philosophy to develop as the basis of all university learning in the four faculties that comprise a major university, namely, arts, theology, medicine, and law. (Grant 2007, 146)

Nevertheless, this is not to say that their legal autonomy left them entirely free of all ecclesiastical control but, as Grant points out, they also received some ecclesiastical benefits (Grant 2007, 145).

There is general agreement in the literature that the medieval university is a wholly new institution. Cobban argues it is

> an indigenous product of western Europe [and that] Classical civilization did not produce the equivalent of these privileged corporate associations of masters and students with their statutes, seals, and administrative machinery, their fixed curricula and degree procedures. (Cobban 1975, 21)

It is apparent, he therefore insists, that there can be no "organic continuity between the universities which evolved towards the end of the twelfth century and Greek, Greco-Roman, Byzantine or Arabic schools" (Cobban 1975, 22). Grant arrives at the same conclusion writing: "The universities that had emerged by the thirteenth century in Paris, Oxford, and Bologna were different from anything the world had ever seen. Nothing in Islam, China, or India, or in ancient civilizations of South America, was comparable to the medieval university" (Grant 1996,172); and, again:

> The key event that made the new intellectual life of Western Europe different from anything else that had gone before is the emergence of the university as a unique and vital institution. Not only was it unique in the history of Western Europe, but it also was unique in the history of the world.
> (Grant 2007, 144)

For Toby Huff, "[t]he uniqueness of the European university can be seen on three levels: legal and social organization, curriculum, and philosophical and metaphysical commitments" (Huff 1993, 161). The legal revolution made possible a radical organizational and curricular transformation of the educational institutions of medieval Europe by creating politically and religiously neutral intellectual space, as Huff explains, "within which men could entertain all sorts of questions about the constitution of the world" (Huff 1993, 338). Also vital in this respect, however, was the need for the curriculum to move beyond simply the teaching of the Seven Liberal Arts and the meager knowledge of what was known as Greek science summarized in the works of the Latin Encyclopedists; it was able to do this with the reintroduction of the works of Aristotle. As Huff notes: "By incorporating the natural books of Aristotle in the curriculum of the medieval universities, a disinterested agenda of naturalistic inquiry had been institutionalized" (Huff 1993, 336). Christopher Beckwith describes this matter more dramatically: "The sudden influx of cultural borrowing [of the Aristotelian tradition] from the Islamic world was fundamental to the development of science in medieval Latin civilization" (Beckwith 2012, 5). Beckwith is fully aware that the Greco-Roman and Islamic developments of a "scientific tradition" never constituted fully scientific cultures, but he justifiably makes the claim that "the insights of great Classical Arabic writers are ultimately what got Europeans so excited about science" (Beckwith 2012, 6). The uniqueness of the medieval university, I think, is implicit in Beckwith's comments on the importance of Aristotle's logic and the adoption of what he calls the "recursive argument method" that first appeared in Classical Arabic thought involving breaking down any topic or problem into its analyzable parts and subjecting each part to exhaustive debate from all perspectives. This logical form of argumentation, of course, was ultimately abandoned in favour of empirical and theoretical argumentation, but it was nevertheless a step on the way to the emergence of modern science with the Scientific Revolution in seventeenth-century Europe (Beckwith 2012, 24, 159, et passim). Hence Huff's summary:

> When all of these elements were finally assimilated into the discourse of the universities by the end of the thirteenth century, along with the formal elements of the Aristotelian corpus, a powerful methodologically sophisticated intellectual framework for the study of nature had been institutionalized.
> (Huff 1993, 337).

The recovery of Aristotle and the birth of an academic (science-like) theology

The recovery of Aristotle's works in the eleventh and twelfth centuries was an enormously important development in European thought. It amounted to the recovery, at least partially, of the Milesian epistemic objective of obtaining knowledge of the physical world for its own sake and an adoption of empirical observation and reason as the avenues for achieving it. This renewed interest in the natural world and the reliance on the autonomy of reason in achieving it does not amount to modern science, but it was certainly a step in that direction. In this respect, medieval thought deviated from the Platonic-Augustinian philosophy that dominated the Church's mode of thought from the time of the Fathers to the twelfth-century Renaissance. Nevertheless, there are also important similarities of both the Platonic and Aristotelian uses of Pre-Socratic thought with respect to religion.

Whereas Socrates simply ignored Milesian/Ionian "scientific thought" in his turn to religion as provider of meaning for human existence, Plato constructed a complex metaphysical system—drawing on various Pre-Socratic philosophers in the process—to provide a rational justification for Socrates's kind of religious knowledge. Plato created a hybrid mode of thought by integrating Milesian rationality with Greek myth, and in making use of Plato for their own apologetic purposes the early Church Fathers and their successors inadvertently injected elements of Milesian rationalism into Christian thought, which, in his nineteenth-century book *The Influence of Greek Ideas and Usages Upon the Christian Church*, English theologian Edwin Hatch laments. As Hatch sees it, whatever elements of Milesian thinking stuck to Plato in his recovery of the Greek religious tradition were absorbed by Christian thinkers. Hatch argues that this changed the centre of gravity of the Christian Faith, making it no less a philosophy than a religion (Hatch 1890, 125). Even though Hatch believed the Church moved in this direction "from an instinct of self-preservation," he also believed that it "checked the progress of Christianity" (Hatch 1890, 349) because whatever victories it won, he asserts, it did so by preaching, not Greek metaphysics, but the love of God and the love of man. He could not, that is, bring himself to believe "that the dominance of the metaphysical element in it will be perpetual" (Hatch 1890, 349).

Plato's metaphysics did not simply disappear after the twelfth-century Aristotelian renaissance but the influence of Greek philosophical thought upon the Church became even more perilous. Indeed, as Émile Durkheim showed, in taking on this mode of Greek thought, the Church carried within itself "the germ of that great struggle between the sacred and the profane" (Durkheim 1977, 26). In striving for knowledge of the natural world for its own sake, in other words, it placed in jeopardy the revelatory knowledge of the supernatural world. But this time, instead of enveloping knowledge within the framework of a rationally justifying metaphysics, it set out to create an academic form of theology that could encapsulate knowledge of the supernatural world within the bounds of human rationality, placing knowledge of God on the same level as the knowledge of the world and its contents. The conflict between Peter Abelard and Bernard of Clairvaux over the role of reason in religion early in the twelfth century is a perfect example of Durkheim's claim, although there are contemporary theologians who dispute Durkheim's assessment.

British philosopher Gillian Evans, retired professor of medieval theology and intellectual history at Cambridge University, for example, holds a contrary view regarding the ultimate import of the relationship of Greek—Aristotelian—philosophy to Christianity. She sets out her view in her *Old Arts and New Theology: The Beginning of Theology as an Academic Discipline*. Despite recognizing an underlying conflict of purpose that produces substantial differences between traditional monastic theology (represented in Bernard of Clairvaux) and the new discipline (represented in Peter Abelard), Evans seems to think they are ultimately reconcilable.

This is also the position taken by Jean Leclerq in his account of the development of Christian thought in this period in his *The Love of Learning and the Desire for God*. For Leclerq, monastic and scholastic (Aristotelian) theology are complementary, with both groups pursuing, as he puts it, "the intelligence of faith" (Leclerq 1962, 190). According to him, theology's task is to give form to faith—a process or activity in which the truths of the Christian revelation are "interpreted, developed and ordered into a body of doctrine" (Leclerq 1962, 190). Scholastic theology, he continues, "has recourse more frequently to the philosopher, monastic theology contents itself more generally with the authority of the Scripture and the Fathers." Thus, although there may be two theologies, he insists that they "draw in common on Christian sources and both enlist the aid of reason" but the fundamental sources in both cases is/are the same. Leclerq also recognizes that this is not a negligible difference because just "[a]s the monk's language differs from that of the schools so also do their thought processes differ from those of scholasticism" (Leclerq 1962, 201). He spells out this relationship at length as follows:

> *Littera sordescit, logica sola placet* [*the letter is vile; logic alone pleases*]: the entire conflict [between monastic and scholastic theology] is rooted in this antithesis. The new style results from the predominance accorded certain disciplines: the accent is no longer placed on grammar, the *littera*, but on logic. Just as they are no longer satisfied with the *auctoritas* of Holy Scripture and the Fathers, and invoke that of the philosophers, so clarity is what is sought in everything. Hence the fundamental difference between scholastic style and monastic style. The monks speak in images and comparisons borrowed from the Bible and which possess both a richness and an obscurity in keeping with the mystery to be expressed.... The Scholastics are concerned with achieving clarity: consequently, they readily make use of abstract terms, and they never hesitate to form new words, the *profanes vacuum novitates* (unholy chatter) which St. Bernard, for his part, avoids.
> (Leclerq 1962, 199–200)

Despite Leclerq's emphasis on the unity of theology in this period, and of the complementarity of its two modes of thought, he felt compelled to justify this claim of harmony. Indeed, what he had earlier claimed to be an essential difference between the two—the emphasis on logic instead of grammar, and a move away from the authority of the Scriptures and the Fathers—he attributes in his conclusion wholly to the different environments in which "the same religious reflection was exercised" (Leclerq 1962, 251). Leclerq urges the reader not to oppose the two milieus of the two theologies too sharply; to recognize that highlighting the monastic method does not discredit the scholastic approach; that the two are complementary aspects of one theological enterprise and, finally, to see that the difference between the two is not fundamental.

Gillian Evans paints a picture of the relationship between the monastic and scholastic traditions similar to that set out by Leclerq. She points out, for example, that there is a strong element of devotion and mystical piety in the monastic study of the bible which is far less in evidence in the use of rational methods of interpretation applied to the scriptures by the "new" school of theologians, if at all. What was assumed indispensable in the *lectio divina* of the monastic community was a mere adjunct to the subject for the scholastics in the cathedral schools and universities. She is fully aware that bringing reason to bear on understanding scriptural and dogmatic matters created a good deal of friction between the monastic and scholastic scholars. The aim of academic theology was to create a subject matter that was teachable in the way that the subjects of the trivium and quadrivium were teachable, which it did by reducing theology to a system of rules. That, moreover, allowed a rapid overall mastery of theology that stood in stark contrast with, and in opposition to, the tradition of a slow absorption of these matters in the monastic context. Consequently, as Evans noted, "[t]he study of the arts provided not only a stimulus to orderliness but also a good deal of contradiction of purpose" (Evans 1980, 45).

The contradiction of purpose that Evans identifies is particularly obvious in the tension and conflict between Abelard and Bernard of Clairvaux. Bernard's objection is not so much to the way Abelard went about his theologizing but to specific errors into which he was supposedly led by applying techniques of the arts to scripture and dogma; a rarified distinction if not a specious one. Paradoxically Evans also maintains that Bernard objected to this method of doing theology as providing a "specious facility in handling deep questions" (Evans 1980, 45). The following description by Evans is an admirable summary of the essence of the debate: "The old school of the study of the Bible had not required any extensive grammar of the secular arts—nothing, in fact, beyond a little elementary grammar. But the new breed of academic theologians approached ancient mysteries with a new confidence, with the aid of techniques which were unfamiliar and even incomprehensible to traditional biblical scholarship. They assumed that the knowledge they had would serve as well in theology as it did in the liberal arts. Bernard accused Abelard of precisely this attempt to set himself up as a theologian when his expertise as a scholar lay in dialectic, and even the gentle Anselm, himself no enemy of dialectical method sensibly applied, accused the *dialectici haeretici* of approaching the study of the Bible without reverence and without respect for a proper procedure which was different from their own" (Evans 1980, 58–59). Albert Victor Murray reached the same conclusion in his analysis, *Abelard and St. Bernard: A Study in Twelfth Century "Modernism"*:

> Bernard is antagonistic to Abelard because he insists on making everything intelligible, because there is nothing that he will not make a subject of dialectical discussion because he has no reverence and looks into the secret things of God...because to him faith is a matter of opinion and because he has no use for authority. (Murray 1967, 140)

It may be true as Evans argues, that Bernard did not object to the use of the arts if kept to the role of "handmaid" to theology. But that kind of subordination of the arts to the purposes of the *lectio divina* is precisely what is excluded by the nature of the arts. Thus it is no wonder that Evans must ultimately admit that a conflict between monastic and scholastic theology existed even where the arts—that is, reason and dialectic—were not abused, and that Bernard is wholly opposed to Abelard because he sees a fundamental irreconcilability between the arts and theology. The scriptures and commentaries on them by the Fathers, Bernard maintained, contained mysteries that are simply too profound for Abelard's type of treatment of them and can only be understood via the *lectio divina*. It is not surprising, therefore, after an assessment of the respective intellectual qualities and abilities of Bernard and Abelard, to find Evans exclaiming "that the two scholars are entirely at cross-purposes in the methods of approach" (Evans 1980, 89). Moreover, in a discussion of the same matter in her book on *The Mind of Bernard of Clairvaux* she writes: "These two methods of approach, those of Bernard and the *lectio divina*, and of some of the professional academics of the day, are so different as to run in opposite directions from entirely different starting points" (Evans 1983, 76). Contemplation was entirely divorced from abstract rational thought, and emotion was given little or no place at all in the new theological classroom. The theological enterprise had come to be subordinated to the laws of thought that applied to all other subjects in the curriculum. Knowledge of God, it seemed, had come to supplant all other traditional theological goals or—though Evans does not make the point so strongly—were reduced to epistemological ones. Furthermore, as Evans puts it, "[i]t was only those aspects of knowledge about God which lent themselves to the new technical procedures which become the subject-matter of academic theology" (Evans 190, 105). Knowledge of God was now available to any educated person, regardless of their possession of spiritual gifts; a matter to which Bernard reacted sternly, according to Evans, for it was perceived as leading the faithful astray. Thus Evans, though suggesting the essential continuity of the new theology with the old, rejects the claim that Bernard was a bigoted opponent of Abelard. Nevertheless, somewhat like Durkheim, she recognizes that Bernard saw the new theology as "no merely superficial threat to the security of orthodox faith in the minds of the faithful, but to strike at its very foundations with both subtlety and force" (Evans 1983, 141). Curiosity—making of theology a search for intellectually respectable knowledge—is for Bernard both an abuse of reason and a threat to the Faith.

Leclerq's understanding of the aim of the scholastics and their contribution to the mission of the Church is, at least on first look, less critical. He maintains simply that the scholastics acquired a taste for certain intellectual activities useful to them in their daily activities, whereas spiritual preoccupations predominated in the cloisters. But this does not fully describe Leclerq's understanding of medieval scholastic thought. He recognizes, for example, that for the monastics, wisdom is far more than mere knowledge and that they had a profound anxiety that sacred doctrine would, in the hands of the scholastics, decline into being no more than "a mere liberal discipline" (Leclerq 1962, 203). Like Evans after him, Leclerq tries to argue that this is only a distrust of the abuse of logic and dialectic, but the matter cannot be disposed of that simply, for the question of what constitutes the essential character of the new reason/logic is precisely what is at stake here.

The scholastics, as Leclerq acknowledges, wanted to obtain knowledge of God; impersonal and universal knowledge of God. He was aware, that the scholastics drew on secular learning for a way of expressing such knowledge in a set of rationally justifiable epistemic claims. As he sees it, they sought "to organize Christian erudition by means of removing any subjective material so as to make it purely scientific" (Leclerq 1962, 225). But Leclerq is fully aware that Bernard and the monastics saw this as a reduction of theology "to nothing more than a rational science like any other" (Leclerq 1962, 215), and therefore as destructive of the Faith. An indication of the implicit adoption of such a conclusion by Leclerq is obvious in his description of the monastic style in liberal studies: "The monastic humanists are not like those of the Renaissance, torn between two cultures. They are not partially pagan. They are wholly Christian, and in that sense, are in possession of the *sancta simpicitas*" (Leclerq 1962, 151). However, in so far as the scholastics did not possess that same *sancta simplicitas* (holy simplicity) they were, it would appear, at least partially pagan, and it seems to me, that the monastics were clear-sighted enough to see that that was so. Moreover, even Leclerq holds that true reverence for God's mysteries requires an additional value to be "superimposed on the scientific method" if they are to be understood (Leclerq 1962, 212). As he explains:

> Theological research [with the scholastics] was approaching the dangerous point at which it might escape the limits set by faith. In trying to submit

God's mysteries to reason, one could be tempted to forget their transcendency and yield to a kind of naturalism. In the effort to explain the realities of religion would they not reduce these realities to something which reason could understand? (Leclerq 1962, 208)

Yet to superimpose any limit upon that reason espoused by the scholastics was precisely what the scholastics saw, and rightly so, as destructive of it; it would make of it something essentially other than what it really is. As Marie-Dominique Chenu points out in "The Masters of the Theological Science," in a collection of his essays entitled *Nature, Man and Society in the Twelfth Century: Essays in New Theological Perspective in the Latin West*, the monks "had cultivated and made magnificent use of the seven secular arts, but only after purging them of their arrogant ways and, according to the current image, reducing them to handmaids" (Chenu, 1968, 304). To submit to such superimposition is tantamount to continuing with the "prolongation of the patristic age" embodied in Bernard and the monastic tradition (Leclerq 1962, 114). Consequently, Leclerq is fully aware that in removing all trace of subjectivity—as, for example, in the "active reading" of scripture that made possible "absorption" of its meaning not dependent on reason—and adopting a purely scientific method, the scholastics surreptitiously espoused a form of naturalism in contradiction with the Christian Faith.

An axial shift: From revelation to reason

Andrew Ede and Lesley Cormack note in the first volume of *A History of Science in Society: From the Ancient Greeks to the Scientific Revolution*, that Aristotle's philosophy "provided an all-encompassing study of the physical world including physics, astronomy, and biology, and of the spiritual and social world using metaphysics, logic, and politics" (Ede and Cormack 2012, 93). Just as Platonism had constituted the dominant force shaping the intellectual life of the Church since the second century, Aristotelianism became the major influence in the intellectual life in the Middle Ages. Aristotle, that is, was the authoritative foundation on issues about the material realm of human existence as well as on spiritual concerns. Although his philosophy was invoked both to determine and preserve orthodoxy, as Ede and Cormack point out, it eventually became the impetus for the development of alternative natural philosophies because of its commitment to the primacy of natural over supernatural explanations in its understanding of the physical world. As they argue:

> At the heart of Aristotle's system were two fundamental ideas. The first was a system to provide a complete description of natural objects. The second was

a system to verify knowledge that would satisfy the demands of proof necessary to convince people who lived in a competitive, even litigious society. The combination of these two components produced an apex of Greek philosophy in the Middle Ages. No aspect of Aristotle's philosophy depended on supernatural intervention, and only one entity, the unmoved mover, existed outside the system of intrinsic or natural action.

(Ede and Cormack 2012, 16)

Given the legitimation of the study of natural philosophy in the context of the medieval university, Aristotelianism became, ironically, a battleground between religion and reason over control, so to speak, of what constitutes legitimate knowledge. Étienne Gilson's attention to this battle in his *Reason and Revelation in the Middle Ages* is particularly insightful.

According to Gilson, there are three "spiritual families" responsible for "the copious philosophical and theological literature in the Middle Ages": the Tertullianists, the Augustinians, and the Thomists (Gilson 1938, 5). He sees the Tertullian Family as extremist because of their belief that (biblical) Revelation, (which Gilson always writes with an upper case R), provides all the knowledge necessary to the religious (Christian) life. For them, there is an absolute opposition between reliance on the word of God and the reliance on reason as one's source of knowledge. Gilson sees Bernard as a member of this Family; as a partisan "of exclusive otherworldliness in the order of knowledge" (Gilson 1938, 14). Such partisans, he argues, appeared "wherever and whenever churchmen were interested in scientific and philosophical studies to the point of becoming actively engaged in the task of fostering their progress" (Gilson 1938, 14). Gilson notes that Bernard had no use for those—like Peter Abelard—who were "slaves of curiosity and pride" (Gilson 1938, 12) but fails to recognize that Abelard could stand as exemplar of an alternative extremist "spiritual family" of Aristotelian rationalists.

Gilson's second school of medieval thinkers is the Augustinian Family comprised of scholars who were ready "to blend religious faith with rational speculation." Exemplars of this family include second-century theologians like Justin Martyr, Origen, and Clement of Alexandria. They, and Augustine after them, Gilson explains, opened "a new era in the history of western thought" by providing "a rational interpretation of the Christian revelation" in terms of Platonic philosophy as updated by Plotinus (Gilson 1938, 22). But Gilson also recognizes that this does not actually harmonize Revelation with reason because, as he puts it, it amounts to a "transfiguration of the Greek ideal of philosophical wisdom," bursting the Platonic frame "under the internal pressure of its Christian contents" (Gilson 1938, 22–23). As he also noted: "No Greek philosopher could have ever dreamt of making religious faith in some revealed truth the obligatory starting point of rational thought" (Gilson 1938, 17). Nevertheless, Augustine's position differs significantly from that of the Tertullianists in that he did not reject reason. Unlike Bernard, according to Gilson, Augustine was fully aware that it is impossible "to condemn Dialectics without making us of it" (Gilson 1938, 11).

Gilson's third "spiritual family" are the Thomists, who, he maintains, affirmed a purely philosophical wisdom based on principles of natural reason, spelled out in Aristotle and his Muslim interpreters, that made possible a harmonizing of faith with reason. This is possible because Thomist philosophy, he argues, is independent of revelation while being "open to the supernatural light of Revelation" (Gilson 1938, 39). Thomist philosophy, that is, recognizes two kinds of truth or knowledge: revealed Truth that is attainable by reason alone—such as knowledge of the existence of God, knowledge of his attributes, knowledge of the existence of the human soul and immortality, among other similar matters—and revealed Truth that entirely surpasses human reason—such as knowledge of the Trinity, of the incarnation, and of redemption. The first kind of knowledge functions as "necessary presuppositions to matters of faith" and the latter constitute "articles of faith" which "can be proved provided they be believed first" even though "philosophical reason alone utterly fails to prove them" (Gilson 1938, 86).

It is difficult to see this description of the relationship between Revelation and reason as establishing the claim that there is a harmony between them, and Gilson acknowledges that there were many thinkers in this period who also failed to see any possibility of such harmony. For example, the alleged Thomistic synthesis was disrupted "under the lasting pressure of Averroes and of the Latin Averroists" who were committed to a strict and exclusive reliance on reason in the justification of knowledge claims (Gilson 1938, 94). One can agree with Gilson that there are at least three modes (schools) of thought at play in Medieval Europe: one reliant exclusively on faith in Revelation producing a mythopoetic/religious kind of thought; one reliant exclusively on observation and reason as the foundation for all knowledge claims; and a hybrid mode of thought that, paradoxically, attempts to blend faith-based (revelational)—and, therefore, non-rational— knowledge with rational justification.

In an essay on "Civilizational Complexes and Intercivilizational Encounters," historian and sociologist Benjamin Nelson arrives at a similar conclusion about the achievement of the intellectual community in the Middle Ages. Rather than modes of thought, however, he argues—somewhat ambiguously—that one finds in this period the emergence of three basic types of "consciousness." His types 1 and 3 correspond closely to my discussion of mythopoetic and rational modes of thought (Nelson 1981a, 96-99). In his essay on "Sciences and Civilization 'East and West'": Joseph Needham and Max Weber," he labels Type 2 as "Faith-Consciousness" which does not, I think, constitute a basic type because it is not wholly different from Types 1 and 2. Rather, it is a hybrid mode that draws on or from the other two and therefore amounts to a hybrid consciousness, or mode of thought, that incorporates a hint of rationality enveloped in a mythic form of existence. He maintains in that essay that

> [h]istory affords many illustrations of the limited institutionalization of universalism or rationality (or dialectic) within restricted spheres. We must not be surprised, therefore, if we find institutions apparently devoted to science or logic in many traditionalist societies. (Nelson 1981b, 185)

Platonized Christianity is, according to Nelson, one example of this kind of distortion. He perceptively remarks that "Faith-structures of consciousness are already a premonition of a next phase in the development of consciousness, the move toward rationalization of the contents of faith; that is, the systematic analysis of the contents and evidences for the faith, the appearance of a science called theology" (Nelson 1981a, 98).

Nelson sees a breakthrough occurring in the twelfth century, which he refers to as an axial shift, that recaptures philosophy's Greek heritage. That shift was one away from the "tribal society" as is exemplified in Ionian philosophy which moved "from [that kind of] particularism to universalism in spheres of science and philosophy" which he describes as

> a comprehensive breakthrough in the moralities of thought and in the logic of decision which open out the possibilities of creative advance in the direction of wider universalities of discourse and participation in the confirmation of improved rationales. (Nelson 1981a, 98–99)

For Nelson, the religious and ethical universalism in Christian thought that began to emerge in this century and is particularly evident in the emergence of theology as an academic discipline, is of tremendous importance in creating those conditions necessary for establishing modern philosophic/scientific thought. The twelfth century, according to Nelson, sees the crystallization of a new structure of consciousness that he refers to as a "rationalizing-and-rationalized structure of consciousness" which transcends the "faith-structure of consciousness" and "sacro-magical structure of consciousness" (Nelson, 1981b, 184). This century "is the time," he writes, "when monastic theology gives ground to scholastic theology, and the time when new images and horizons of science, self, person, society, the cosmos, action, justice, forms of rule, institutions of law and learning take on a cast that have ever since been distinctive and primary features of the Western European world" (Nelson 1981b, 184).

Nelson presses this interpretation of the significance of the revolutionary intellectual development of the twelfth and thirteenth centuries even further in his "Eros, Logos, Nomos, Polis: Shifting Balances of the Structures of Existence," showing them to be "the seedbeds of the control structures of Western social and cultural organization" (Nelson 1981c, 217). For Nelson, the victor in the Abelard and Bernard encounter was Abelard, and his move from a "faith-structure of consciousness" to a "rationalized-structure of consciousness." Abelard, that is, is a major architect of the structure of the rational consciousness of modernity—the cause of the axial shift implicit in his need to know what he believed. Nelson summarizes that axial transformation as follows:

> The early scholastic writers, including Anselm, said that they believed in order to know. *Credo ut intelligam; fides quaerens intellectum* [I believe in order to understand; faith seeking understanding]: such were their telling expressions. Those who apply these expressions often enough, those whose faith seeks understanding, find themselves imperceptibly shifting on their axes; they discover themselves passing from wanting to know in order to believe to wanting to know for the sake of knowing. (Nelson 1981c, 219)

The revolutionary character of the Milesian experiment in thought is certainly evident in the emergence of scholastic (academic) theology from the matrix of the monastic religious thinking of the day.

Conclusion

Early Christian philosophical theologians had adopted a form of Platonic thought in their attempts to make sense of and justify their revelational knowledge about a spiritual reality beyond the grasp of human reason. This blended form of thought was the Platonization of the Christian faith. This was only the first of two processes of what has been called the Hellenization of Christianity; the "baptism" of Aristotle by Thomas Aquinas was the second. In each case these Christian intellectuals introduced into Christianity philosophical elements which, though superficially complementary to the Faith, ultimately undermined the Revelational knowledge foundational to its existence. Thus I am in agreement with Durkheim's assessment that the second Hellenization of the Christian Faith carried with it "the germ of that great struggle between the sacred and the profane" (Durkheim 1977, 26).

In this light, it is not at all surprising to find that Durkheim considered the Faith to be very much at stake in the Abelard-Bernard controversy. It was not at stake in that the scholastics, any more than the monastics, were deliberately casting doubt or aspersion on the truth of the Christian religion, but rather because the very need to examine the Faith implied doubt. The need to understand the Faith, even without question as to whether it might be false was, Durkheim points out, a remarkable innovation that both stirred doubt and released the germs of that mode of thought first introduced by the Milesians that freed thought from myth. The very right to examine the Faith claimed by the scholastics also implies a diminution of that Faith. As Durkheim concludes:

> the moment one introduces reason, criticism and the spirit of reflectiveness into a set of ideas which up to that time has appeared unchallengeable it is the beginning of the end; the enemy has gained a foothold. If reason is not given its fair share, then from that moment that it has established a foothold somewhere it always ends up casting down the artificial barriers within which attempts have been made to contain it. This was the achievement of scholasticism. (Durkheim 1977, 75)

It took some time, however, before those barriers came down. As Ede and Cormack write: "The Aristotelian system had proved extremely fruitful as a research program, since it provided an all-encompassing study of the physical world including physics, astronomy, and biology, and of the spiritual and social world using metaphysics, logic, and politics" (Ede and Cormack 2012, 93). It is no surprise, therefore, that, as they put it, "[b]y the beginning of the fourteenth century the study of Aristotle in the Thomist Tradition was in complete ascendancy" (Ede and Cormack 2012, 79). But they, like Durkheim, also note that the creation of the university ultimately legitimized a broader intellectual debate that, ironically, having been "created to determine and preserve orthodoxy became the site for alternative natural philosophies in later centuries" (Ede and Cormack 2012, 66). That expansion of the intellectual life of Europe comes to the fore in the Renaissance and the Scientific Revolution of the sixteenth and seventeenth centuries.

— 6 —

The Renaissance, Scientific Revolution, and Enlightenment

Introduction

In *A New Science: The Discovery of Religion in the Age of Reason*, Guy Stroumsa argues that we will fail to understand fully the nature of the modern study of religion if we persist in believing that it is in the second half of the nineteenth century that the most dramatic developments in the study of religion took place. He maintains rather that "the period between Renaissance and Romanticism is the crucial one in European intellectual history for the first emergence and early formation of the modern study of religion" (Stroumsa 2010, viii). It is this period of European history, he claims, that made possible "a new paradigm of religion"—a new conceptual framework of the study of religion—which in turn "permitted an intellectual revolution" (Stroumsa 2010, 4), and particularly so in regard to making room for a historical and critical approach to ancient texts, including religious texts. He writes: "[T]he main argument of this book [is] that the study of the Bible was central to the birth of comparative religion in early modernity" (Stroumsa 2010, 4).

Before looking more closely at Stroumsa's claims about the modern study of religion, I think it important to understand just how intellectually complex the period of history between the Renaissance and Romanticism was. This includes not only what Stephen Toulmin calls "the modest skepticism" of Renaissance humanism, but also the Scientific Revolution, and the Radical Enlightenment that Peter Gay refers to as "an age of criticism" and Jonathan Israel calls "a revolution of the Mind," with considerable differences in their assessments of the import of these developments for the modern study of religion. Consideration must also be given to the import of what historians refer to as "the age discovery" that, as G. N. Clark put it in the 1950s, amounted to "the most momentous of current events, not only for their intrinsic interest and their material results but for less tangible and even greater reasons" (Clark 1954, 62). The full importance of these developments for understanding the emergence of a scientific study of religion is primarily a matter of the Radical Enlightenment's idea of intellectual progress—the idea of the growth of genuine knowledge—even though the Enlightenment was not only of epistemic or scientific significance; it also had an "emancipatory" objective that influenced economic, political, technological, and legal aspects of society leading to the overturning of its traditional power structures. Despite the emancipatory interest of the Radical Enlightenment, it must still be kept in mind that the Scientific Revolution of the seventeenth century invented a way to measure, manipulate, and explain natural phenomena based simply upon human reason and thereby also provided for the possibility of explaining social and cultural phenomena on the same basis.

The Renaissance

The fourteenth-century Renaissance clearly marks a new development in European thought in that it deviated considerably from the culture of traditional Christian orthodoxy. As Ede and Cormack observe, the Renaissance "witnessed a flowering of intellectual and artistic activity that started in Italy during the fourteenth century and was emulated in other parts of Europe over the next 200 years" (Ede and Cormack 2012, 92). As Arthur Herman points out, in the Renaissance re-discovery of Aristotle, the Florentines discovered freedom as an essential aspect of being human, and in the process created a new, secular ideal of human social existence involving the pursuit of excellence for its own sake (Herman 2013, 268–269). In constructing a "studia humanitatis" to support this ideal, the educational objectives shifted from traditional interest in the trivium and quadrivium, and the more recent developments in natural philosophy (Aristotelian science), to a focus on history, rhetoric, moral philosophy, and the reclamation of Greek and Roman literature. The social and moral ideals of the ancient world, even when they deviated from Christian orthodoxy, were deemed most suitable to the new ideal, and the Renaissance intellectuals were committed to a continuation of those ancient goals. Most important for the period, Stroumsa argues, was the recovery and repair of the texts of the ancient Greek and Roman worlds, taken as models for expressing their own aims, goals, and desires. The ancient science of philology, with its critical concerns related to correcting texts that had become corrupted over the centuries, was a primary focus of attention.

Stroumsa sees Isaac Casaubon's critique of the Corpus Hermeticum in the late fifteenth century as pseudepigraphical in nature, and of particular importance because it amounted to undermining the "holistic conception of religious history, to make room for the historical and critical approach to ancient texts and hence the early history of religious and philosophical ideas" (Stroumsa 2010, 4). He then attempts to show, that by the end of the eighteenth century, the new modern era of religious studies was able to emerge on entirely different epistemological foundations. As he claims, the modern study of religion was the result of offering "a new understanding of religion that had no real precedent in the Middle Ages or during the Renaissance" and he calls this "birth of the modern comparative study of religions…the discovery of religion" (Stroumas 2010, 5).

More recently, Stephen Toulmin argues a contrary understanding of the Renaissance in his *Cosmopolis: The Hidden Agenda of Modernity*. It is important, however, to recognize that in many ways the Renaissance, as Peter Gay has argued, is only "a prelude to modernity" insofar as it rested uncritically on the authority of the "ancients," as Richard Foster Jones notes in *Ancients and Moderns: A Study of the Scientific Revolution in Seventeenth-Century England* (1982 [1936]), even with respect to Aristotle's natural philosophy. As Ede and Cormack point out, it is certainly true that there was a "flowering of intellectual and artistic activity" in Europe in this period, but, as the early critics of the Renaissance argue, it drew its information about the world entirely from the books of ancient authors. As Jones describes the criticism, this dependence on the ancients was "to lose oneself in a nebula of fruitless words which produced only the sensation of knowledge and not its reality" (Jones 1982, 19). Francis Bacon, among other such critics, objected to the implicit theory among Renaissance thinkers of the decay of intellect and thought since the time of the ancients. That theory (presumption), the critics maintained, amounted to an obstacle to progress in gaining knowledge of the world that would be securely tied to the physical world through sense-observation rather than to ancient beliefs (Jones, 1982, 51 and 268). Thus, even though the Aristotelian system had been extremely fruitful as a research program in the past, and remained of great apologetic value to the Church, it was about to come to an end.

Toulmin is not ignorant of the consensus about the emergence of modernity on the basis of shared assumptions about rationality that were enunciated by those seventeenth-century philosophers who constructed a new scientific way of thinking about nature and society. He recognizes that their attempt to frame their questions about nature independently of the context in which they were operating is not wholly wrong, but he argues that such decontextualization of rationality as the product simply of the ivory tower, so to speak, was naive. The espousal of reason as limitless, emphasis on global and universal epistemological objectives, and the quest for certainty, he insists, simply blinded the seventeenth-century thinkers to the modest skepticism of Renaissance intellectuals—that is, to the Renaissance culture of reasonableness and religious tolerance—that connected humans and the natural world. According to Toulmin, therefore, the seventeenth-century thinkers constituted something of a "counter-Renaissance" movement in that they "looked not just for a way to give knowledge the certainty that Montaigne and his fellow-skeptics denied it: they also wanted to build up a fresh cosmology from scratch" (Toulmin 1990, 83). Their science was not just an abstract enterprise but a worldview with a cosmopolitan function.

Toulmin focuses his attention in this book on what he considers the weaknesses of the modern age. Even though the modern age has yielded striking technological successes, it has also, he insists, led humanity into its deepest failures. Toulmin's agenda, therefore, is to counter "the current widespread disillusion with the agenda of Modernity and salvage what is still humanly important in its project" (Toulmin 1990, xi).

Toulmin recognizes that there is not full agreement among scholars even as to the meaning of the concept of modernity, yet he claims that there is an underlying consensus about what modernity is, namely, shared assumptions about rationality introduced by seventeenth-century philosophers who adopted a new scientific way of thinking about nature and society. He admits that in several respects this standard view is not wholly wrong but is in some need of elaboration and correction. Thus, he writes:

> ...one aim of seventeenth-century philosophers was to frame all their questions in terms that rendered them independent of context, while our own procedure will be the opposite—to recontextualize the questions these philosophers took most pride in decontextualizing. The view that modern science relied from the very start on rational arguments, divorced from all questions of metaphysics or theology, again assumed that the tests of "rationality" carry over from one context or situation to another, just as they stand; i.e., that we can know without further examination what arguments are rational in any field, or at any time, by reapplying those that are familiar in our own experience. (Toulmin 1990, 21)

As far as Toulmin is concerned, the problem with the standard view of the modern age is that it fails to recognize that the seeds of Modernity lie in the Renaissance and not simply in the philosophical developments of the seventeenth century. That attribution constituted something of a counter-

Renaissance by emphasizing global and universal concerns rather than local and temporal interests in the practical side of life. The Renaissance, he maintains, rejected trust in limitless reason:

> The contrast between the practical modesty and the intellectual freedom of Renaissance humanism, and the theoretical ambitions and intellectual constraints of seventeenth-century rationalism, plays a central part in our revised narrative of the origins of Modernity. By taking the origins of Modernity back to the 1500s, we are freed from the emphasis on Galileo's and Descartes' unique rationality, which was a feature of the standard account in the 1920s and 1930s. The opening gambit of modern philosophy becomes, not the decontextualized rationalism of Descartes' *Discourse* and *Meditations*, but Montaigne's restatement of classical skepticism in the *Apology*, with all its anticipations of Wittgenstein. Montaigne claimed in the *Apology* that "unless some one thing is found of which we are completely certain, we can be certain about nothing." (Toulmin 1990, 42)

Toulmin agrees with Montaigne that there is no general truth about which certainty is possible, and he concludes that we can claim certainty about nothing.

For Toulmin, then, the key features of the modern age are the result of a dual origin—of "two distinct beginnings"—in Renaissance humanism and seventeenth-century Rationalism, and he attempts to justify this claim by means of historical explanation of the emergence of each. The modest skepticism of the Renaissance, he claims, can be accounted for by the period of relative economic prosperity and political stability that characterized the late fifteenth and sixteenth century. That prosperity and stability allowed for, even if it did not directly cause, a culture of reasonableness and religious toleration in which the natural and the human were intimately connected. Contrary to the standard view of the seventeenth-century rationalists' "Quest for Certainty" as the result "of pure, detached intellectual study," Toulmin claims that the quest was a response "to a specific historical challenge—and the consequent "breakdown of public confidence in the older cosmopolitical consensus" (Toulmin 1990, 70 and 71). He writes:

> ...the Cartesian program for philosophy swept aside the "reasonable" uncertainties and hesitations of the sixteenth-century skeptics, in favor of new, mathematical kinds of "rational" certainty and proof. In this it may (as Dewey and Rorty argue) lead philosophy into a dead end. But for the time being, that change of attitude—the devolution of the oral, the particular, the local, the timely, the concrete—appeared a small price to pay for a for-

mally "rational" theory grounded on abstract, universal, timeless concepts. In a world governed by these intellectual goals, rhetoric was of course subordinate to logic; the validity and truth of "rational" arguments [are] independent of who presents them, to whom or in what context—such rhetorical questions can contribute nothing to the impartial establishment of human knowledge. For the first time since Aristotle, logical analysis was separated from and elevated above the study of rhetoric, discourse and argumentation.
(Toulmin 1990, 75)

The work of the seventeenth-century rationalists, claims Toulmin, is neither the product of the ivory tower nor was it simply concerned with matters epistemological and scientific. He writes: "They looked not just for a way to give knowledge the certainty that Montaigne and his fellow skeptics denied it: they also wanted to build up a fresh cosmology from scratch" (Toulmin 1990, 83). Their science, he insists, was not just an abstract science as they and their successors claimed—they, in effect, produced a worldview with a cosmological function, namely, the justification of the modern social order. Their scientific work, he maintains, "was done as part of 'forms of life' or 'life worlds' very different from those within which it now goes on" (Toulmin 1990, 137). That worldview, he goes on, was based not simply on confidence in Cartesian or Newtonian physics but rather "rested on other, parallel subtexts, whose meaning had little to do with deducing mathematical theorems, or explaining natural phenomena" (Toulmin 1990, 117–118). In summary, Toulmin writes:

> The comprehensive system of ideas about nature and humanity that formed the scaffolding of Modernity was thus a social and political, as well as a scientific device: it was seen as conferring Divine legitimacy on the political order of the sovereign nation-state. In this respect, the worldview of modern science—as it actually came into existence—won public support around 1700 for the legitimacy it apparently gave to the political system of nation-states as much as for its power to explain the motions of the planets, or the rise and fall of tides. (Toulmin 1990, 128)

Toulmin concludes, then, by saying that the thought of the seventeenth-century rationalists was not wholly at odds with the human concerns of the Renaissance humanists. Consequently he sees it as feasible to reconcile the legacies of the humanities and the exact sciences, although he does recognize that this will require an admission that "the agenda of 'modern thought' overreached itself"; that is, that "Descartes' foundational ambitions are discredited …" (Toulmin 1990, 175 and 167). Hence his own project is to carry modernity "back to a time before Galileo and Descartes and giving the Renaissance humanists credit for originality [and] even 'modernity'..." (Toulmin 1990, 82). Toulmin then goes on to claim that recording the twin legacies of the Renaissance and the Enlightenment will "open up all kinds of new possibilities" for contemporary thought (Toulmin 1990, 143) by replacing the rationalists' notion of science with an understanding of science which "subordinates it to the needs of citizens and communities" (Toulmin 1990, 200–201).

Toulmin is justified in his claim that the intellectual life of the Renaissance created a register of critical thought not apparent in the medieval period preceding it. He is wrong, however, to think of the "scientific revolution" that occurred in these centuries as the result of pure ratiocination; a mere metaphysical construct, and as the following brief account of the Scientific Revolution will show, the epistemic objective of the natural sciences could not have been achieved had they been subordinated "to the needs of citizens and communities."

The scientific revolution

Recent histories of the development of the sciences in early modern Europe have raised doubts about whether there really was a "Scientific Revolution." Peter J. Bowler and Ivan Rhys Morus, for example, in their *Making Modern Science, a Historical Survey: Episodes in the Development of Science* claim that an increase in our knowledge of scientific practice in the Middle Ages, and the historical discoveries of other cultures, made important contributions to scientific learning in early modern Europe. They suggest that the revolution metaphor is inappropriate because it implies that this enterprise was an entirely new—even unique—approach to understanding nature. As they put the matter in their Introduction:

> Historians' views of the Scientific Revolution—and particularly of its unique status—have undergone considerable revision in recent years.... Historians now are far less happy to accept that it makes sense to talk at all about "science" during the seventeenth century. There is a recognition that in actuality seventeenth-century men of science and natural philosophers (as they would describe themselves) engaged in a whole range of activities that may or may not fit comfortably with modern notions of science.
>
> (Bowler and Morus 2005, 24)

Recognizing clear continuities between modern scientific approaches to understanding the natural world, and ancient modes of natural philosophy, does not undermine the claim that new methods in the study of natural phenomena could set that enterprise on a significantly different footing—sufficiently different to be considered momentous, even if not absolutely different. In one sense, everything and every historical development is connected in some sense, however vague, to every other historical development. Bowler and Morus's comment that some of the modern "scientists" engaged in this "revolution" actually tried to trace this development back to Hermes Trismegistus and magic. But they also recognize that this does not undermine the claim, for example, that the new knowledge of the "scientific revolution" was not only new, but was also quite different in how it was obtained. Bowler and Morus, therefore, quite clearly recognize that "in the end, a new kind of activity that we call science did emerge, resulting in an explosion of new methods, theories, organizations, and practical applications" (Bowler and Morus 2005, 17). Unlike Bowler and Morus, I think this "explosive" difference of intellectual activity of the post-Renaissance scientists from the scholars engaged in "a kind of scientific" thinking that preceded them, is precisely what justifies calling this development the Scientific Revolution.

John Henry make this point succinctly in his essay "Religion and the Scientific Revolution," in the *Cambridge Companion to Science and Religion*:

> Historians typically use the expression "Scientific Revolution" to refer to that period from the early sixteenth-century to the late seventeenth, when something recognizably like modern science coalesced out of previously distinct traditions as natural philosophy, the mathematical sciences, and Renaissance magic. (Henry 2010, 39)

That revolution is often described as exemplified in Copernicus' *On the Revolution of the Celestial Spheres* (1543). P. M. Harman summarized the revolution in his book, *The Scientific Revolution* in this fashion:

> By around 1700 educated men conceived the universe as a mechanical structure like a clock, the earth was regarded as a planet revolving around the sun, and the mysteries of nature were supposed to be open to investigation by means of experimentation and mathematics. (Harman 1983, 1)

But these views stand in stark contrast to Stephen Toulmin's attack on modern science as rationalistic and strangely independent of any and all historical and cultural influence; a failure to understand the world as it is and creating one the rationalists prefer.

This is not to say that science is not itself a cultural product—an artifact of sorts—but only that the natural world which is the object of its interest is not a cultural artifact. As Alan Chalmers points out in his book *Science and Its Fabrication*:

> The natural world is the way it is independently of the class, race, or sex of those who attempt to know it, and the scientific merit of the theories that constitute our attempts to characterize it should be similarly independent of these factors. (Chalmers 1990, 115)

Again, he writes:

> The natural world does not behave in one way for capitalists and in another way for socialists, in one way for males and in another for females, in one way for Western cultures and another for Eastern cultures. A large scale nuclear war, made possible by modern science, would destroy us all, whatever our class, sex, or culture. (Chalmers 1990, 112)

Chalmers is well aware of the historical and sociological fact that there is "a wide range of kinds of knowledge," as he puts it, to which individuals (and cultures, so to speak) have laid claim. Even though he does not think it likely that we will ever be able to find a characterization of the concept of knowledge "that captures the features of them all," he insists "that it is possible and important to distinguish the aim of producing scientific knowledge from other [epistemic and non-epistemic] aims and objectives" (Chalmers 1990, 25 and 95). However, it seems to me, although I will not argue the matter here, that Peter Watson is correct in understanding that science alone can provide "the basis for comprehending other forms of knowledge" (Watson 2016, 313) which is essential for establishing a scientific study of religious thought and behavior.

In his book on *The Invention of Science: A New History of the Scientific Revolution* David Wooton, like Alan Chalmers, acknowledges that science is a cultural artifact. He is fully aware that there were, and perhaps still are, systems of knowledge that some erroneously think of as scientific, as well as other non-scientific knowledge claims. But he, like Chalmers, differentiates them from the system of knowledge produced by the Scientific Revolution; he does not, that is, accept postmodernist interpretations that see all forms of, or claims to, knowledge as wholly culture-bound. Wooton argues that the only pre-Revolutionary scientific knowledge "which functioned like a modern science" was astronomy, which was ultimately "transformed in the years after 1572 into the first true science" (Wooton 2015, 1). Asking what made it science Wooton writes:

> It had a research programme, a community of experts, and it was prepared to question every long-standing certainty (that there can be no change in the heavens, that all movement in the heavens is circular, that the heavens consist of crystalline spheres) in the light of new evidence. Where astronomy led, other new sciences followed. (Wooton 2015, 1–2)

This intellectual revolution clearly transcended the Aristotelian philosophy of nature that had dominated European thought and, according to Wooton, "transformed the nature of knowledge and the capacities of humankind" (Wooton 2015, 13). Consequently, Wooton claims "that the seventeenth century idea of natural science underwent a fundamental revision, and by the end of the century the idea that had taken shape was basically the one that we still have" (Wooton 2015, 49).

Wooton's basic question is: "What exactly was it that enabled seventeenth- and eighteenth-century science to make progress in a way that previous systems of knowledge could not?" (Wooton 2015, 4). His answer is that progress was made possible by employing observation, experiment, and theory in the quest for knowledge of the natural world. In contrast to Toulmin's account of modern science as a quest for certainty, Wooton shows that "the …founding of modern science was accompanied by an escape from the old notion of true knowledge (*scientia*) and its replacement by the concept of theory…" (Wooton 2015, 397). This new science, that is, was conscious of being incomplete which, as Wooton points out, is what made epistemic progress possible. Indeed, insofar as the Scientific Revolution made knowledge possible, it "is not absolute but progressive, not definitive but provisional" (Wooton 2015, 398); it "offers reliable knowledge (that is, reliable prediction and control) not truth" (Wooton 2015, 570), and is "different in kind from anything that had gone before" (Wooton 2015, 457). He is fully aware that this new avenue to obtaining knowledge of nature is "flawed, profoundly contingent [and] culturally relative" but shows that "the postmoderns notwithstanding, we have learnt to develop reliable knowledge, even though we as human beings have continued to be fallible as ever" (Wooton 2015, 541 and 568). Despite all this, he adds, "[t]he new language and the new ideas of [modern] science have now survived for 300 years …, and there is nothing to suggest they are likely to go out of fashion soon" (Wooton 2015, 566). Thus, he fittingly concludes that:

> Science—the research programme, the experimental method, the interlocking of pure science and new technology, the language of defeasible knowledge—was invented between 1572 and 1704. We still live with the

consequences, and it seems likely that human beings always will. But we do not just live with the technological benefits of science: the modern scientific way of thinking has become so much part of our culture that it has now become difficult to think our way back into a world where people did not speak of facts, hypotheses, and theories, where knowledge was not grounded in evidence, where nature did not have laws. The Scientific Revolution has become almost invisible because it has been so astoundingly successful.

(Wooton 2015, 571).

Wooton is aware that there are historians who will find retrospective histories like his suspect. In a preemptive response to such criticism, he writes:

Historians who refuse to engage in it narrow the intellectual scope of history unnecessarily and arbitrarily; indeed history written without the benefit of hindsight (if such a thing were possible) would not be history at all, but rather to adopt Foucault's term 'genealogy.'" (Wooton 2015, 551)

Michael Hobart's more recent *The Great Rift: Literacy, Numeracy, and the Religion-Science Divide* takes up the same challenge of accounting for the rise of modern science in Europe, even though Hobart's primary concern is to understand the basis of the ultimate conflict that emerged between religion and science. Despite this difference, Wooton and Hobart have both keyed in on the absolutely fundamental role of mathematics in the genesis of the Scientific Revolution, which I will spell out here.

Wooton points out in his work that a core principle in the history of science is that "a revolution in ideas requires a revolution in language" (Wooton 2015, 48). Wooton has in mind here the transition from the use of conventional language to the use of mathematics to describe the procedures available to explore and solve problems in accounting for nature. This, he argues, characterizes the radical difference in the approach to nature between the Aristotelians and opponents of the philosophers like Galileo, and if one asks how this transition occurred, Wooton writes, "the answer is through perspective painting, cartography (and related sciences of navigation and surveying) and ballistics" (Wooton 2015, 205), which he describes as instruments for thinking that had long been in preparation. This is why he asserts that "[h]istorians of science have often (and rightly) suggested that the key to the Scientific Revolution is 'the mathematization' of nature" (Wooton 2015, 199) and he provides the following brief description of this development:

The Scientific Revolution was first and foremost, a revolt by the mathematicians against the authority of the philosophers. The philosophers controlled the university curriculum (as a university teacher, Galileo never taught anything but Ptolemaic astronomy), the mathematicians had the patronage of princes and merchants, of soldiers and sailors. They won the patronage because they offered new applications of mathematics to the world.

(Wooton 2015, 209).

Hobart provides a more detailed account of the import of this mathematization of the natural world based on a proper understanding of the two distinct information technologies—literacy and numeracy—that characterize the history of human thought. The first information age, Hobart argues, was born of literacy; it was a world based on the assumption that words captured and communicated both knowledge about the world as well as beliefs about the world, or worlds, beyond the natural. As Hobart explains, it was alphabetic literacy that made possible "the higher reaches" of Greek thought: "science, religion, and philosophy were all based on the technology of alphabetic literacy and the classifying temper it propagated" (Hobart 2018, 6). This mode of thought also dominated intellectual activity in medieval Europe. The second information technology was based on relational numeracy, that is, on "seeing numbers as relations, rather than merely as collections of things or objects…" (Hobart 2018, 6). This gave rise to what Hobart calls the analytic temper which supplanted alphabetic literacy in the quest for knowledge of the natural world. In Galileo's time, he argues, this "enabled fresh readings of ancient mathematics" catapulting "premodern mathematics into a highly abstract and relational world" which ultimately made possible getting to the deep substructures of the natural world by way of "reverse engineering" the phenomena of nature (and, ultimately, even of history and culture, including religion) (Hobart 2018, 7). Hobart writes,

> Once gaining a toehold in European thought and culture…modern numeracy and analysis burrowed into the core scientific thinking about nature and from there generated their modern progeny, the bifurcation of science and religion. (Hobart 2018, 15)

He designates Galileo's work as "The Moment of Modern Science" because it was Galileo who first exemplified the inside of "the emerging, analytic temper" (Hobart 2018, 237). This does not so much concern what Galileo discovered as how he made his discoveries—by distilling "relations from the ephemera of moving bodies" (Hobart 2018, 244). Wooton makes the same claim:

> With Galileo's discovery of the parabolic path of projectiles (1592) and the law of fall (1604) the sublunary world began to be mathematically legible, and Newton went on to show that the same physical principles were at work in the heavens and on Earth. (Wooton 2015, 199)

This, Hobart maintains, amounts to "reverse engineering" the phenomena of nature and getting to the substructures of the natural world. He writes:

> We still don't know why they work, but properly understood and manipulated and applied, empty symbols and their rule of combination can capture nature's most recondite secrets, beginning with motion itself.
> (Hobart 2018, 252)

In this sense, Galileo and other contributors to the creation of modern science carved out a type of knowledge of nature that could be achieved by way of analysis of intersubjectively available data that could be expressed in abstract mathematical generalizations that would be tested by way of empirical observation and experimentation. Thus, Hobart concludes:

> After Galileo words would have less and less to do with the means, technically speaking, of scientific discovery and explanation ... [because] at the most basic, reductionist levels of explaining how natural phenomena work, words fail; mathematical symbols and formulas and the reverse engineering of analysis take over. (Hobart 2018, 39–320)

It is important here also to note Hobart's claim that this kind of scientific knowing is incommensurable with religious thought, dominated as it is by the classifying temper—by the literary technology of information—and is, to use Hobart's term, "inexorably distant from religious belief" (Hobart 2018, 316 and 317). Wooton had arrived at a similar conclusion. "Initially," Wooton writes,

> key figures of the new science hoped that would help prove the reality of supernatural activity; after the publication of Newton's Principia...the result was quite the opposite: the new science seemed to legitimize a new scepticism. (Wooton 2015, 429)

It is also important to note that Hobart admits that nobody really knows why mathematics works like this; that it is "a mystery of sorts." But, he claims that "the uncertainties and mysteries of science and religion are as day to night, and from the moment of modern science's inception, the gulf between these two has inexorably grown wider and deeper" (Hobart 2018, 317–318).

The radical Enlightenment

As I have already noted, unlike Toulmin, Peter Gay sees the Renaissance as a mere prelude to modernity. Insofar as the Renaissance was a period of lively, even chaotic, intellectual activity, and even though that activity deviated considerably from Christian orthodoxy at the time, and its appropriation of classical thought made criticism possible, it did not amount to an age of criticism; it did not, that is, usher in the disenchanted, secular view of the world characteristic of modernity. Gay writes: "[I]t is the indispensability of the sacred that differentiates the Middle Ages at its most scientific and skeptical from ages of criticism" (Gay 1967, 237). One does see here a curiosity about the world that has some semblance to that of the period of modern science, but it is not a curiosity that seeks for explanations of the world "from a critical stance of philosophical doubt but from a devout longing for closeness to the divine center" (Gay 1967, 232). The Renaissance did nevertheless provide an important impetus to the thought of the seventeenth-century philosophers who, Gay claims, saw it as a period of great new beginnings in that it prepared European intellectuals to approach their own Christian faith with skeptical detachment and to read pagan philosophers with sympathy.

In such a context, Gay argues, the philosophers were able to develop new instruments for understanding the world that would eventually make possible a view of the world as a natural system. This is the beginning of a disenchantment in the minds of Christians that will continue to grow into a fully-fledged critical rationalism. Evidence for this, he claims, is overwhelming: "Polite literature, serious music, and political controversy all grow more secular in subject matter and forms of expression" (Gay 1967, 339). Gay is not ignorant of the religious quality of these centuries, evident in a continued association of religion with science, for example, but insists nevertheless that during this time "... religious institutions and religious explanations were slowly being displaced from the center of life to its periphery" (Gay 1967, 338). This was clearly indicated, he argues, by what he refers to as the treason of the clerks: accommodations made to this mode of thought by the church itself; its concessions to criticism, science, and philosophy creating a bland piety without social force (Gay 1967, 346). As Gay points out, "[t]he origins of ideas may be a clue to their function [but] they do not determine it" (Gay 1967, 323). The seventeenth-century philosophers he therefore writes, "saw the Renaissance as the first act of a great drama in which the Enlightenment itself was the last—the great drama of the disenchantment of the European mind" (Gay 1967, 279). "[T]he scientific battles of the seventeenth century," that is, "were fought out with the vocabulary and the conceptions of pagan antiquity" (Gay 1967, 306) even while the philosophers rejected the very idea of a classic text and saw themselves as pioneering thinkers without ancestors (Gay 1967, 308).

Gay notes that the worldliness of the seventeenth-century philosophers was not quite the secularism of the Enlightenment, neither was its

Christianity that of the Renaissance. These philosophers still sought a compromise between Christianity and classicism, and therefore, between piety and worldliness—a compromise Gay refers to as a period of "pagan Christianity" and describes as a time of secular forces that explode whatever unity the Christian system had possessed (Gay 1967, 256). But the philosophes, he writes, could not grant "that philosophical Christians or Stoic Christians were men with a coherent world view, and it was precisely this failure that freed the Enlightenment from diffidence and made it revolutionary" (Gay 1967, 320). Gay describes the new world such thinking ushered in as follows:

> It is a world of intense energy, of great hopes and great pride coupled with respect for rigor and passion for method. Rapidly and with accelerating pace, the study of nature, especially of astronomy and dynamics, grew into an autonomous pursuit, and by the time of Newton, science had triumphantly proved itself a progressive field of inquiry: each theory was a provisional statement inviting modifications; each experiment was a threat—a welcome threat—to prevailing formulations. By the force of logic, science began to cut its ties to philosophy and to assume a posture at first equal, and then hostile, to theology. (Gay 1967, 309)

Gay sees Hume as the epitome of this development because he

> was willing to live with uncertainty, with no supernatural justifications, no complete explanations, no promise of permanent stability, with guides of merely probable validity; [and what is more], he lived in his world without complaining, a cheerful Stoic .... [He] makes plain that since God is silent, man is his own maker: he must live in a disenchanted world, submit everything to criticism, and makes his own way. (Gay 1967, 419)

For Gay, then, the project of the Enlightenment was the pursuit of modernity which he describes as essentially a recovery of intellectual nerve in that it attempted to move beyond the fatalism characteristic of the medieval Christian world. "The ancients," he writes, "had felt helpless before the forces of nature and man's irrationality, and the philosophers of antiquity had rationalized this impotence in systems pervaded by a profound pessimism" (Gay 1969, 84). The philosophers, however, developed a new style of thinking which involved the search for wholly naturalistic explanations of phenomena; they rejected the infusion of theological, metaphysical, and aesthetic concerns characteristic of much of ancient "science."

It is not that the philosophes wholly rejected classicism but rather that they kept "their respect for their ancestors within proper bounds" (Gay 1969,

125), and placed greater emphasis upon reason and the growth of knowledge which provided them with "an expansive sense of power over nature and themselves" (Gay 1969, 3). The world was being emptied of mystery by the advance of knowledge. As Gay sees it,

> [t]he sacred was being hollowed out from within by the drying up of religious fervor, the call for good sense, the retreat of Augustinian theology, the campaign against "enthusiasm," and the advance of rationalism among the clergy of all persuasions. (Gay 1969, 27)

The sacred and religious fervor was being replaced by a secular social conscience and good manners (Gay 1969, 39). Reason, industry and humanitarian sentiment were now seen as the means of securing a good life without servitude. The birth of modernity in the Enlightenment, therefore, involved a new way of thinking not only about the natural world but also about humanity and society. For Enlightenment intellectuals, scientific detachment was combined with a reformist involvement that involved a critique of tradition and the demise of traditional social hierarchies which in turn created the need for the "moral sciences" of political economy, history, sociology, psychology, medicine, and so on, which would advance freedom and humanity. In addition to a scientific cosmology, therefore, Enlightenment thinkers "called for a social and political order that would be secular, reasonable, humane, pacific, open, and free...: (Gay 1969, 397), and a critical social science that would "unmask pleasing dreams for the sake of realistic programs [and] fictions for the sake of reality" (Gay 1969, 335).

An understanding of Hans Blumenberg's analysis of the nature of the modern age in his *The Legitimation of the Modern Age* (1966) will help clear away the concerns critics may have of Modernity and the Enlightenment that ushered it in. Blumenberg's view of the character of modernity is in many respects like that held by Peter Gay, although he does not appear to have as high an evaluation of its human benefits; Blumenberg, that is, does not see the modern age as superior to others in coming to understand the place of human existence in the world. For Blumenberg, scientific rationalism cannot be a sufficient guide to human action simply because it cannot determine ends. It therefore requires supplementation, and in this opens itself up to other sources of wisdom including myth, religion, and metaphysics.

Despite that evaluation, however, Blumenberg recognizes modern European thought to be significantly different from that of Antiquity and the Middle Ages in its understanding of the importance of human self-reliance, self-assertion, and an unwillingness to rely on divine providence.

The Moderns, that is, adopt a rational approach to the resolution of human problems rather than passively accept a promise of salvation; they relate, therefore, to a natural world that is open to scientific explanation rather than to a supernatural world which is not, and it is to this break with traditional thought to which Blumenberg devotes his attention in *The Legitimation of the Modern Age*. Whereas in *The Genesis of the Copernican World* (1987) Blumenberg looks at the links between the Copernican revolution in astronomy and cosmology, in *The Legitimation of the Modern Age* he devotes himself to refutation of the claims of the Romantics and other critics of Modernity who deny its rupture with the traditional mode of thought and existence in the Middle Ages. Thus Blumenberg rejects the claim that the import of modernity is really little more than the secularization of Christian ideas. He describes these charges as follows:

> The occasion for talk of the legitimacy of the modern age does not lie in the fact that this age conceives of itself as conforming to reason and as realizing this conformity in the Enlightenment but rather in the syndrome of the assertions that this epochal conformity to reason is nothing but an aggression (which fails to understand itself as such) against theology, from which in fact it has in a hidden manner derived everything that belongs to it.
> (Blumenberg 1966, 97)

In contrast to such claims Blumenberg argues that modernity constitutes a break with the dominant theme of divine omnipotence in the Middle Ages, and that it is an affirmation of the contingency of the world which involves a critical commitment to rationality both in knowing the world and living in it. Blumenberg does not deny that the modern age has some connection with the Middle Ages, but he insists that it is not such a continuation of it. Modernity, as Blumenberg asserts, accepted "a mortgage of prescribed [residual] questions...as its own obligation..." (Blumenberg 1966, 65). Thus, he writes:

> What mainly occurred in the process that is interpreted as secularization ...should be described not as the transposition of authentically theological questions...into secularized alienation from their origin but rather as the reoccupation of answer positions that had become vacant and whose corresponding question could not be eliminated. (Blumenberg 1966, 65)

In this, the Enlightenment took over the explanatory functions of Christianity in the same way Christianity had taken over the explanatory functions from Antiquity (Blumenberg 1966, 69). According to Blumenberg, this is characteristic of what he calls "epochal thresholds"—that is, periods during "the phases of more or less rapid change in the basic rules for the procurement of very general explanations" (Blumenberg 1966, 66).

According to Blumenberg, then, even though the moderns recognized the values of the legacy of Antiquity, they nevertheless rejected the "fundamental Renaissance thesis of the unsurpassibility of ancient literature" (Blumenberg 1966, 125). Thus, he insists that "the modern age is neither a renewal of the ancient world nor its continuation by other means..." (Blumenberg 1966, 126). Nor is the modern age merely a continuation of Christianity; it emerges rather as a response to the crisis of Christianity in providing a comprehensive understanding of human life through reason and theory, which in turn depended upon a transition from a "naive" to a "self-conscious" curiosity about the world (Blumenberg 1966, 237). This, he insists, gave rise to an unrestricted cognitive drive whereas the Middle Ages had tied knowledge to happiness. Blumenberg writes:

> From a central affect of consciousness there arises in the modern age an indissoluble link between man's historical self-understanding and the realization of scientific knowledge or the confirmation of the claim to unrestricted theoretical curiosity. The "theoretical attitude" may be a constant in European history since the awakening of the Ionian interest in nature; but this attitude could take on the explicitness of insistence on the will and right to intellectual curiosity only after it had been confronted with opposition and had had to compete with other norms of attitude and fulfilment in life.
> (Blumenberg 1966, 232–233).

The success of this "theoretical curiosity," and the search for knowledge free from all restriction in respect to her "human existential interest posited as absolute" (Blumenberg 1966, 233), therefore, is a chief characteristic of the modern age. As Blumenberg observes: "...when, as in the modern age, a form of life first begins to depend on science for the conditions of its possibility does the problem of knowledge as such become so elementally acute for it that the problem of the possibility of life poses itself even before that of happiness in life" (Blumenberg 1966, 271). As he elaborates in his conclusion:

> Truth has become the result of a renunciation for the modern age..., a renunciation that lies in the separation between cognitive achievement and the production of happiness. This separation could be accepted as a temporary one as long as the integration of theoretical accomplishments still seemed attainable or indeed insofar as one considered one's own present situation to be quite near to the summit of the ascent. But this separation also begins—with increasing doubt about the convergence of knowledge and happiness—

to be set up as an ideal: Lack of consideration for happiness becomes the stigma of truth itself, a homage to its absolutism. (Blumenberg 1966, 404)

Conclusion

Developments in the intellectual life in Europe in the Middle Ages were, in many ways, unique in history. There were significant socio-political developments that made possible some expansion of intellectual life beyond the boundaries of the Church. Nevertheless, despite the advances in modes of analysis and argumentation, as well as the emergence of alternative natural philosophies, these advances did not amount to a revolutionary break from ecclesiastical control. This is reasonably described, however, as an enlargement or maturation of thought making possible a mode of thought entirely independent from religion and the Church. I think, that is, that we see in this period of European intellectual history the first clear steps, so to speak, in the emergence of what Ernest Gellner calls "the Western epistemic tradition" (Gellner 1974, 32) which, but only implicitly at this stage of growth, seeks knowledge of the world and its contents for its own sake. The unacknowledged assumption of "the diplomatic immunity" (Gellner 1973, 178) of the value placed on possessing such knowledge from all other values will ultimately trigger a revolutionary shift in European thought and culture. We see in this intellectual shift the vestibule of the modern age.

— 7 —

The Age of Discovery and the Protestant Reformation

Introduction

The taxonomy of religions in the Middle Ages was very limited. In addition to Christianity, only the Jews, Pagans, and Muslims constituted the intellectual and socio-political context of the rise of Christianity. In the fourth century the Church Fathers were engaged in polemics against numerous pagan systems of thought and in justifying the suppression of pagan worship. During the later period of Christian dominance in Europe, Christian intellectuals were involved in producing apologies for Christianity over against the Jews and Muslims. But an expansion of that taxonomy in the early modern period of European history constituted a major change in European attitudes to religious belief.

David Wooton points out in his *The Invention of Science: A New History of the Scientific Revolution* that the voyages of discovery brought about an amazing expansion in Europe's knowledge of the world, including its diversity of religions. As he puts it, whereas "the known world in the first half of the fifteenth century was more or less identical to the world known to an educated Roman at the time of Christ, by the beginning of the sixteenth century it was clear that there were extensive inhabited territories that had been unknown to the Greeks and Romans." This, of course, "created a new enterprise that intellectuals could engage in: the discovery of new knowledge" (Wooton 2015, 110). The new knowledge that interests Wooton is knowledge of the physical world and he rightly claims that this scientific enterprise "required that certain social and technical preconditions be met: the existence of reliable methods of communication, a common body of expert knowledge and an acknowledged group of experts able to adjudicate disputes" (Wooton 2015, 106). But the epistemic revisions that the voyages of discovery demanded were not limited simply to the sciences but also to belief in general. As G. N. Clark observes in his mid-twentieth century assessment of "The Early Modern Period" of European history, these discoveries "altered the tenor of life in Europe itself…[They] had great, immediate, and ever-growing effects on the region of the mind…Every thinker was confronted by new facts and new mysteries…" (Clark 1954, 73–74). In a more recent assessment, historian Joyce Appleby describes the import of the voyages of discovery for European society; new information that came back with those voyagers "upended the grand Christian narrative of the origins of life and the place of our planet in the universe" (Appleby 2013, 14). Indeed, she argues that it "nudged Europeans toward modern ways of thinking," not only about the planet but also about the people that inhabited these new lands (Appleby 2013, 42). As she argues: "The existence of previously unknown places peopled with unlikely inhabitants posed intellectual puzzles for the leaders of Christendom…[creating] an impact on humanists as well as the protectors of Christian dogma" (Appleby 2013, 59–60).

It is clear then that the discovery of the new world created a range of epistemological problems for European intellectuals, but none greater than for theologians. Theologians—and Christians in general—were aware of different belief-systems and other religions but, as Appleby explains, "this new kind of diversity didn't seem to fit in at all," making Christianity appear "a local and particular religion like those that flourished elsewhere" (Appleby 2013, 70 and 71). The recently invented printing press, of course, was a means of spreading this information far and wide, generating discussions and conversations often bordering on the heretical. "The existence across the Atlantic of strange people with truly weird mores," as Appleby notes, "shook Christian confidence in the universality of their religion, which until now had only been marred by the existence of stubborn Jews and heretical Muslims" (Appleby 2013, 92). She continues: "Like Aquinas with Aristotle, Christians had to meld their new experiences with the precedent-shattering voyages of the fifteenth century into their old dogma in order to answer concerns of potential converts as well as doubts that they themselves might harbor" (Appleby 2013, 98). She argues that the increasing interaction of ordinary citizens with the educated elite in society "created a broad receptivity to the novel propositions that were challenging centuries of learning" about the natural world but especially so about the significance of the increase of knowledge about the wide variety of spiritual beliefs and practices (Appleby 2013, 127 and 177). The publication of the seven volume *Religious Ceremonies and Customs of the World* by Bernard Picart and

Jean-Frédéric Bernard (1723–1737) that treated these new religious traditions sympathetically, she adds, became "part of the new modern consciousness [that] was a heightened awareness that society had not been handed down by some divinity but was rather the product of human beings themselves" (Appleby 2013, 179).

Appleby sums up her analysis of the import of the Age of Discovery on European thought in the following paragraph:

> [O]ver the course of four centuries, studying natural phenomena became an activity defining western modernity while loosening the hold of religious dogma over scientific enquiry....[F]inding a new continent with its own array of human cultures delivered a monumental shock to Europeans because the phenomena of the New World could not be absorbed into the existing cosmological knowledge of the sixteenth century, provoking people to think anew their assumptions and categories. (Appleby 2013, 256)

A social and intellectual revolution in the understanding of religion: Early Modern Europe

Picart's and Bernard's eighteenth-century *Religious Ceremonies and Customs of the World* was not the first examination of the epistemic implications of the diversity of conflicting religious beliefs in an expanded cultural world. Jean Bodin's work of 1593, *Colloquium of the Seven about Secrets of the Sublime*, as Sam Preus points out in his *Explaining Religion: Criticism and Theory from Bodin to Freud*, was already an extended work that provided a critical treatment of the epistemic and spiritual tension created by the new diversity of religious thought in Europe. Although not published in full until the nineteenth century (1857), the Latin manuscript—*Colloquium Heptaplomeres de Rerum Sublimium Arcanis Abditis* (1588)—circulated (covertly) in the late seventeenth century and more widely in the eighteenth century in more than a hundred copies of the manuscript. As Preus argues, this book made possible a critique of religion by revealing the tensions and questions raised about the truth of religion(s) which Bodin describes in imagined conversations among a Catholic, a Jew, a Muslim, a Lutheran, a Calvinist, a philosophical naturalist, and a skeptic. As Preus sees it, this made it possible for Bodin to seek a way outside of the religious frame of mind to settle the question of the truth of religion. Though not explicitly rejecting revelation, Bodin put reason above revelation in dealing with the social and political implications of such religious diversity for society, which undermined the generally accepted biblical model for the organization of reality. This was a very unusual position to take up at the time. As Preus puts it, Bodin nevertheless realized that making intellectual headway in such a situation required going radically beyond the mutually contradictory claims, credentials, and paradigms of the religious traditions; it required a new criterion for assessing religious claims, an Archimedian point outside the conflict. (Preus 1987, 3–4)

Bodin's *Colloquium*, Preus claims, moved European thought in this direction by setting up "a confrontation, on equal ground, of contradictory paradigms, in the attempt to find new common ground," of "reasoned argument alone, operating in a detached setting where no authority should prevail except their own consensus or, lacking that, harmony in their agreement to disagree" (Preus 1987, 4). For Preus, Bodin's lodging of this indirect critique of religion merits him a place in the history of the development of the modern (scientific) study of religions and religion. But such merit belongs not simply to Bodin in Preus's judgment. Preus writes:

> It is perhaps no accident that the first class of "professionals" that broke ranks in the religious wars and focused on religion itself as a problem—of truth, of conscience, and of social order—were outsiders, not theologians but diplomats. Prior to Bodin one thinks of Machiavelli and Thomas More (the *Utopia*); and, after Bodin, Herbert of Cherbury and Thomas Hobbes. All of them made creative contributions to the analysis of religious motivation and behavior, and of the role of religion in society, and all for the sake of a tolerable postmedieval social order. (Preus 1987, 5)

Bernard Picart and Jean-Frédéric Bernard were not theologians, or even diplomats; they were, respectively, an engraver and a publisher, but they also merit a place in the history of the emergence of a scientific study of religion. They were refugee publishers who entered the book trade not only to make a living but also to think through the problems of religion and society in their troubled times. As Lynn Hunt, Margaret C. Jacob, and Wijnand Mijnhardt make clear in their *The Book that Changed Europe: Picart's and Bernard's Religious Ceremonies of the World* (2010), Picart and Bernard established that "[f]rom the sixteenth century onward the discovery of new worlds had compelled early modern society to come to terms with much greater religious and cultural variety" than Europe had experienced earlier (Hunt *et al.* 2010, 124). They argue, however, that like the theologians and diplomats Preus refers to, Picart and Bernard were concerned to support voices arguing for religious toleration, and believed this could best be done by "offering a global and culturally relative depiction of religious diversity" revealed in travelogues describing new peoples and new religions (Hunt *et al.* 2010, 7). They write:

Toleration, in their view, did not lead ineluctably to disbelief, rather it opened the door to uncensored knowledge, to deeper reflection on the significance of the religious impulse, and to a sense of kinship rather than hostility to other people's beliefs and practice. (Hunt *et al.* 2010, 21)

However, even though Picart and Bernard were not intent on dismissing religion as illusory, they clearly wished to "cast a " and secular light" on religion. As Hunt *et al.* put it, in summing up what was known about religion and giving that knowledge a new political significance, Picart and Bernard created a new genre of literature that, in pointing to the multiplicity of confessions within Christianity itself, created doubt about the value of established religion and encouraged readers to try to understand the character (i.e. logic) of other religions and to establish some distance from their own beliefs. In what they call the "astonishing afterlife" of Picart's and Bernard's book (Hunt *et al.* 2010, 19), they show that "these ideas seeped gradually into the European intellectual water table" (Hunt *et al.* 2010, 43) and in that sense "helped create the field of comparative history of religion" (Hunt *et al.* 2010, 19 and 43).

Hunt *et al.* base their assessment of the scientific import of Picart and Bernard's work on several major contributions they think were made by the publication of Picart's and Bernard's *Religious Ceremonies of the World*. They point out first that these two collaborators rejected the religious or theological approach to understanding religion. For example, they were not interested in questions as to which religion was superior to all others (Hunt *et al.* 2010, 11). They rejected the religious manifestos of priests (and/or politicians) (Hunt *et al.* 2010, 95). As they write: "Bernard's Machiavellian loathing of the anti-intellectual priesthood and his abhorrence of superstition seeps from the pages of his *Moral Reflections*" (Hunt *et al.* 2010, 119), and they argue that Picart and Bernard maintained that religion was not "an unchanging system of beliefs but a discrete entity concerned everywhere with the gods or the heavenly" (Hunt *et al.* 2010, 2). An important aspect of this rejection of a religio-theological approach to understanding religion(s), they claim, was Picart and Bernard's objective of cultivating a healthy attitude of doubt (and critique) that would distance people from their own beliefs, and thereby increasing the possibility of seeing the beliefs of others from their points of view (Hunt *et al.* 2010, 18). As Hunt *et al.* remark,

> [t]hey wanted to confront their audience with a radically new religious education that would turn the traditional religious surveys...upside down: they wanted to show the public that acquired religious ceremonies and customs had obscured the universality of religion. They aimed at transforming preju-

dice into inquisitiveness, because they were certain that knowledge would lead to the acceptance of deviant religious teachings and practices.
(Hunt *et al.* 2010, 126)

Picart and Bernard's concern with doubt about and critique of then current religious certitudes are the foundations of the emergence of objectivity in research about human, and particularly religious, affairs. Their aim, it appears, was to help people to distance themselves from their own cultures and from their own personal religious beliefs and commitments as essential in coming to understand the beliefs, commitments, and practices of others. As Hunt *et al.* explain: "Religious belief and practice became an object of study for these men rather than an unquestioned way of life...They published to foster an open and critical discussion about religion" (Hunt *et al.* 2010, 24). Freedom of conscience on religious matters was essential to obtaining the objectivity they thought essential for understanding others. For them, freedom of thought (i.e., religious freedom of conscience) was essential to truly understanding others. According to Hunt *et al.*, "Religious toleration was an essential tool in the search for religious truth" (Hunt *et al.* 2010, 20).

Picart and Bernard's primary aim was simply to present the facts about the discovery of new forms of religious thought and practice. They undertook a careful literary and historical study of them, "compiling, adapting and synthesizing the best information available about religious practices around the globe" (Hunt *et al.* 2010, 17). Hunt *et al.* show that Picart and Bernard made sure that their book "could be received as an unbiased compendium of the most up-to-date writings ..." on religions then known. Of particular importance in their work was the undertaking of a global survey of religious practices that included the recent discoveries of "new peoples and new religions" (Hunt *et al.* 2010, 4). Their work in this respect, therefore, laid the foundations for what in the nineteenth century was called "comparative religion." They emphasized the importance of accuracy and balance in their portrayal of religions in order to establish "the credibility of their comparative method [and that] meant demonstrating the intrinsic interest and merit of pagan and heathen practices" (Hunt *et al.* 2010, 213). Hunt *et al.* write: "[O]n the one hand, Bernard and Picart want to align idolatry with a universal story of the decline of natural religion, exemplified in particular by the corruption of Roman Catholicism; but on the other hand, they want to show the intrinsic interest of all the varieties of religious practice around the world" (Hunt *et al.* 2010, 240).

Hunt *et al.* also attribute to Picart and Bernard the creation of the modern concept of religion. They maintain Bernard, in his early book *Moral*

Reflections (*Reflexions Morales* 1723), seemed "to be sketching the existence of some sort of universal religiosity that simply gets expressed in different forms, and its origins appear to be entirely human" (Hunt *et al.* 2010, 36). In *Religious Ceremonies of the World* they maintain that Bernard "was giving new meaning to the category itself. He was contributing to an intellectual shift of major importance in the European conceptualization of religion" (Hunt *et al.* 2010, 286). About Picart they write: "[His] images, especially when read alongside Bernard's text, essentially created the category 'religion'" (Hunt *et al.* 2010, 155).

Finally, Hunt *et al.* assert that Picart and Bernard were involved in theoretical analysis of religions in various guises. They claim that such theorizing is implicit in their support of the new science over against scholastic Aristotelianism (Hunt *et al.* 2010, 57) and in their application of the notions of the uniformity and regularity of nature in their "reconstruction of the development of the religions of the world" (Hunt *et al.* 2010, 4). As they argue,

> Bernard and Picart were developing their approach at an important turning point in European understanding of non-Western religions. The almost obsessional focus on linguistic etymologies, allegories, and attempts to trace the diffusion of Egyptian beliefs, Judaism, and even early Christianity that had characterized sixteenth- and seventeenth-century scholarship now increasingly gave way to more sustained effort to get at the internal logic of exotic beliefs. (Hunt *et al.* 2010, 228)

Bernard tried to get at that internal logic, they write, by postulating "a universal human nature as the root of religiosity" (Hunt *et al.* 2010, 128) involving a universal psychological impulse generated by human physiological anxieties. Bernard used his survey of the religions of humankind, they claim, to "test his hypothesis about the presence of universal principles at the heart of true religious behavior" after the manner of Francis Bacon's approach to science that called for a systematic collection of empirical case histories for this purpose (Hunt *et al.* 2010, 130).

Even though Picart and Bernard were still in some sense religious, and wanted to assist people in discerning "within religious diversity itself the truths one could honestly live by and cherish" (Hunt *et al.* 2010, 21), and even though "new European attitudes of racial superiority" re-emerged after them, Hunt *et al.* maintain that their work "reflected an unusual moment in European intellectual and religious history" (Hunt *et al.* 2010, 160). They lament the fact that neither modern anthropology nor comparative religion recognized the significance of their work for later nineteenth-century intellectual developments in the formation of the scientific study of religion(s). They write:

> [Picart and Bernard] sought, wherever possible in word and image, to slip out from under the biases found in most accounts of religion and then to search for the universals seen in the religions of Europe, Asia, the Americas, and Africa. They blended encyclopedic erudition with the style of late Baroque realism, using engravings to give aesthetic pleasure and enlightened perspectives. They brought art into the service of curiosity and tolerance while setting new standards for documentation and the citation of evidence. (Hunt *et al.* 2010, 309)

Hunt *et al.* know that all this makes Picart and Bernard only "a stepping-stone" toward the modern scientific study of religion, but they suggest that not recognizing their contribution to that enterprise, is to fail to understand a critical episode in its establishment.

A social and intellectual revolution in understanding religion in America

James Turner makes a similar claim for the rise of the scholarly—not, significantly, scientific—study of religion in his *Religion Enters the Academy: The Origins of the Scholarly Study of Religion in America*. He describes this development as follows:

> In the later eighteenth century, the study of [East] Indian languages would take on a momentum of its own. This would lead in the nineteenth century to the scholarly study of Indian cultures, and these inquiries would finally open to Euroamerican eyes the varied religions of the North American Indians. By 1900 these non-European religions would form a small subordinate part of the new discipline of religious studies. (Turner 2011, 12)

In his later book—*Philology: The Forgotten Origins of the Modern Humanities* (2014)—he makes a similar claim regarding the origins of what he calls the comparative study of religions. He writes:

> Comparative religions seems—obviously but deceptively—to owe its existence to European imperialism. Certainly, imperial ventures brought deeper, broader awareness of beliefs and practices of subject peoples. Such knowledge of other religious systems enabled emergence of the discipline.
> (Turner 2014, 170)

According to Turner, the various academic approaches to the study of religion—and especially so in the USA—were humanistic disciplines engaged in understanding and articulating religious thought and belief.

There is historical evidence that supports Turner's claims about this new intellectualist approach to the study of religion that emerged from the expanded typology of religions emerging from the Age of Discovery. However, Turner seems simply to ignore that the Scientific Revolution had invented a way to measure, manipulate, and explain natural phenomena based simply on human reason, and that this provided for the possibility of explaining religious thought and behaviour on the same basis.

Although Turner states that interest in non-European religions played only a small and subordinate role in the emergence of what in North America is generally referred to as "religious studies," his description and analysis of that interest seems to imply a greater role for it. He asserts rather baldly that "we owe academic religious studies to the deists" (Turner 2011, 14)— who greatly influenced American thought toward the end of the eighteenth century—because their use of the notion of "natural religion," as embodying universal truths that can be found in every religion, inspired a comparative study of religion. As he writes: "In beating Christians about the head with non-European religions, deists may have encouraged the comparative investigation of religions, although disinterested scholarship was not their forte" (Turner 2011, 16). The early nineteenth century, he argues, brought with it an increasing interest in non-European religions in several quite different arenas: the "scholarly side effects" in America of British hegemony in India; the missionary activities of evangelical Protestants in Asia; and, as already noted above, interest in Indian religious/spiritual thought and practice. He is aware that these early encounters with non-European religions in America were not disinterested studies of those religious traditions but rather polemical and apologetic enterprises. He refers to Hanna Adams (1755–1831), for example, as a pioneer of the study of religion because she was seriously engaged with non-European religions from the 1820s and on. He claims, that is, that she "had no trouble recognizing something properly called religion in Native American Cultures" (Turner 2011, 28).

By approaching Amerindian religious traditions as worthy of understanding, Adams pushed American thought beyond its comfortable religious boundaries just as the Age of Discovery had much earlier influenced European thought about religion. However, although Adams, along with other intellectuals in nineteenth-century America, foreshadowed the emergence of "religious studies" in the United States, Turner claims that it would be a mistake to see her as "a serious precursor of modern religious studies" (27), as did Louis Henry Jordan in his (1905) history of the field, because she lacked an understanding of the scholarly academic world and, more importantly, she used her understanding of Amerindian religiosity as a tool to improve the Unitarianism to which she was committed. That is, her motivations were not in a disinterested scientific knowledge of the Amerindian traditions but were motivated rather by theological quarrels within the Christian tradition.

Turner's ambivalence about Adams's contribution to the emergence of "religious studies" in American academic institutions is somewhat odd because the scholars who followed after Adams are no more interested in non-European religions simply out of Enlightenment curiosity than was she. As he sees it, there were Christian reasons "to care for them" that characterizes the comparative study of religions between 1820 and 1875 (Turner 2011, 32). Turner shows that most of the early American comparativists, that is, examined other faiths only to repair what they perceived as deterioration of the Christian tradition or to expand their Christian theology in an idealist fashion as a universal religion. James Freeman Clarke (1810–1888) is but one example of many whom Turner points to as indicative of this development, drawing particular attention to Clarke's *Ten Great Religions: An Essay in Comparative Theology* (1871).

Compared to Hanna Adams, however, Clarke's work, Turner points out, was scholarly, as was that of other Unitarians (Transcendentalists or not) and for this reason, it appears, Turner believes that "these Unitarian writings, inflected by Transcendentalism" provide "the first real foundations for the academic study of religion in the United States" (Turner 2011, 51). Turner knows that this ultimately is but a version of liberal nineteenth-century Protestantism that wanted to show that all religions are aspects of the progress of humanity, but he claims that it was this mode of theological scholarship that eventually led "to the creation in America of an academic discipline dedicated to studying all religions" (Turner 2011, 32), even though he acknowledges that most of it focused on preparation of persons for missionary activity (Turner 2011, 32, see also 53). However, "[w]hen exactly they got a proper discipline for studying it was never clear. No great event stands out to mark the birth of the academic study of religion" although Turner credits the history of religions program at the University of Chicago with providing the first respectable program for the study of religion separated from ministerial training. But even here he notes that it remained closely tied to Christian biblical studies and theology (Turner 2011, 57, see also 61). Nor was there any agreement on what it should be called: history of religion(s), science of religion, religious studies, religion, comparative religion, etc.

For Turner then, the "religious studies" that emerged from the earliest interest in non-European religions was and is a humanistic discipline, intellectualist in orientation that was and is "a historically minded, text-based study oriented toward articulated religious or ethical propositions" but essentially a religio-theological enterprise (Turner 2011, 65–66).

The final chapter in Turner's book on the emergence of the study of religion in American universities is given over to an examination of William James's Gifford Lectures, published as *The Varieties of Religious Experience* (1902). Turner certainly recognizes that James' attempt to understand religion is wholly alien to the development of the academic study of religion in the United States just described. According to Turner, James's lectures had nothing to do with comparative religion and the distinction between world and local religions or with the historical development of religions. Nor was James interested in providing a psychological explanation of religion. He was especially opposed to the materialistic reductionism of psychologists like James H. Leuba in his *A Psychological Study of Religion* (1912) and the simple empirical data collecting of Starbuck in his *The Psychology of Religion* (1899). According to Turner, moreover, James was dissatisfied with what he called "the science of religion" because he found it "aloof from real lived religious experience" (Turner 2011, 79). William James, that is, considered religion a vital aspect of life and, as Turner remarks, James "longed…'to find evidence for the operation of immaterial and spiritual elements within nature [the natural world]'" (Turner 2011, 77). For James, the core of religion is to be found in religious experience which he saw as "the ultimate source of and reason for…all religious thought and behavior" (Turner, 2011, 79). James was, consequently, opposed to scientific materialism in general as a form of intellectual imperialism, claims Turner, and he was especially dissatisfied with physiological psychology of religion in particular. According to Turner, therefore, James wished "to foster a new science, with a broader vision of what 'reality' comprised"—that is, a science that was open to the possibility of a reality beyond the physical world (Turner 2011, 74 and 78).

Turner may be right in claiming that James wanted to shake up the academic study of religion as it existed in his day, and that his objective in *Varieties* was his "strenuous effort at intellectual reform" (Turner 2011, 79). Nevertheless, Turner's claim that the book was an enduring presence in religious studies is questionable. Indeed, Turner acknowledges that professional religious studies students have generally neglected James—at least by Christians, on the one hand, who were theologically concerned about the value of the study of religion on their own faith and, on the other hand, by students in the field committed to European models for a scientific study of religion, which James appears to have repudiated (Turner 2011, 80). Nevertheless, Turner claims that with the change of name of the professional association for "academic" scholars of religion from the National Association of Biblical Instructors (NABI) to the American Academy of Religion (AAR) "*Varieties* became relevant to the field" and that James, therefore "stretched the map of religious studies in America" (Turner 2011, 81).

The change from NABI to AAR amounts essentially to a change of name, not of the character of the enterprise (or enterprises) that are sponsored by the AAR. The AAR represents "the academic study of religion" as it is for the most part carried out in colleges and universities in the United States (and Canada), but that study is not non-confessional. However, the character of its confessional commitment has changed from a capital-C confessionalism, which espouses particular doctrinal claims about supernatural agents, to a lower case-c confessionalism that acknowledges the existence of some kind of religio-moral reality beyond the physical realm and naturalistic explanation, but open to humanistic understanding. The AAR—at least the vast majority of its membership—is not agnostic on this matter and is, therefore, engaged in the quest for an encounter with that spiritual reality.

An emerging scientific ethos for the study of religion

James Turner presents a persuasive argument regarding the influence of the discovery of other religions on the traditional theological study of religion in classical and medieval Europe. The plurality of religions and their gods undermined the typical theistic (Christian) view of the universe that had dominated European thought until then. But this plurality did not undermine a general belief in the existence of a transcendent truth beyond the physical world. This truth was seen as being expressed differently in the plurality of religions of which Europeans became aware from the voyages of discovery. As Turner argues, this information provided the foundation for a humanistic study of the reality of the spiritual experience of humankind throughout history. As Turner has it, such a humanistic study revealed the existence, truth, and meaning of spiritual experience by revealing its universality. Turner, moreover, points out that such a humanistic study of religion still exists as a scholarly undertaking in contemporary American educational institutions which has also taken root in other scholarly contexts worldwide.

Such humanistic studies of religion, however, were not the only approach to understanding or explaining religions that was generated by the discovery of other religions. The Scientific Revolution of the sixteenth and seventeenth centuries that explained natural phenomena based simply upon human reason eventually provided the impetus for explaining social and cultural phenomena, as well. The natural sciences, that is, provided a model for a new and coherent intellectual tradition for the study of religions and religion that not only broke away from the religio-theological paradigm within which that study had been ensconced until the seventeenth century, but also differs radically from the humanistic approach described by Turner. Preus traces out the development of that naturalistic framework in both his *Explaining Religion: Criticism and Theory from Bodin to Freud* (1987) and in *Spinoza and the Irrelevance of Biblical Authority* (2001). Guy Stroumsa makes a similar claim about the emergence of a scientific approach to understanding and explaining religion in his *A New Science: The Discovery of Religion in the Age of Reason* (2010).

Preus in his *Explaining Religion* argues that a naturalistic paradigm for the study of religions emerged from their conflicting truth claims. He makes use of Thomas Kuhn's notion of paradigm shifts (Kuhn, 2012, 89) to identify a series of minor revolutions in thought about religion, the cumulative effects of which establishes the reasonableness of a naturalistic paradigm. The history of those minor revolutions, he maintains, can be divided into two periods. The first period, represented in Jean Bodin's work, involved a progressive advance of criticism of the absolute character of conflicting religious truth claims and an increasing degree of detachment from religious presuppositions and commitments in the study of religions. Rationalist and historical approaches—represented by Herbert of Cherbury and Bernard Fontenelle—characterized the second period. According to Preus, this period involved an increasing awareness of the social nature of religion that resolves the paradox of religion's intellectual obsolescence and social persistence. Preus shows that David Hume marks a watershed between these periods because Hume represents the self-conscious substitution of a scientific for a theological approach in the study of religion. As Preus notes, with Hume "a line of criticism definitely ends and construction of alternative theory begins" (Preus 1987, 84). For Hume, that is, the concern in this field of study was no longer to be focused on the problem of the legitimation of religion, but rather on its explanation. Religious truth claims, that is, could not be shown to be true in any literal sense; they had been surpassed as knowledge and its explanation, therefore, had to be sought elsewhere, which gave rise to a wide range of explanatory accounts of why devotees believe such truth claims. Such explanations of why devotees believed religious truth claims is what distinguishes a scientific study of religion from the study of religion in the framework of the humanities with its apologetic intentions. Thus, Preus writes: "Hume's thoroughgoing naturalism, his clear vision of religion as part of a science of humankind, and his development of alternatives to all the contemporary theological explanations of religion together warrant the paradigmatic role he is accorded here" (Preus 1987, 100).

Preus extends the argument presented in *Explaining Religion* in his *Spinoza and the Irrelevance of Biblical Authority* (2001) by tracing the rise of the critical, historical, and comparative study of scriptures. This development, he argues, undermined the dominance of insider theological interpretation of the scriptural texts supported by the political establishment of an official "public interpreter of scripture" that had legal authority in society at that time. Spinoza opposed the notion that scripture had any authoritative role in public policy and law, and insisted that scripture be studied with the same critical methods applied to any other ancient texts. According to Spinoza, such traditional methods of interpretation could only cause division in the church and a curtailing of liberty in society. Preus writes that:

> Spinoza's remedy was to recast the Bible in a new intellectual framework—naturalistic and historicist—in service of his campaign for liberty. Deprived of its halo of infallibility and subject to the same critical scrutiny due any ancient book, Spinoza's Bible would also lose its political relevance. But such analysis, Spinoza hoped, would force the theologians to take into account a domain whose relevance they had not recognized: that of historical facts.
> (Preus 2001, 22)

It was not only the advance in philological and historical scholarship that placed a heavy burden on the interpreters of scripture. There was an explosion of knowledge and new ways of knowing in the emerging scientific revolution which placed great strain on the notions of revelation, of the infallibility of, the canonical authority of, scripture, and of "saving knowledge" and associated religious knowledge claims. These developments, Preus points out, "excluded claims to knowledge that had no regard for the public criteria of reason and evidence that were being honed in the quest for more exact knowledge and made available to wider and more critical scrutiny through the medium of print" (Preus 2001, 29). For Spinoza "[k]nowledge was knowledge, and only one authority presided over its domain: that of evidence and reasoned judgment" (Preus 2001, 38). In this, claims Preus, Spinoza echoes a distinctive feature of Francis Bacon's admonition to natural philosophers to question conventional beliefs and open themselves to natural histories in all areas of learning. Bacon and the Moderns, as Richard Foster Jones (1965) has shown, could only free themselves from opinions learned from books and social convention by rejecting Classical authorities. As Preus observes: "Acutely aware of the social dimension of knowledge,

Bacon charged that trying to develop genuine knowledge by relying on allegedly universal common notions amounted in fact to relying on 'the common stock of opinion'" (Preus 2001, 164).

Preus claims that Spinoza "completely displaced the status and function of theology in the study of religion" by showing that the origin and meaning of scripture "could be accounted for without remainder through human history alone…" (Preus 2001, 208). Thus Preus concludes that: "Although it was not his intention, he [Spinoza] laid the foundation for what is now an established academic discipline that applies the same historical, critical, and comparative method to the explanation and interpretation of scripture and biblical religion as one applies to any other religious text or system" (208).

In *A New Science: The Discovery of Religion in the Age of Reason* Guy Stroumsa also presents an argument to support the claim "that the study of the Bible was central to the birth of comparative religion in early modernity" (Stroumsa 2010, 4). According to him, the emergence of a genuinely scientific approach to the study of religion was dependent on three major historical events: the discovery of the other-than-European religions in the Americas and East Asia; a renewed interest in antiquity and the growth of modern philology; and the fallout from the Protestant Reformation and the wars of religion that followed on that historical movement.

Although the discovery of new religions was not in itself a major factor in the development of a scientific study of religion according to Stroumsa, he nevertheless, like Hunt *et al.*, argues that this discovery "provided the trigger without which the new discipline could not have been born" (Stroumsa 2010, 22). This "revolution in knowledge," as he describes it, permitted "a radical transformation in the perception of religious phenomena" which "entailed the urgent need to redefine religion as a universal phenomenon." This transformation made possible a comparative study of religions that would eventually reflect the unity of humankind (Stroumsa 2010, 3). Whereas the term religion before the seventeenth century functioned as a binary concept, with religion being either true or false, Stroumsa maintains that the discovery of the multiplicity of the forms of religion "permitted …the development of a single concept of religion" that could accomplish that task and make possible a non-polemical and therefore more secular and objective study of religions (Stroumsa 2010, 7). Stroumsa does not here provide a full-fledged overview of this intellectual development but attempts to get his point across in a series of case studies. These include the missionary activity of the Jesuits who, in order to accommodate the mores of the people whom they wished to convert to Christianity, invoked the notion of civil religion. By doing so, they discovered equivalences between and among religions and cultures that gave rise to the notion of natural religion which, in turn, made possible a type of comparative study of religions. As Stroumsa puts it, the concept of civil religion "permitted these scholars to overcome the limits of Christianity" (Stroumsa 2010, 38).

Stroumsa sees this move by the Jesuits amounting to a Thomas Kuhn-like paradigm shift in the study of other religions that was created by the adoption of "a modicum of critical attitude toward religion on the part of enlightened Christians" (Stroumsa 2010, 38). In a study of the work of Joseph Justus Scaliger (1540–1609), he maintains that we can see a transition from concern with theological matters to interest in academic research aided by sheer intellectual curiosity. In this process, the Bible became an object of intellectual and academic interest like other ancient Near Eastern religious texts. He writes:

> A better understanding of ancient Israel helped explain other religious systems, including polytheistic ones, while other religions shed new light on that of Israel. At the time, the religion of biblical Israel still held a place of honor in intellectual reflection, which it would gradually lose throughout the eighteenth and nineteenth centuries. (Stroumsa 2010, 49)

A similar conclusion seems warranted, he claims, from a study of the philological work of the French biblical scholar Richard Simon (1638–1712) on Judaism (1678). Simon's work suggested that Christianity and Judaism are essentially the same religion because they hold essentially the same beliefs, which Stroumsa sees as an "overgrowth...due to a lack of historical criticism and common sense on the part of the rabbis" (Stroumsa 2010, 75). This emphasis on the importance of honest history, and the import of the multiplicity of religions for understanding of religion was, then, both a result of commitment to the autonomy of reason and a contribution to it—an essential element in the growth of a scientific study of religions. In the seventeenth century scholars still tried to incorporate newly discovered civilizations into a biblical *Heilsgeschichte* (salvation story), even though they did not take scripture literally. That bibliocentric framework, however, was lost in the eighteenth century, claims Stroumsa, where "one perceives a move from the 'genetic' analysis of ancient Near Eastern and Mediterranean religions to a comparative analysis of religions around the world" (Stroumsa 2010, 88). Stroumsa continues: "The application of philological methods to the biblical texts combined with ethnological observation led to a major breakthrough in the study of ancient religions. It permitted the historicizing of religious truth and a strong rejection of the symbolic thought that had been so much in fashion during the Renaissance" (Stroumsa 2010, 88). In discussion of Iranian religions and Islam, Stroumsa shows the processes of detheologization that made possible a more modern study of religion, and how the rejection of revelation as a category in this field "legitimated an identical approach to all religions as purely human phenomena ..." (Stroumsa 2010, 142).

The Protestant Reformation

As unlikely as it may seem, the Protestant Reformation or, rather, the fallout from the Reformation helped create conditions under which the scientific study of religious phenomena was ultimately to emerge. That fallout is what historian Brad S. Gregory referred to as the emergence of Christian denominationalism and the birth of secularism. Gregory refers to this as the Reformation's "unintended consequences" in his *The Unintended Revolution*, with the subtitle *How a Religious Revolution Secularized Society* (2012) and in his *Rebel in the Ranks: Martin Luther, the Reformation, and the Conflict that Continues to Shape Our World* (2012). The denominationalism produced by violent disagreements among Christian theologians on matters of doctrine reinforced the devaluation of the epistemic credibility of religious belief implicit in the discovery of a plurality of non-European religions. Gregory maintains that the Reformation not only contributed to the secularization of the state—that is, establishing the principle of the separation of church (religion) and state—but also to the "secularization of knowledge" which made possible the formation of critical attitudes toward religions and religiosity. According to Gregory, these developments created the conditions that made possible the scientific study of religious phenomena.

Gregory maintains that around 1500 there was some unity in European society regarding, as he puts it, "truth claims that were held to be God's answers to the Life Questions, and thus applicable to everyone" (Gregory 2012, 84). He acknowledges that there were local differences that made Christianity in that period of history variegated and diverse, but that this all occurred within an overall framework of unity amounting to a "social, political, intellectual, and cultural totality" based on the Bible (Gregory 2017, 5). Religion in that period of European history, that is, was "more than religion." It was intimately interconnected with every other aspect of society. As Gregory remarks in his later book, *Rebel in the Ranks*

> If religion had been just religion, these fissures might not have mattered too much. But in the sixteenth century religion was never just religion, so the ruptures and rifts made worlds of difference. Religion wasn't separate from the exercise of power or one's duties to others, or the buying and selling of

goods, it wasn't separate from education or morality. It touched everything, which meant disagreements about it threatened to disrupt everything.
(Gregory 2017, 139–140)

The Reformation, therefore, adopting the principle of *sola scriptura* as an alternative foundation for Christian belief and practice, introduced what Gregory calls a hermeneutical heterogeneity that "proved doctrinally contentious" [generating an] unwelcome pluralism of competing Christian truth claims" (Gregory 2012, 93 and 100). These intra-Christian tensions ultimately resulted in widespread violence throughout Europe, with each denomination (Catholic, Lutheran, Calvinist) competing for political control of society. The Protestant solution to the doctrinal tensions and religious violence it often spawned, claims Gregory, came by way of privatizing religion, which made possible toleration of the hyper-pluralism that had emerged. Indeed, Gregory argues that these religious disputes ultimately inspired an atheistic secularism that could "accommodate doctrinal disagreement and insulate public life from religious influence" (Gregory 2017, 14). That development, of course, called for a clear distinction between church (religion) and state which made it possible for the state to protect both individual rights and accommodate a plurality of Christian denominations by prescinding from theological debate, that is, "transcending" religion by relying on reason to resolve disputes in the public realm. However, that reliance on reason, Gregory argues, made possible the perception of religious beliefs as irreducibly subjective and arbitrary (Gregory 2012, 175) and therefore a purely personal choice and, for that reason, irrelevant to the public life of the community, and this, ultimately, made possible disestablishing the church (religion) and the emergence of purely political institutions to look after the common welfare of the nation. As Gregory writes in *Rebel in the Ranks*: "To find persuasive answers to questions about politics, law, morality, and society, disagreements about God [religion] would have to be set aside" (Gregory 2017, 13), and it would be necessary "to insulate public life from religious influence" (Gregory 2017, 14).

Many see the Peace of Westphalia of 1648 that ended thirty years of religious strife in Europe as providing a new system of political order based on the co-existence of sovereign states each with the guaranteed right to establish the faith of its people—i.e., to determine the religion (denomination) of its own state. But Christians living in principalities where their denomination (Catholic, Lutheran, Calvinist) was not the established church were guaranteed the right to practice their faiths publicly (at allotted days and hours) and in private whenever they wished. Despite the truth of Gregory's assertion that "[c]onflicting claims about Christian truth were no more settled in 1648 than they had been in the 1520s" (Gregory 2017, 210), the Peace of Westphalia nevertheless had a significant positive effect in reducing the amount of violence on the continent. This was a step in the direction of the secularization of the state in early modern Europe and the secularity of modern democratic states today. The present-day adoption of the principle of the separation of church and state is an extension of that seventeenth-century development.

For the most part one can agree with Gregory that the Protestant Reformation created a plurality of Christian denominations; that it emphasized individual choice as regards religious commitment; that it redefined and narrowed the scope of religion, separating it from life in the public realm; and, ultimately, that it led to the separation of church and state in modern democratic societies. However, his claim that the Reformation was "a religious revolution that led to the secularization of society" (Gregory 2017, 213) is problematic in that it fails to differentiate society from the state. In his *Rebel in the Ranks* he insists that the Reformation led to a diminution of Christianity's influence on "Western societies" (Gregory 2017, 2). But he notes later that by secularization (not secularism) he does not mean the elimination of religion or "merely a decline in the number of people who attend worship services or pray or say they believe in God." Rather, he writes that by secularization he refers specifically to the declining influence of religion in public life—"all those areas of human life that in the Middle Ages and the Reformation era Christianity was supposed to inform politics, law, economics, education, social relationships, family-life, morality, and the culture at large" (Gregory 2017, 217). According to Gregory, "by construing religion narrowly, it separates religion from the rest of life" (Gregory 2017, 241) and this makes possible not only freedom of religion but also freedom from religion (Gregory 2017, 235). Gregory best sums up his thesis in the following sentence from *Rebel in the Ranks*: "individual, secularized freedom of the early twentieth-first century is the long-term, unintended outcome of the Reformation era" (Gregory 2017, 261).

Gregory further claims that the Reformation's influence on the "secularization of knowledge," "framed not only...the logical demand of rational coherence, but also...the methodological postulate of naturalism and its epistemological correlate, evidentiary empiricism" (Gregory 2017, 299). This secularized knowledge has come to characterize the modern research university which rejects all revealed knowledge claims and therefore rejects theology as a legitimate university discipline. Gregory acknowledges that theology remained a Faculty in most European universities but insists that, because it was given no influence on other academic subjects and disciplines, its exclusion amounts to an "ideological secularism that has been progressively institutionalized in modern Western universities since the early twentieth century" (Gregory 2017, 306–307).

Gregory is right in his assessment that such secularization "has dominated the most important forum in Western society for the consideration of religious truth claims on their own terms in relationship to the rest of knowledge" (Gregory 2017, 359). But that is precisely what has been conducive to a scientific study of religion. He is also correct in noting that science as secularized knowledge has not provided "a convincing rational substitute for religion with respect to the Life Questions." However, it is precisely because the sciences are not in competition with religion in this regard that makes it possible to engage in a scientific study of such phenomena.

Conclusion

The period of European exploration and its discoveries, and subsequently the Protestant Reformation, further rooted the modern epistemic tradition that emerged with the social and intellectual developments in the fourteenth-century Renaissance and the birth of the Scientific Revolution. The discoveries of a plurality of religions beyond the traditional religious alternatives to Christianity—Paganism, Judaism, and Islam—inspired a curiosity about the "new" religions that ultimately generated critical approaches to understanding all forms of religiosity, including Christianity itself. The Reformation ultimately led to a radical reorganization of society in its initiation of a process of separating Church and State. With the emergence of an age of critical thought and the creation of a public realm free from control by religious authorities, the non-religious study of religion became a real possibility for the first time in history although it did not immediately come to fruition. Unlike Strousma, I think that the modern—scientific—study of religion did not emerge until the late nineteenth century. Stroumsa, however, maintains that the most dramatic developments in the non-religious study of religion occurred in "the period between the Renaissance and Romanticism," not in the late nineteenth century (Stroumsa 2010, viii). I have no quarrel with him that Richard Simon's seventeenth-century work can justly be called "the first nonpolemical comparative study of Judaism and Christianity," or that a "radical transformation in the perception of religious phenomena occurred during this period, or "that the study of the Bible was central to the birth of comparative religion in early modernity," or that the study of religion during this period depended upon the emergence of "a new understanding of religion that had no real precedent in the Middle Ages or during the Renaissance" (Stroumsa 2010, ix, 3, 4, and 5). I agree, for example, that these developments point us to some of the historical conditions that ultimately made possible the modern/scientific study of religion, but they did not actually ground such a study. Stroumsa's title, *A New Science*, is not justified, as he actually acknowledges periodically throughout the text by referring to the study of religion in this period as "the early modern study of religion" (Stroumsa 2010, 12). He notes, for example, that "early modern scholarship on religion remained, by and large, an enterprise of Christian believers" (Stroumsa 2010, 10). The ideal of a fully scientific study of religion did not emerge until the late nineteenth century, and the socio-political conditions necessary for its full establishment did not come into full play until well into the twentieth century.

There can be no quarrel with Stroumsa about the science-like import of the application of philological and historical methods to the study of religious (biblical) texts and to the study of religions. This permitted the historicizing of claims to religious truth and the undermining of apologetic considerations that had been dominant in the Middle Ages. But it did not altogether transcend the search for religious truth. As Stroumsa acknowledges, this period of history in the study of religion promoted

> a will to search with the light of knowledge rather than of theology for the truth in religious matters and in the history of religion. These scholars believed that such a truth could be found through historical, comparative investigations. (Stroumsa 2010, 90–91)

— 8 —

Crossing a Threshold in the Scholarly Study of Religion

Introduction

In *The Science of Religion in Britain 1860–1905*, Marjorie Wheeler-Barclay has provided a detailed description of "an unprecedented burst of activity" in the study of religion as "an appropriate subject for disinterested scholarly investigation" (Wheeler-Barclay 2010, 2). She sees this scholarship "as the first attempt...to create a coherent field of study that would treat religion purely as an element in human culture," and she maintains that "[b]y 1860, a number of trends had converged to stimulate the creation of a new field of religious studies" that she refers to as "[t]he Victorian 'science of religion'" (Wheeler-Barclay 2010, 2, 36, and 247). Despite the label she gives it however, she argues that these Victorian developments "did not achieve the status of an autonomous academic discipline during the nineteenth century." In fact, she claims that the Victorians "could not establish a truly scientific study of religion" because they were, for the most part, engaged in a discourse about religious issues. As she puts it: "Theirs was a truly engaged scholarship...intended as a vital contribution to the contemporary debate on Christianity" (Wheeler-Barclay 2010, 2). Victorian scholarship on the comparative study of religion, however, was not simply an apologetic enterprise because, Wheeler-Barclay claims, it involved participation of scholars engaged in research within an academic/university context.

There can be no doubt, as I pointed out in the previous chapter, that a disinterested—but not genuinely scientific—study of religion predated the nineteenth century. For this reason, as I pointed out in the previous chapter, I find Guy Stroumsa's reference to this scholarly enterprise as "the early modern study of religion" more appropriate than his reference to it as a "new science," and I think it also characterizes most of Victorian scholarship on religion. The early modern study of religion clearly gained independence from close ecclesiastical control and made use of a wide variety of methodological tools borrowed from other social-scientific disciplines in their accounting for religious thought and behaviour. It did not, however, establish a strictly scientific study of religious thought and behaviour. Wheeler-Barclay recognizes that with Müller there was an annunciation of sorts of the birth of a "new science" of religion—despite the Romantic influence supporting Müller's commitment to religious truth. Wheeler-Barclay claims that the desire for such a science is implicit in Müller's support of Huxley's "drive to eliminate the privileged status of theological studies at the universities and to promote more original scientific research at those institutions" (Wheeler-Barclay 2010, 56.) But she also points out that although Müller may have given the new science "an impulse, a shape, a terminology and a set of ideals," as Sharpe had also claimed, (Sharpe 1986, 45), there was little agreement of scholars engaged in studying religion on matters of the objective of such study, on its subject matter, or on its methodology. She points out, for example, that Andrew Lang's "distrust of positivism and materialism" was "much more widely shared among his fellow workers in the field than is usually recognized" (Wheeler-Barclay 2010, 105). According to her, William Robertson Smith, a significant figure in this history, used "scientifically respectable methods in attempting to account for archaic societies." However, with his seeking the principle of progressive revelation in history, he opposed "most of the thinkers whose works had shaped the British version of the science of religion" (Wheeler-Barclay 2010, 162). Similarly, Jane Ellen Harrison, even though an atheist who adopted a sociological approach in her study of religion, ultimately adopted "the study of religion as part of a personal search for meaning and spiritual fulfillment." For Wheeler-Barclay, "the Victorian science of religion [was]...an engine of reform rather than demolition," thereby turning "the Victorian science of religion on its head" (Wheeleer-Barclay 2010, 217 and 227). On the other hand, Lewis Farnell, (a fellow-classicist), pointed out that this was "passionately partisan scholarship", not "the quiet unprejudiced temper of science" (Wheeler-Barclay 2010, 231). According to Wheeler-Barclay, therefore, the longed-for science of religion sought in Great Britain during the last few decades of the nineteenth century "never achieved the unity of an academic discipline" (Wheeler-Barclay 2010, 247). I agree with Wheeler-Barclay's analysis and her conclusion. However, by distinguishing a foundation on which to establish such a science from actually establishing that science, I agree with Leonardo Ambasciano, in his *An Unnatural History of Religions: Academia, Post-Truth, and the Quest for Scientific Knowledge*, that "[t]he Victorian Science of Religion played a major part in the establishment of a truly scientific approach to religion" in the twentieth century (Ambasciano 2018, 55).

Eric Sharpe has pointed out in his *Comparative Religion: A History*, that Friedrich Max Müller has earned recognition by historians of the "field of Religious Studies" as "the father" of the modern scientific study of religion because of his persistent advocacy for such a discipline. Sharpe acknowledges that Müller was not the only one to advocate such a scientific enterprise but that he was the more universal figure in the field to do so. He was, moreover, the earliest to advocate the establishment of such a science in the "Preface" to his *Essays on the Science of Religion* (1867). His *Introduction to the Science of Religion* (1873), first delivered to the Royal Society in London in 1870) was informally adopted as the foundation document for the new science of the comparative study of religion (or Comparative Theology) as he referred to it. While giving preeminence to Müller as founder of the field, Sharpe points to the Dutch historian of religions, Cornelis Petrus Tiele, as a co-founder of the Science of Religion. As Louis Jordan, in his 1905 history of the field, *Comparative Religion, its Genesis and Growth*, argued: Tiele "'did infinitely more or this new discipline as one of its Prophets and Pioneers than he was ever privileged to do for it as one of the Founders and Masters.'" Sharpe quotes Tiele's further judgment, as found in Jordan:

> as the foundation of the new Science had only just been laid, he [Max Müller] could but submit the plan of the building to his readers and hearers...[his *Introduction to the Science of Religion*] dealt with the preliminaries rather than with the results of the Science and was an apology for it more than an initiation of it. (Sharpe 1986, 45)

Understanding the full import of these claims will require some knowledge of the peculiar character of the sciences in Great Britain and of the emergence of the research university in the nineteenth century and its eventual global influence.

Science, society, and the modern research university

In speaking of what Wheeler-Barclay has called the Victorian Science of Religion, Eric Sharpe remarks in his *Comparative Religion: A History*, that an academic discipline "comes of age when it first attains the dignity of a University Chair, and the comparable privileges of scholarly journals, lectureships and congresses" (Sharpe 1986, 119). It is abundantly clear that there have been many individual scholars in pre-Victorian times who, as Sharpe has put it, regarded themselves as engaged in the scientific study of religious thought and behaviour, but did not establish such an enterprise as a university-approved discipline. It is true, as Sharpe points out, that "the last quarter of the nineteenth century and the first few years of the twentieth century saw a gradual, if local, change in the climate of university opinion, as a number of universities and colleges in the West (Europe and America) made some efforts to provide for the teaching of the new subject" but also notes that "it was difficult to introduce comparative religion on a par with other academic subjects" (Sharpe 1986, 119). In addition to the already existing chairs in theology Sharpe, in his chapter on "The Quest for Academic Recognition," recounts a history of the establishment of Chairs (departments) of the comparative study of religion, but not as a distinctively new scientific enterprise. This is due in part because British science, as David Knight has argued, constituted something like a "local culture." As he puts it: "A feature of British science which marked it as separate, or provincial even, was its emphasis on natural theology. Science in France had emerged as a distinctive activity or profession, justifying itself; in Britain it had not, and claims of utility meant both usefulness in industry and support for belief in a Creator and Designer, and, thus, in a God-given morality" (Knight 1986, 31). British scientists and scholars, that is, had not fully adopted the European notion of the modern research university, built upon the foundations laid for it in the founding of the University of Berlin in 1809. Clarifying this will contribute to an understanding of why the Victorian science of religion is not strictly scientific as Wheeler-Barclay argues yet, as Ambasciano argues, it played a major role in the establishment of a genuinely scientific study of religion.

The aim of the University of Berlin, as Thomas Albert Howard put it in his *Protestant Theology and the Making of the Modern German University* was "to sever the centuries-old tie between confessionally defined Christianity and university education" and to do science for the sake of science alone (Howard 2006, 130 and 176). The universities of the eighteenth century were "an antiquated hold-over from the Middles Ages" and were unable to adjust to new social and cultural forces in society such as the emergence of new sciences throughout the seventeenth and eighteenth centuries outside the university framework and their development in separate academies. In light of these new forces, the epistemic sterility of the traditional university foreshadowed its demise. In response to this threat the founders of the University of Berlin repudiated the confessional character of the older universities, rejected its association with the idealist notion of improving human character, and expanded its curriculum to accommodate the new sciences.

Howard argues that the University's founders had in effect adopted a new *Wissenschaftsideologie* which he describes as follows:

> The ideal of *Wissenschaft*...became increasingly dissociated from the pedagogy of *Bildung* and from the synthetic and monistic tendencies of idealism. Instead, it became closely tied to growing positivist assumptions, empirical research, and seemingly inexorable forces of academic specialization, differentiation, and professionalization. (Howard 2006, 273)

Committed as it was to critical scholarship and interminable innovation—"to increase the domain of knowledge through research and publication and to instruct students how to do the same"—Howard claims that this amounted to the creation of "the secularized research university that we recognize today." This development harboured "Weber's conception of academic work as the unremitting accretion of value-neutral scientific knowledge" (Howard 2006, 81, 4, and 273).

For Howard the motive force behind the emergence of the modern research university lay in the fact of the antiquated character of the university, associated as it was to confessionally defined Christianity, and its inability to provide some order to the fragmented character of knowledge produced by new sciences in the seventeenth and eighteenth centuries. For Chad Wellmon, in his *Organizing Enlightenment: Information Overload and the Invention of the Modern Research University*, that impetus came from the demise of the "epistemic authority," which he calls the "Bibliographic Order" and the "Empire of Erudition" that reigned in Europe during the seventeenth and much of the eighteenth centuries. As Wellmon puts it:

> most eighteenth-century writers considered print and its various forms—from encyclopedia and lexica to periodicals and newspapers—to stand in for a certain desire for the control and mastery of knowledge. The technology of print made knowledge manageable, accessible, and available.
> (Wellmon 2015, 45)

For these eighteenth-century scholars, epistemic authority was lodged in print, but the prolific increase in the availability of print-information as sources of knowledge in the later eighteenth century threatened the hope of finding "a unified authoritative account of it," creating what Wellmon calls epistemological anxieties about what culturally counts as authoritative knowledge (Wellmon 2015, 41, 7). The gap between the realms of print information and the knowledge that could overwhelm the human capacity to navigate it was perceived as an epistemological crisis which "the class of erudites"—"humanist scholars as a social class"—attempted to avert by formalizing the information "into bits of bibliographic information," amounting to the "conflation of knowledge with the technologies of knowledge" which "made the homogeneity of the empire of erudition and a 'comprehensive' account of knowledge conceivable" (Wellmon 2015, 77). Wellmon points out that "[as] the empire began to fracture under the expansion of print technologies...scholars began to seek out new ways to imagine the unity and authority of knowledge. They sought different technologies and new metaphors for conceiving of the norms and practices underlying authoritative knowledge" resulting in such activities as the creation of the encyclopedia as a device for information management (Wellmon 2015, 77). As Wellmon puts it, "Erudition stood in for what counted as real, authoritative knowledge: a thorough, detailed familiarity with an established core of humanist learning and a rejection of intellectual specialization" (Wellmon 2015, 48). This response to the information-overload and epistemological crisis, however, would not be successful.

Whereas at the beginning of the eighteenth century "the erudite scholar... embodied true knowledge and learning" by the middle of that century "the pedant had become a satirical persona (Wellmon 2015, 34). The German intellectuals, Wellmon argues, uniquely settled on the research university as a solution to the epistemological fragmentation of knowledge by institutionalizing, as he puts it, the "practices, concepts, and methods designed to generate a particular kind of knowledge with its own authority and norms" (Wellmon 2015, 35). "The research university," he writes,

> was imagined as a technology that could reconnect an objectified world of knowledge, which so many feared had begun to exceed rational control, with the subjective development of individual persons. If classical conceptions of science sought to harmonize the individual with the cosmos, the research university sought to harmonize the individual with science as a distinct social sphere, a community dedicated to science. It sought to form scientists. (Wellmon 2015, 44)

Whereas "the authority of the medieval university originated from the church and the authority of the Enlightenment university rested on the state," the modern research university, Wellmon argues, "represented a distinct community; it was the bearer of a particular practice and culture that embodied a distinct and authoritative form of knowledge" (Wellmon 2015, 153). Where the earlier universities saw their task as the formation of moral character in their students (*Bildung*)—which romantic influence on the early development of the research university in part espoused—Wellmon shows that the founders of the University of Berlin insisted that its initial task "was to develop the 'character' of the student by introducing him to a particular way of relating to science as a unified, distinct realm of knowledge" (Wellmon 2015, 98). Research, that is, was seen as a new type of formation. Thus, Wellmon writes that "it was only when science was institutionalized as a practice guided by a stable ethos, a new form of consciousness into which persons could be formed, that it truly became modern science," an enterprise committed to "the endless, unceasing pursuit of knowledge" (Wellmon 2015, 108, 112, and 224). In this, Wellmon is in full agreement with Howard regarding the rejection of the traditional idealist notion of *Bildung*. Wellmon is aware of, but not worried about, the fact that *Wissenschaft* as modern specialized science also manifests the problem of epistemic fragmentation because the founders of the research university were never committed to the idealist and romantic notion of the unity of all knowledge. Thus, in summary, Wellmon points out that the research university

> represented a new conception of epistemic authority grounded in the formation of a disciplinary self and the practice of science. The research university came to represent not just another content delivery device, another more efficient technology for disseminating information, but rather an institution and community that bestowed epistemic authority and legitimated knowledge.
> (Wellmon 2015, 122)

He concludes by reiterating that the modern research university "had come to represent a new and distinct form of epistemic authority, and the disciplinary-self had come to embody the virtues and habits of this authority" (Wellmon 2015, 26); thereby "[g]rounding the university in a distinct culture of science was an innovation of the German research university" (Wellmon 2015, 154 and 209).

Although Wellmon focuses little attention on the effects the modern research university had on theology and the possibility of a Science of Religion, Howard did not altogether neglect this issue. It comes as no surprise that he recognizes that with the expansion of the research university "the presence and prestige of theology continued to be eroded," and he is puzzled over the continued "renown of nineteenth-century German academic theology." He seems to suggest that this might be clarified in seeing that academic theology might overlap with "a more general philosophical and historical understanding of 'religion'" that may have contributed to the emergence of "a new discipline, 'the science of religion' or *Relgionswissenschaft*" (Howard 2006, 269, and 270). Drawing on the views of Paul de Lagard at Göttingen and Franz Overbeck at Basel, he is doubtful that theology could be transformed into such a discipline. Nevertheless, he surmises, interestingly, that with the secularization of knowledge in the modern research university "the logic of science demanded a critical historical investigation of religion in general, shorn of all residual attachments to any particular religion and its supporting institutions" (Howard 2006, 380). These observations describe *in nuce* the idea of the scientific study of religious thought and practice envisioned by Müller in Britain, Tiele in Holland, and the Reveilles in France. For them, it appears that a scientific study of religion was a new intellectual and academic enterprise they nominated Science of Religion—a phrase they used as a synonym for "comparative religion" and "history of religion." As Sharpe puts it, they were aware that the new discipline would have to "satisfy the demands of history and science" (1986, 26). None of the three saw it as an outgrowth of, or connected with, theology. Indeed, as I pointed out earlier, Wheeler-Barclay has shown that Müller, for example, supported Huxley's drive to eliminate theology from the curriculum of the university. Nevertheless, Wheeler-Barclay claims that this generation of scholars of religion did not establish a science of religion, largely because they failed to insulate their science from their religious convictions. I believe the evidence will show the contrary.

My argument will not be that scholars like Müller, Tiele, or the Reveilles, actually established a Science of Religion but that they made possible its eventual emergence with and after the First International Congress of the History of Religions in Paris in 1900. Strong support for such a science will be especially clear in the case of Müller for whom the commitment to science transcended even his commitment to the truth of religion. I will argue, however, that all of them were able to compartmentalize their scientific from their religious commitments because they believed that, in the final analysis, these two intellectual and epistemic endeavours would fundamentally come to the same conclusion about the ultimate character and meaning of the world and its contents. Whether they were right or not, this compartmentalization of scientific and religious beliefs made it possible for the idea of a Science of Religion to gain purchase in the minds of students of religion in the last half of the nineteenth century. This was the conclusion to which the Dutch scholar of religion, Pierre Daniël de la Saussaye, came in his 1887 *Lehrbuch der Religionsgeschichte*, translated as "Manual on the Science of Religions" (1891). As Arie Molendijk notes in his *The Emergence of the Science of Religion in the Netherlands*, de la Saussaye commented that "Science of Religion is a new science which has assumed an independent existence during the last decades" (Molendijk 2005, ix). Molendijk justifiably points out that "[i]t is difficult to locate the beginning of the scientific study of religion because...so much depends upon one's own viewpoint and where emphasis is put," but he is, I think, in general agreement with de la Saussaye, acknowledging that when "[s]een in terms of the encounter between comparativism and empiricism...much is also to be said for locating the beginnings of the science of religion in the second half of the nineteenth century" (Molendijk 2005, 19 and 21). He insists, moreover, that "[i]t is certain that scholars such as Müller and Tiele thought of themselves as establishing a new field of research" (Molendijk 2005, 20). He also points out that Albert and Jean Réville, greatly influenced by Dutch scholarship in this regard, shaped the study of religion to a large extent in France. Significantly, Molendijk notes the importance in this history of "[t]he Paris conference of 1900" which, he states, "is generally considered to be the first truly scientific congress in the field" (Molendijk 2005, 258).

Max Müller, Cornelis Tiele, Albert and Jean Réville and the science of religion

It is clear from the illustrious lives of Müller, Tiele, and Réville that they were not only accomplished historians, but also deeply religious persons engaged in religious practice, ministerial activity, and inter-religious dialogue. It is also abundantly clear that they pointedly distinguished their religious commitments and activities from their scientific research on religious thought and practice, including their own. Each publicly announced that the aim of his scholarly activities in the comparative study of religion was to achieve scientifically respectable, objective knowledge about religions and religion. Each also persistently distinguished this work from theology which they seemed to think an intellectual exercise inappropriate in the modern university. Rather than producing an apologetic defence of their religious faith, or in engaging in interreligious dialogue or other religious ministries, knowledge alone was their objective in the study of religion.

In his *Comparative Religion: A History*, Sharpe argues that these scholars, neither individually nor collectively, "established" a Science of Religion as we understand that notion today. He writes that "the science of religion [at the end of the nineteenth century] was not yet sufficiently established as an independent entity, being still viewed largely in the perspective of Christian apologetics" (1986, 140). Nevertheless, he admits that the International Congress of the History of Religions associated with Universal Exposition that took place in Paris in 1900 was a harbinger of the emergence of such a science. Instead of organizing a world's parliament of religions like the one held at the World's Exposition of Chicago in 1893, this group of scholars led by Albert and Jean Réville—a student of Tiele—thought it more important to display what the study of religion ought to be. As J. Réville put it, they believed "it was incumbent upon them to assure to the study of religion/religious studies their rightful place in the great concert of congresses of the Universal Exposition" (J. Réville 1900, 272). Therefore, they arranged for a congress on the strictly historical study of religions, which dissociated it from the apologetically-tinged study of religion that had held sway in the universities. Tiele and Müller acted as honorary co-chairs of the congress, and Sharpe's judgment that "[o]n the whole the organisers were justified in calling it the *first* congress of the history of religions. Since it was the first such congress devoted exclusively to the scientific study of religions" indicates that from this point on, as Sharpe puts it, there would be two "comparative religions." As Sharpe describes it, there was a "comparative religion" that "scholars used...to describe a type of historical scholarship, cool and uncommitted" and one described as apologetic or crypto-apologetic that "enthusiasts used to describe a means to an end" (Sharpe 1986, 253). Neither group was entirely in control of the field through the nineteenth century. Müller, Tiele, and the Reveilles, as an analysis of their publications will reveal, were members of the "cool and uncommitted" kind of scholarship despite their religious beliefs and commitments. Because, as Sharpe has argued, Müller was the more "universal figure" among historians of religion in the nineteenth century, I begin this account of the emergence, if not establishment, of the Science of Religion with Müller (Sharpe 1986, 35). He was a most consistent and persistent advocate for the development of such a "Science of Religion" from the mid-1860s to his death in 1900, and for its right to a place among the other sciences in the university. In my account, I differ from Sharpe who suggests that Müller's religious involvements with Christian missionaries, and his support of the 1893 World Parliament of Religions in Chicago and its support of interreligious dialogue, made it very unlikely that Müller could have clearly separated these matters from his concerns "about the method by which it is appropriate to study the phenomena of religion" (Sharpe 1986, 38).

Friedrich Max Müller

Before delving into Müller's publications, one must be cognizant of some important cultural developments in nineteenth-century Britain. One must take seriously, for example, the widespread interest in science and the intense concern about the dangers it portended for religion. The founding of the British Association for the Advancement of Science (now the British Science

Association) in the nineteenth century had popularized scientific knowledge which often clashed with religious belief. Given the association of the sciences with the university, it seemed the locus of epistemic authority had shifted from the church to the university and that knowledge itself was secularized. In some sense, the university came to "own" the sciences. Given that cultural milieu, Müller was aware that garnering support for the idea of studying religions scientifically would be an uphill battle. In the Preface to his *Essays on the Science of Religion* in 1867 he wrote: "I doubt whether the time has yet come for attempting to trace, after the model of the Science of Language, the definite outlines of the Science of Religion" (Müller 1881 [1867], xi). He was aware that such study might well require Christians to give up some cherished doctrine, or modify some other aspect of his or her faith, because the aim of the Science of Religion was neither to support nor attack religion but simply to provide knowledge about it. "In order to maintain their scientific character," he writes, historians of religion "must aim at truth, trusting that even unpalatable truths, like unpalatable medicine, will reinvigorate the system into which they enter" (Müller 1881, xxvi). To maintain the scientific character of conclusions reached, he writes: "they must be independent of all extraneous considerations..." (Müller 1881, xxvi).

Within the space of a few years from advertising his interest in the scientific study of religions in *Essays on the Science of Religion*, Müller provided an overview of the new discipline in his 1870 lectures to the Royal Society in London, published in 1873 as his *Introduction to the Science of Religion*. "I chiefly wanted to show," he writes, "in what sense a truly scientific study of religion was possible, what materials there are to enable us to gain trustworthy knowledge of the principal religions of the world and according to what principle these religions may be classified" (Müller 1893, 145). He again acknowledges that the title of this science will jar many who think religion is simply "too sacred a subject for a scientific treatment" (8) and confesses that he at one time had "shared the same misgivings" because such a science will entail "losses of many things we hold dear" and "[t]hat it will change many of the views commonly held about the origin, the character, the growth, and decay of the religions of the world" (Müller 1893, 4, 8, and 12). However, despite such losses, he maintains that the scientific study of religion "does not entail the loss of anything that is essential to *true religion* [and] that the gain is immeasurably greater than the loss" (Müller 1893, 8, emphasis added). More significantly though, he insists on the importance to him of overcoming such fears because what he "holds even dearer than the truth" [of religion] is "the right of testing the truth" (Müller 1893, 8).

There is clear indication here that Müller believed getting to the truth *about* religion is relevant to remaining religious, indicating that the scientific study of religion must remain free of religious bias. He is also convinced, paradoxically, that such losses, will not undermine or falsify religion itself. Müller proclaims his continuing belief in the value of religion, insisting that if there are not "daily lessons of a Divine teacher and guide" or "no increasing purpose in the succession of the religions of the world, then we might as well shut up the godless book of history altogether, and look upon men as no better than the grass which is to-day in the field and to-morrow is cast into the oven" (Müller 1893, 151). There is no contradiction here because even though he is aware that what he calls "Comparative Theology," a synonym for "Science of Religion," could falsify not only a favoured doctrine or two but reveal religion as a whole to be nothing but hallucinations and a universal disease (as he acknowledges in his third set of Gifford Lectures) he gives every indication that he does not believe that will happen (Müller 1898c, 92). According to him "[i]n Comparative Theology...we have simply to deal with the facts such as we find them. If people regard their religion as revealed, it is to them a revealed religion, and has to be treated as such by every impartial historian" (Müller 1893, 74), but only as a psychological, not an ontological, reality. That is why he insists that his readers "will have observed that [he] ha[s] carefully abstained from entering on the domain of what [he] call[s] Theoretic as distinguished from Comparative Theology," a domain which, for him, amounts to engaging in philosophy of religion or philosophical theology. Interestingly, if not paradoxically, he also expresses his personal conviction that his Comparative Theology will produce something of value for Theoretic Theology when the Science of Religion has completed its work (Müller 1893, 151 and 136). This is even the case, he explains in his Hibbert Lectures, if religions "can be explained by a mere appeal to sense and reason in the ordinary meaning of those words" for in that case this would but reveal religion to be a natural phenomenon or rational religion, as he calls it (Müller 1878, 27). At best, Müller's argument here lacks clarity and cogency, and his belief of an ultimate coherence between Comparative and Theoretic Theology—between science and religious faith—is without foundation.

Although Science of Religion is not the focus of his Hibbert Lectures *On the Origin and Growth of Religion as Illustrated by the Religions of India*, Müller nevertheless presents those lectures as an example of such an objective scientific study of religious phenomena. For such an undertaking, he argues, one must avoid both attacks on and defences of religion and recognize that the notions of revelation and religious intuition constitute "contraband of thought" (Müller 1878, 218 and 220). He maintains that the science of language could provide a model for the science of religion in recognizing that one ought not to proceed on the basis of the assumption of the existence of one true religion any more than one could proceed scientifically to study language on the basis of the existence of one true language. In studying religion, one must collect facts about religions and classify them in hope of discovering what are the real antecedents of religion just as one does for the study language. In the case of religion that means getting to "the sensuous and material beginnings of those ideas which constitute the principal elements of religious thought" (Müller 1878, 221). He suggests that one can see in the philosophic theorizing of religion by ancient Greek philosophers the "beginning of the science of religion" but acknowledges that the Science of Religion of which he speaks "is but a desire and a seed" (Müller 1878, 5 and 377). Although Müller expresses the hope that these lectures will inspire "other and stronger labourers" whose work can establish this new science, he continued to champion the cause for another two decades, insisting that the Science of Religion be included as appropriate subject matter for research and teaching in the university (Müller 1878, 377).

Müller was aware that many in the university were likely to see the scientific study of religion as a threat to their faith and that it would be met "with anything but a friendly welcome on the part of educational reformers," as he puts it in his second volume of his Gifford Lectures on *Physical Religion* (Müller 1898b [1891], 330). He was fully aware, as he noted in his *Introduction to the Science of Religion*, that religion, and especially Christianity, would be considered too sacred to be subjected to scientific analysis and criticism. As he put the matter in his third set of Gifford Lectures, *Anthropological Religion* delivered the following year:

> To expect that religion could even be placed beyond the reach of scientific treatment, or honest criticism, shows an utter misapprehension of the signs of the time, and would, after all, be no more than to set up private judgment against private judgment. (Müller 1898c [1892], 8)

Müller also responds in these lectures to the complaint that a Science of Religion is unlike the natural sciences and therefore does not deserve a place in the university curriculum. His response to such criticism is of special importance in that he shows his understanding of the role of the modern research university as committed to producing knowledge for its own sake. In *Physical Religion* he writes:

> So far as these attacks are directed against all scientific studies which cannot at once show what they lead to, or produce useful and marketable results, no defence seems to me necessary. We surely know by this time how often in the history of the world the labours of the patient student, jeered at by his contemporaries as mere waste of time and money and brains have in the end given the world some of its most valued possessions. (Müller 1898b, 330)

Müller is clearly enunciating here a mantra of the value of the modern research university as seeking knowledge for its own sake, indicating that the university had, at least informally, become the new locus of epistemic authority. Müller reiterated this message in his *Anthropological Religion*:

> [W]e might still claim for the history of religion the same right to a place among our academic studies which is conceded to other historical studies. If at our schools and universities we teach the history of literature, of art, of the various branches of physical science, surely the history of religions ought to form a recognized department in the teaching of every university. Knowledge has a value of its own even if it should not be of practical or marketable utility. Even if religion were nothing but hallucinations as we have been latterly told, an accurate knowledge of the causes and different phases of this universal disease might prove useful for a final cure.
>
> (Müller 1898c, 91–92)

This passage clearly indicates the strength of Müller's commitment to the study of religion as an impartial and truly scientific enterprise. Early in his proposal for a Science of Religion he noted for his readers that such an enterprise would likely require giving up favoured doctrines or religious beliefs but would not "entail the loss of anything that is essential to true religion" (Müller 1973, 8). But in this passage, he recognizes that studying religion in an impartial and neutral fashion could bring one to seeing religion as delusional rather than the rock on which it can be founded. Ultimately, for Müller, the Science of Religion must leave religion open to the logical possibility of a completely reductionist explanation. As he put it in his Hibbert Lectures, if religion "can be explained by a mere appeal to sense and reason in the ordinary meaning of these words, let it be done" (Müller 1878, 27). It is in that sense that the Science of Religion is comparable to the natural sciences and deserves its own department in the university. The historian of religion, he writes, should "try to decipher and understand [the facts] as we try to decipher and understand the geological annals of the earth, and to discover in them reason, cause, effect, and, if possible, the close geological coherence which alone can change empirical fact into scientific knowledge" (Müller 1898d, vi).

But Müller did not give up his Christian faith. Despite his radical scientific views and his acceptance of the sciences, and the university that houses them as new loci of epistemic authority, he expressed a belief that after this "toilsome journey the historian of religion arrives in the end at the same summit which the philosopher of religion has chosen from the first as his own" (Müller 1898d, 542). In his *Introduction* he argues that "Comparative Theology," that is, the Science of Religion, must be kept distinct from "Theoretic Theology," that is, philosophy of religion or philosophical theology, and maintains that he has not, in his scientific activity, engaged in "Theoretic Theology." Nevertheless, he left himself some wiggle room by claiming that "Comparative Theology," philosophy of religion and theology, has "its right place at the end, not the beginning of Comparative Theology" (Müller 1873, 146–147). But espousing this view is itself, or seems to be, engagement in "Theoretic Theology" that involves Müller in a contradiction of sorts by affirming as ultimately fundamental the existence of two mutually exclusive sources of knowledge. Nevertheless, by pragmatically compartmentalizing them, he effectively provided a foundation for a strictly scientific study of religion worthy of inclusion in the curriculum of the modern university.

Cornelis Petrus Tiele

Eric Sharpe has claimed that this "Dutch Egyptologist" is the only serious contender, along with Müller, "for the title 'the father of comparative religion.'" I find myself in agreement with Sharpe's judgment that Tiele "was perhaps the continental equivalent of Friedrich Max Müller in England" (Sharpe 1986, 35 and 121). However, Sharpe also notes that "[i]t must not be forgotten...that many of the founding fathers of comparative religion were liberal Christians ..." concerned with "the problems of living religion" (Sharpe 1986, 148 and 252). The question that needs answering, therefore, is whether the religious commitments of these founding figures distorted their understanding of the nature of the Science of Religion as a religiously independent intellectual enterprise. Sharpe suggests as much in claiming that some of them were "quite happy that comparative religions should be an applied, as well as a pure, science" (Sharpe 1986, 252). But Müller explicitly rejects such a notion in his *Introduction*, noting that scholars who study medicine leave the application of it to others, and he advises the scientist of religion to invoke a similar division of labour in their work. He sees the need for this division of labour in distinguishing the scientist *qua* scientist from the scientist *qua* citizen. He writes:

The Western Epistemic Tradition and the Scientific Study of Religion

> In practical life it would be wrong to assume a neutral position between... conflicting views [of religion and morality]. Where we see that reverence due to religion is violated, we are bound to protest; where we see that superstition saps the roots of faith, and hypocrisy poisons the springs of morality, we must take sides. *But as students of the Science of Religion we move in a higher and more serene atmosphere.* (Müller 1893, 7; my emphasis)

Tiele, like Müller, was also religious, and I have no doubt that Molendijk is right in his claim that Tiele "wanted to know more about religion as such"—that is, the essence of religion beyond its various material and historical expressions—but disagree with his claim that this shows that Tiele "emphasized the philosophical character of the new science" (Molendijk 2005, 80 and 127). As I read Tiele's work, I think his philosophical objectives, like Müller's, belong to his personal religious goals rather than being an aspect of the science of religion as he conceived it. Tiele distinctly says as much in his *Outlines of the History of Religions: To the Spread of the Universal Religions*: the objective of the discipline is "to show how religion, considered generally as the relationship between man and the superhuman powers *in which he believes*, has developed in the course of ages among nations and races, and, through time, in humanity at large" (Tiele 1892 [1877], x and 2; emphasis added). Oddly, Molendijk actually seems to agree with this interpretation, writing that "Tiele did not want to enter into a metaphysical discussion about transcendent issues, but to research the constituent elements of religion as such," insisting that the superhuman is not the subject of research (Molendijk 2005, 128 and 129). This is the essential message of his mature deliberations on the nature of the scientific study of religion in his two-volume Gifford Lectures *Elements of the Science of Religion, Morphological (Vol. I) and Ontological (Vol. II)*: that it is not the superhuman powers, but the human belief in them, that is the focus of the intellectual interest of the historians of religion *qua* scientist.

For Tiele, the Science of Religion should be ranked as an "independent science"—free from ecclesiastical and religious influence. Its subject matter, like that of the other sciences, is intersubjectively available to all practitioners in the field. As he puts it in volume one of *Elements of the Science of Religion*, "religions are simply objects of investigation" (Tiele 1897, I, 9). Belief in the gods is available for critical investigation, but the gods themselves are not. Consequently, Tiele does not understand by religion some metaphysical reality but rather a peculiar set of beliefs, customs, and social institutions. He writes: "The object of our science is not the superhuman itself, but religion based on belief in the superhuman; and the task of investigating religion as a historical, psychological, social, and wholly human phenomenon undoubtedly belongs to the domain of science" (Tiele 1897, I, 5). For Tiele, it is by way of an empirical study of the history of the changing forms of religions that the laws of historical development can be discerned. What is perceptible, and what general statements follow from what is perceived, is what constitutes the character of the scientific study of religions which is to be clearly distinguished from all discussion of realities beyond the perceptible. The latter Tiele sees an exercise of faith, and for him "[b]etween knowledge and faith," there "exists a difference in kind" (Tiele 1897, II, 36). It is not that he thinks empirical knowledge and faith to be completely unrelated, but he is adamant that science does "not go beyond demonstration of the finite causes and the fixed laws which govern physical and mental life," whereas faith ascends "to one or more supernatural causes, in which everything finite has its origin" (Tiele 1897, II, 38).

It is true that Tiele believes the scientific study of religion has at least an indirect spiritual benefit because, he asserts, along with providing knowledge about religions it also reveals its limitations in relation to the knowledge of what he calls "religion itself." Although he claims that religion itself provides benefits to humankind whereas science is "solely concerned with gaining knowledge," it is not the duty of the science of religion to supply an apology for religious belief and practice or for "religion itself" (Tiele 1897, II, 245). He writes

> It would fall beyond the province of our science to prove that this belief in the infinite within us is well-founded and to vindicate the right of religion to exist. Our science is psychological, and its task is *merely* to search for the origin of religion in man's spiritual life. We leave the rest to Apologetics and Dogmatics, and on the theoretical side, to Metaphysics, or that general philosophy which seeks to fathom the deepest foundation of all things.
> (Tiele 1897, II, 234–235)

Thus, for Tiele, the scientific student of religion, by definition, must remain neutral on the question of the "truth of religion"; as he puts it: "Though not called upon to prove the truth of religion, our science is not entitled to pronounce it an illusion" (Tiele 1897, II, 235). Putting it this way, Tiele appears to restrict the scientific approach to the study of religion, in a way that Müller did not, by suggesting the new science could not move beyond description and classification of religions to a full non-religious explanation of religion. This, however, does not amount to engaging in religious apologetic or in surreptitiously subverting the growth of this new science as did the later phenomenologists who attempted to re-integrate or blend a scientific with a crypto-theological approach to understanding religion by way of a supposedly new phenomenological method suited to what they intuited as the peculiar nature of religious phenomena.

Albert and Jean Réville

The end of what Sharpe describes as the formative period in the development of the Science of Religion, culminates in what he describes as "[t]he first genuinely scientific congress of comparative religion" (Sharpe 1986, 142 and 138) held in Paris in 1900 under the leadership of the father-son team of Albert and Jean Réville. Known as "The International Congress of Historians of Religion," Sharpe continues with his description: "it was the first such meeting devoted exclusively to the scientific study of religion.... In fact it reflected very accurately the methods and concerns of the Sorbonne" (Sharpe 1986, 140–141). Arie Molendijk claims that this congress indicates that the science of religion had become a truly international phenomenon by the end of the nineteenth century with the Dutch having had a major role in that development, in part by way of their influence on the Révilles (Molendijk 2005, 264). He points out, for example, that "the Dutch influence on the Fifth Section (*sciences religeuses*) of the École Pratique des Hautes Études in Paris was...unmistakable" given the appointment of Albert Réville as its President in 1886, and Müller's influence on Albert Réville is also obvious, given his Introduction to Réville's *Prolegomenon of the History of Religions*. At the end of Müller's career Sharpe claims that "the foundations of the new science had been laid: perhaps not as firmly as Max Müller himself believed, but none the less capable of being built upon" (Sharpe 1986, 46), and the Paris Congress shows that judgment is well borne out, although whether such a science has ever been firmly established is a matter that will be taken up in the conclusion to this volume.

Albert Réville's commitment to the new science of religion comes out clearly both in his early *Prolegommenon* and later in his Hibbert Lectures, *Lectures on the Origin and Growth of Religion as Illustrated by the Native Religions of Mexico and Peru*. In the former work he sounds very much like Müller in both showing his religious commitment in finding that "[i]n religion, man has always sought, *and with reason*, to worship another than himself," while, like Müller, recognizing that even if religion is an illusion, the "illusion remains as the historical fact, and we seek to know exactly what constitutes it" (A. Réville 1884a, 18). In the Hibbert Lectures he writes: "Gentlemen, in these lectures I shall be loyal to the principles of impartial scholarship to which I understand this Chair to be consecrated. Expect neither theological controversy nor dogmatic discussion of any kind from me. It is as a historian that I am here, and as an historian I shall speak" (A. Réville 1884b, 5). It is under the inspiration and leadership of Albert and his son Jean Réville that the Paris Congress of the History of Religions was organized along scientific lines, with both Müller and Tiele serving as Honorary Presidents for the event. Albert's opening address to the Congress shows the firsts signs of establishing the idea of a new science under consideration in several European centres in the last decades of the nineteenth century. He said,

> The history of religions, like all histories, is possible only through the collective labour of all those who devote their strength to it, and it will never be possible to say that it has been done completely, definitively, and without the possibility of revision. But what can be said is that its broad outlines have been traced.... We neither exaggerate nor do we depreciate the place which we occupy in the field of general scientific progress.... Our Congress will probably not create a great stir among all those philanthropic, economic, industrial, scientific and artistic meetings, whose programmes speak more directly to the preoccupations of the multitude. But he would indeed be deaf who did not hear the voices energetically demanding, in the field that we have chosen, light, more light, and still more light.... In spite of all that still separates us from the ideal goal which draws us, the nineteenth century will have the honour of bequeathing to the twentieth, in respect of the History of Religions, a capital which cannot but grow. If we are sincere lovers of truth, this must be a sufficient ambition for us. (quoted in Sharpe 1986, 141)

In a brief post-Congress account of the Paris meeting, Jean Réville reported that the organizers had considered it "incumbent upon them to assure to the study of religion/religious studies their rightful place at the great concert of congresses of the Universal Exposition" that took place in Paris that year (Jean Réville 1900, 272). The ambition of this group of historians of religion was to disseminate this intellectual enterprise "to scholars in all nationalities"—an enterprise that Réville and his academic colleagues clearly distinguished from previously dominant religio-theological and philosophical approaches to the study of religions. As he put it:

> The desire of the organizers of the Congress [was] that this [scientific] initiative taken by them in connection with the...Exposition of 1900 shall be the point of departure of a regular series of congresses of the same character to meet every two, three, or five years for the purpose of giving to the general history of religions the stimulus necessary to assure to it for all time the place it should rightfully occupy in our modern instruction; of aiding in some way to disseminate the results of its researches over the wider and wider spheres of influence, and to give to scholars of all nationalities who devoted their time and powers to labors in this field an opportunity of becoming acquainted with one another and of consolidating their common studies.
> (Jean Réville 1900, 274–275).

Conclusion

The title and the substance of this chapter in the history of the scientific study of religion does more than merely suggest that the emergence of what Wheeler-Barclay has called the Victorian Science of Religion was in a very important sense *the critical episode* in the creation of a Science of Religion. This is not to deny, nor does it undermine, Guy Stroumsa's argument in *A New Science: The Discovery of Religion in the Age of Reason* discussed in chapter 6, that the period between the Renaissance and Romanticism was critical to the early formation of "the modern study of religion." He rightly argues that in this period of European intellectual history we see the emergence of a rational—philological and historical—approach to the study of the Bible that was of critical importance to the birth of comparative religion. However, even though this development increased the number of scholars interested in understanding religions and their ancient texts, it did not give rise to the *idea* of the study of religion as a new science. That was the product of the nineteenth century.

There were many twists and turns in the Victorian development of the notion of a "science of religion" (and its several synonyms). Nevertheless, it was in the second half of the nineteenth century—in Great Britain and Europe—that the idea of such a new science was successfully established in the literature of this field of study and in the academic lexicon. The emergence and establishment of the idea, however, did not at that time guarantee its establishment as a legitimate intellectual enterprise worthy of inclusion in the curriculum of the modern university. This idea is the "capital," as Albert Réville put it, that the international congress of historians of religion in Paris "bequeathed" at the turn of the twentieth century. Jean Réville made very clear that enhancing the scientific study of religion by distinguishing it from the objectives of the 1893 Parliament of the World's Religions, was their primary objective. For them, "Exposition 1900 shall be the point of departure of a regular series of congresses of the same character…for the purpose of giving to the general history of religions the stimulus necessary to assure to it for all time the place it should rightfully occupy in our modern instruction …" (Jean Réville 1900, 274–275).

What progress has been made, if any, by twentieth-century scholars in this field, or even by their twenty-first century successors, is the focus of the next chapter.

— 9 —

Modernity, Postmodernity, and the Study of Religion

Introduction

My objective in this book has been to trace the development of what Ernest Gellner refers to as the Western Epistemic Tradition. This tradition or (episteme), I argue, made possible the idea of a scientific study of religion capable of providing comprehensive non-religious explanations of religious thought and practice from their evolutionary origins to their diverse historical and cultural expressions. Before beginning that journey, I found it essential to clear the field of religious studies of the detritus of generations of debate over definitions of the key terms religion and science. Although I provide a bit of a history of the making of that detritus in Chapter 1 and 2, I take seriously in this book the advice of philosopher of science Karl R. Popper to

> Never let yourself be goaded into taking seriously problems about words and their meanings. What must be taken seriously are questions of fact, and assertions about facts: theories and hypotheses; the problems they solve; and the problems they raise. (Popper 1976, 19)

In Chapter 3, I argued that the emancipation of thought from the grip of mythopoetic thinking, initiated by ancient Greek thinkers prior to Socrates and Plato, first spawned critical philosophical thinking about religion, some of it to purify religious thought and practice (Xenophanes) and some of it polemical, an effort to undermine religious influence in the lives of individuals and society in general (Euhemerus). Some ancient Greek historians appear to have taken a straightforward epistemic interest in the diversity of religions to be found in the ancient Mediterranean world (Herodotus). Unlike the approach to religion by these Hellenic philosophers and historians, however, the Milesian philosophers approached religion in the same way as they approached gaining knowledge about the physical world around them, and even their thought and practice did not amount to being a scientific enterprise as it is conceived today. It nevertheless, transcended the mythic modes of thought of their predecessors. In other words, the Milesians produced a new cultural value of seeking knowledge of the world for its own sake, an essential prerequisite for the subsequent emergence of a scientific mode of thought. In that sense, the proto-scientific mode of thought, introduced by these pre-Socratics was an achievement worthy of being called the First Enlightenment.

In general, there was a decline in such proto-scientific thinking in the Hellenistic period even though there was significant development in such intellectual disciplines as mathematics, geometry, astronomy, biology, geography, and philology. To a limited degree these disciplines influenced religious thought, especially philology and astronomy, but they did not give rise to further scientific approaches to understanding or explaining religious thought and practice. Quite to the contrary, as I show in Chapter 4, the Hellenistic period saw a diminution of confidence in reason and a concomitant resurgence of religion that spawned prophets and sages—a kind of popular clergy as one critic of the period describes them—rather than thinkers. Neo-Platonic modes of thought trumped the naturalistic attitude characteristic of pre-Socratic thinkers and Aristotle, replacing such protoscientific interests with more democratic concerns of ethics and the meaning of life. Although something of the classical period of philosophical thought was ultimately transmitted to later generations of thinkers, no major, and few original, intellectual contributions were made by philosophers in this period of history.

In Chapter 5, I argued that with the closure of the philosophical schools by Justinian in 529 CE, intellectual life in the early Medieval period was dominated by Christianity. Knowledge of religion was essentially the catechetical and devotional teachings of the Church grounded not only in scripture and tradition but also framed by Augustine within a Platonic metaphysic of sorts. The recovery of Aristotle's philosophic corpus in the tenth and eleventh centuries, however, inspired a more scholarly and academic investigation and justification for the knowledge claims espoused by the faithful. The study of religion in this period blended catechetical and devotional study with rational concerns for the justification of the explicit and implicit knowledge claims made by the Church. This ultimately produced an elaborate structure of theological disciplines that made possible a more systematic and comprehensive understanding of the Christian faith and its relationship to the other religions of the antique Mediterranean and early European world. Although an advancement over the early devotional approach to understanding religion, this scholarship did not amount to a science of religion because it was still constrained by religious commitment and belief and, therefore, did not approach the connotation of the modern notion of science. Theology emerged as an academic discipline in this period for the first time in the history of Western thought and contributed to the notion of a study of religion but ultimately hampered the establishment of any scientific study of religion.

In Chapters 6 and 7 I argued against Guy Stroumsa's suggestion that the idea of a strictly scientific study of religion emerged in the period between the Renaissance and Romanticism. However, he is right to have argued that in this period of European intellectual history the emergence of a rational—that is, a strictly philological and historical—approach to the study of the Bible was of critical importance to the eventual birth of the science of religion. Stroumsa's designation of this development as the rise of the modern comparative study of religion is quite appropriate, as is his claim that this development increased the number of scholars interested in a non-partisan understanding of religions and their ancient texts. The fourteenth-century Renaissance, the Scientific Revolution, the discovery of new-world religions, and the Protestant Reformation contributed to the emergence of a new epistemic tradition in European thought and the formation of the secular state made its development possible. As I argued in Chapter 8, however, the *idea* of the study of religion as a strictly (unblended) scientific enterprise—in no way constrained by religious commitment or belief—was the product of the nineteenth century. In this chapter I will show that such a discipline has never been firmly established in our modern research universities in Europe, Britain, America, or elsewhere in the world but that the very idea of it is still very much a matter of scholarly debate.

The study of religion in European and British universities

As I pointed out in Chapter 8, the ambition of the Paris Historians of Religion involved much more than merely ensuring that the history of religions congress they organized in 1900 would continue periodically into the future. It was their aim to inspire their colleagues to disseminate this scientific approach to the study of religion internationally and to assure that such a study of religion, as Jean Réville put it, would "rightly occupy [a place] in our modern instruction" (Jean Réville 1900, 275). To a limited extent this new scientific approach to the study of religion was already ensconced in universities in several European countries. Historian of religions Lammert

Leertouwer, in his essay "C. P. Tiele's Strategy of Conquest" (1989), argues that this was, in part, accomplished in Dutch universities by Tiele's work to free the study of religion from emancipatory objectives. Tiele, he maintained in his account of "Gerardus van de Leeuw as a Critic of Culture", was intoxicated by science, and refused to treat religion "as an academic source of information or as a product of extra-cultural information" (Leertouwer 1991, 57). Even though Arie Molendijk maintains in his *The Emergence of the Science of Religion in the Netherlands* that the new approach to the study of religion was not underwritten by the Dutch Act of Higher Education of the period, he acknowledges that the Dutch approach to the field significantly influenced the study of religion in France (Molendijk 2005, 24).

The American scholars who participated in the Paris Congress for the History of Religions were very much impressed by developments in a scientific study of religion in Europe and inspired to bring them to the attention of their colleagues and university administrators back home. Despite these developments, however, it was not the case that the scientific study of religion was widely established in universities in the Netherlands or elsewhere in Europe. There are far more departments of theology in European universities today than departments for the study of religion, and where departments are hybrids that include both the study of theology and, say, comparative religions, it is the study of theology that usually predominates.

As David Robertson points out in his *Gnosticism and the History of Religions,* there was a major transformation of the study of religion in the Dutch university system with the adoption of phenomenology as a new methodological norm that had as its scientific objective neither religious/faith knowledge nor objective scientific knowledge but "understanding." According to Robertson, phenomenologists seek a special "non-rational" and "esoteric" form of knowledge of the essence of religion whose charm "remains confessional and normative" (Robertson 2022, 162). Not only was the establishment of the scientific study of religion in universities undermined by this so-called new methodology of phenomenology, the very idea of a strictly scientific study of religion as conceived by the Paris historians was effectively colonized by that subtle form of religion. As Robertson shows, the formal institutional founding of the International Association for the History of Religions (IAHR) at the seventh History of Religions Congress held in Amsterdam in 1950, "enshrined phenomenology semi-officially as the de facto methodology of the History of Religions."

In Britain, as in Europe, there was no great impetus for establishing academic departments for the strictly scientific study of religions and religion.

Rather, as Eric Sharpe outlines in his history of the "Victorian 'science of religion,'" it was impossible because what was called the "comparative study of religion" appealed to "two types of mind, the 'scientific' as well as the 'religious.'" As he explains:

> The "scientific" mind was concerned to apply a particular method to a body of data—data taken as a rule to refer only to the workings of the human mind, and not to any type of transcendent reality. The "religious" mind, on the other hand, had as its essential point of departure a stance of faith in the actual existence of a transcendent order of being; and although the emergent data of comparative religion might well come into conflict (or appear to do so) with certain traditional answers to questions of religious authority, these could not contradict the basic stance of faith itself. (Sharpe 1985, 144)

Those of a religious mind have remained the dominant group in British universities where the study of religion was (is) most often found as aspects of already existing departments of theology. The first independent department for the study of religion was not founded until 1967 under the headship of Professor Ninian Smart. Smart considered the kind of study of religion championed by the International Association for the History of Religions as an unhelpful form of scientific purism. As he writes in a 1990 essay in support of creating a new institutional home for the academic study of religion:

> Existing global institutions like the IAHR have done noble and effective things. But you need a more embracing organization with not too much attention to purism. What I mean is that though the overall aim of a World Academy of Religion would be the cross cultural, multidisciplinary and reflective study of religion, it has, to make real progress, to embrace all kinds of committed and non-committed scholarly organizations—it has to embrace Jewish exegetes and Christian theologians, Islamic historians and editors of Vaishnava texts, Marxists historians of atheism and Catholic jurisprudence, liberal New Testament scholars and Sikh professors, and so forth. It has to embrace as much as possible of the scholarship of all sorts going on in the world. (Smart 1990, 305)

Smart's understanding of the study of religion as both polymethodic and multidisciplinary seems to have provided the framework for understanding who, so to speak, belongs in the field of religious studies. As Steven Sutcliffe documents in his *Introduction to Religion: Empirical Studies*—a collection of essays celebrating the fiftieth anniversary of the British Association for the Study of Religions (BASR)—this suggested that the field should be imagined as "an intellectual feast with an open invitation to table" (Sutcliffe 2004, xviii). This was not however widely adopted by the BASR. As Sutcliffe pointed out:

> This has been perceived to be an issue on both discursive and institutional grounds: put simply, if we are to differentiate a *particular* body of scholars and hence develop and refine a set of cumulative explanatory discourses, not to mention an institutional and financial production base, we cannot have a completely "open house." (Sutcliffe 2004, xix)

The primary issue in this regard has been the seamless blending of theology "into the polymethdological spectrum" (Sutcliffe 2004, xix) and the decision of a "Theology and Religious Studies Benchmarking Group 2000" to use the rubric "Theology and Religious Studies" to determine categorization of the study of religion "for funding, staffing, student applications and other disciplinary-administrative [matters]" which made the study of religion look like a junior partner to theology (Sutcliffe 2004). Interesting in this regard is the volume of essays published for the British Academy on the occasion of its centenary in 2002, under the title *A Century of Theological and Religious Studies in Britain* (Nicholson 2003). Sutcliffe's collection of essays, originally presented orally at meetings of the BASR, and published in *Religion: Empirical Studies,* however, provides an alternative, non-religious, way of understanding the field. The publication of the volume *Fields of Faith: Theology and Religious Studies for the Twenty-first Century* in honor of the theologian Nicholas Lash the following year, however, shows that the problem of control of the field in Britain's universities was not resolved by the progressive developments in the BASR.

A science of religion in America?

Insofar as the creation of the International Association for the History of Religions in 1950 adopted the agenda of the 1900 Paris historians of religion for the advancement of a strictly historical study of religion, I argued in Chapter 8, we can talk of the formal *institutional* establishment of the new science of religion. That institution, up to the present, has to some extent kept alive the idea that a scientific study of religion might one day be recognized as a discipline in the curriculum of modern research universities. The American historian of religions Morris Jastrow, for example, saw this as a distinct possibility in the early foothold that this science had gained in universities in Europe at the turn of the twentieth century (Jastrow 1899, 320). Jastrow was aware of the obstacles that had prevented the study of religion from gaining scientific recognition—its newness as a scientific enterprise, the tension and violence religion often generates, and possible conflict with denominational groups, among others—but he insisted that its scientific value demands that this discipline be fostered in the university (Jastrow 1899, 322). He therefore pleaded with senior university administrators to work "toward [providing] *official* recognition of the subject in the Graduate Department [of his university]...(Jastrow 1899, 323). He argued that "not much progress in advancing the historical study of religion at colleges and universities can be expected from now on unless the question of *official* recognition is seriously taken up," and he expressed the hope that American university officials would be inspired by what is happening in this regard in Holland and France (Jastrow 1899, 324, 325). Jastrow reissued his advice to university administrators two years later in his *The Study of Religion*: "If permanent results are to be secured [in the study of religion]," he wrote, "provision must be made for systematic instruction at English universities; and similarly in the United States, where but little has been done by universities to encourage the subject, the example set by Holland and France needs to be largely followed" (Jastrow, 1901, 56–57).

The study of religion as a modern scientific enterprise, however, had played no part in the curriculum of US colleges in the colonial period. Inspired by a medieval philosophy of education, religion virtually dominated student life and consequently effectively determined the structure of American higher education in the colonial period. New philosophies of education emerged in the nineteenth century, however, because of an increasing interest in the natural sciences, which resulted in the removal of biblical and theological scholarship from college curricula and placement in separate college-affiliated seminaries. As Julie Reuben has shown in her book *The Making of the Modern University: Intellectual Transformation and the Marginalization of Morality,* even though this transformed post-secondary education, it did not lead to the secularization of the antebellum college. The integrating ideal of the unity of knowledge—that is, the belief that all knowledge is knowledge of God—remained as an essential element of the undergraduate curriculum, though significantly modified. Talk of "religious studies" in the sense I am using that notion here, therefore, could not have been an element of the college curriculum until the second half of the nineteenth century. As Conrad Cherry argued in his *Hurrying Toward Zion: Universities, Divinity Schools and American Protestantism,* interest in specialization and professionalization in American education created by the continued growth of scientific knowledge, brought about a radical transformation of American higher education. This further segregated science from religion by excluding theological questions and questions of meaning from the framework of scientific inquiry, and even with this transformation of the college into the early modern research university, the concern for achieving scientific truth (knowledge) in new fields of learning did not in fact bring about a wholesale secularization of religious studies in the research universities that succeeded them. As historians are quick to point out, the "university reformers" —the designation used for those who brought about this transformation in higher education in America—even though they rejected sectarianism, still believed in the ultimate harmony of scientific with religious truth, expecting that science would eventually establish that harmony as factual. Thus the "reformers" did not entirely renounce the original vision and aim of the colleges they transformed, but they nevertheless created a new educational context, an environment within which the genuinely scientific study of religion (*Religionswissenschaft*) could emerge. Whether such a study of religion did in fact emerge in that context, however, is still open to debate.

Robert S. Shepard, in *God's People in the Ivory Tower: Religion in the Early American University* points out that the nineteenth-century American university provided "an academic structure for the scholarly study of religion" (Shepard 1991, 42), but in no way does he suggest that it produced a genuine science of religion. A "brief flirtation with the science of religion" at Cornell University, he notes, greatly influenced Morris Jastrow of the University of Pennsylvania to take up a scientific approach, but he acknowledges that this did not lead to the establishment of a discipline comparable to that founded by European scholars (Shepard 1991, 18). Indeed, Shepard argues that the primary focus of students of religion in this period was the Christian faith, and he shows that they were as much concerned with the dissemination of "religious knowledge" as with obtaining knowledge about religion. While admitting that this Protestant-inspired "Christian *Religionswissenschaft*" helped to raise the level of scholarship with respect to religion (in that it pushed the discourse about religion beyond ecclesiastical boundaries), he clearly stresses the "irregularity and fragility of the American university's interests in the scientific study of religion" (Shepard 1991, 9).

Julie Reuben comes to roughly the same conclusion in her book on *The Making of the Modern University*. In the final analysis, the study of religion encouraged in this new educational context was not so much secular and scientific as "desectarianized"; its creation was motivated as much by religion as by science. The "scientific study of religion" for the university reformers, that is, arose naturally from their belief in the ultimate harmony between scientific and religious truth that would issue in scientifically sound religious knowledge. Interestingly, however, Reuben accounts for the decline in the fortunes of the scientific study of religion at the end of the second decade of the twentieth century in terms of the recognition by university leaders that "[the] academic study of religion was not inherently religious" (Reuben 1996, 142). She rightly notes that the number of religious studies programs in American colleges and universities grew rapidly after the Second World War but, whatever the scientific influence of European developments in the field, it is clear that the study of religion in America succumbed to religion, which did little to support its scientific study in the academic setting.

The immediate postwar period was an age of anxiety in which university leaders in America sought ways to engage the university in the battle against fascism, communism, and the threat of a nuclear arms race, and religion was an obvious resource for the task. This was an era that witnessed "a national turn to religion," as Conrad Cherry describes it (Cherry 1995, 104), and the implications of that national mood for the study of religion in the university are clearly exhibited in Merrimon Cunninggim's book *The University Needs Religion* (1947). As in the past, students of religion aligned themselves with the humanists, sharing their concerns for spirituality, morality, and the humanizing of society. As Hart highlights in his *The University Gets Religion: Religious Studies in American Higher Education* (1999), this was clearly a religious revival and not an intellectual reformation, and it contributed to a reappropriation of the mainline Protestant rationale for the study of religion invoked from the 1870s to the 1920s by the university reformers. The postwar leaders, as Hart indicates, "strikingly repudiated the conception of religion and higher education forged by the educational reformers who [had] led the way in creating the research university" (Hart 1999, 130). This spurred a successful theological renaissance in the university, which, in the short run, benefited the growth of "the study of religion" in American colleges and universities by appropriating humanistic values and by encouraging the creation of a "religio-scientific" study of religion that gave less attention to what Hart calls the "sturdier scholarly ideals" (Hart 1999, 132) of *Religionswissenschaft* than it did to the religious and moral quest. Hart writes: "From 1945 until 1970 religious studies established not only its educational but also its institutional identity as a partner with the humanities. While this strategy allowed the discipline to blossom, the field could not shake its Protestant and ministerial genesis and orientation" (Hart 1999, 112). The motive for the study of religion in this period, therefore, was primarily religious; and religion scholars, for the most part, were still playing the role of campus minister (Hart 1999, 133). This is nowhere clearer than in President Nathan Pusey's campaign to restore religion at Harvard; an act which, though "liberal and pluralistic in approach to the subject," was intended to resurrect Harvard's education for Christian ministry. I suggest there is irony in the title of Hart's book—*The University Gets Religion*—because even though scholars claimed to be seeking to establish a respectable academic approach to the study of religion, the academy merely got more religion. This is an irony that seems to have escaped Hart's attention in his earlier analysis of the nature of the study of religion represented by the American Academy of Religion in an essay titled "American Learning and the Problem of Religious Studies" (Hart 1992).

This unobtrusive resurgence of religion in the academic study of religion was encouraged by Mircea Eliade, a historian of religions who imported the European notion of *Religionswissenschaft* into the study of religion in the United States. Eliade was appointed to a position in the Divinity School in the University of Chicago in the second half of the twentieth century. His understanding of the kind of science of religion in which he considered himself engaged was infused with an emancipatory agenda. In his journal *No Souvenirs* he wrote: "The history of religions as I understand it is a 'saving' discipline" (Eliade 1977, 296), and, commenting on psychologist Herbert Fingarette's remark that Freud understood psychoanalysis to have "brought into the most intimate partnership a science of human change and the art of self-liberation," Eliade attributed "a similar function as well to the history of religions" (Eliade 1977, 309–310). For Eliade, that is, the academic study of religion needed to be a humanistic, emancipatory, and salvific enterprise—a very attractive view of the religious studies enterprise that drew an extraordinary number of students to the University of Chicago for graduate studies in religion. Not surprisingly, the University of Chicago became a prolific producer of PhDs in religious studies who became undergraduate instructors in the rapidly developing field of religious studies in the 1960s, which ensured the dominance of Eliade's conception of the field in the United States.

It has been argued by some that the study of religion in American colleges and universities today is essentially a naturalistic enterprise, and that in the mid-to late 1960s religious studies exchanged its originally Protestant religious ambitions for the scientific aspirations which still characterizes the hopes of some scholars in the field today. Two significant developments behind this restructuring of the field have been suggested. The first is the ruling of the Supreme Court justices in the *Abington School District v. Schempp* case (1963) over the role of religion in the nation's public schools, which, according to Hart, "halted abruptly the religious and theological revival of the 1950s and early 1960s" (Hart 1999, 201). The *Schempp* decision purportedly undermined the Protestant establishment by precluding any amalgam of theology and devotion in the academic work undertaken in public colleges and universities without, however, banning the "neutral" study of religion.

The second significant development in the (supposed) secularization of religious studies is the transformation of National Association of Biblical Instructors (NABI) into the American Academy of Religion (AAR) in 1964, which represented not only a reaction against the mainline Protestant influence on the study of religion in the past, but also, it is claimed, a commitment to a scientific framework for the study of religion over the pre-1960s religio-humanistic one. Hart, for example, declares that members of the Academy were concerned with establishing the field on an objective and scientific basis, and that "to be religious was no longer as important for Professors of religion as methodological sophistication and academic achievement" (Hart 1992, 213). Similarly, George Marsden, in his *The Soul of the American University: From Protestant Establishment to Established Nonbelief* (1994) maintains that with the (supposed) change of orientation represented by the AAR, a "normative religious teaching of any sort has been nearly eliminated from standard university education" (Marsden 1994, 5). "While the AAR embraced both the humanistic and the social scientific impulse," Marsden writes, "the latter signaled the dominant direction for the future" (Marsden 1994, 414). Conrad Cherry echoes these claims in his insistence that the members of the AAR who now occupied the field "would gauge their work… by how well it conformed to the canons of the disciplinary specialties in the contemporary university" (Cherry 1995, 116). In his *Princeton in the Nation's Service: Religious Ideals, Educational Practice*, P. C. Kemeny, following Hart and Marsden, claims that the AAR brought about a methodological revolution that gave religious studies an empirical, scientific foundation, eclipsing the non-scientific approaches of a bygone era (Kemeny 1998, 231). If these authors are to be believed, the majority of the students of religion in the United States, in the span of some five years, willingly exchanged their religious identities for the professional identity of scholar and scientist, swapping their moral and religious goals for objective knowledge about religions.

Given the continuing commitment to the fundamentally religious values the AAR espoused with its Protestant heritage, it is clear that neither the AAR, nor the departments of religious studies it "represents," can support a modern, scientific study of religion or any organization committed to such a project. Indeed, a naturalistic study of religion would represent the triumph of science over religion and the humanities. Such a move should be resisted, in fact, as contributing to the dehumanization of culture and society. Consequently, it is precisely because of the expansion of the study of religion in US colleges and universities, and the success of the AAR in shaping the nature of that enterprise, that a modern, scientific study of religion has failed to develop fully in the United States and does not appear likely to do so in the future.

The study of religion in global perspective

There are few educational institutions with specifically designated departments for the study of religion in geographical areas beyond Europe, Britain, and the Americas. The development of a critical scientific study of religion in some non-Western countries was impossible because religion was itself an essential aspect of a cultural identity, and in others, university disciplines were expected to contribute directly to the welfare of society. In colonial states, as in the colonizing states, theology was the matrix out of which the academic study of religion emerged. Theology's influence on the field globally, that is, has been pervasive. As Gregory Alles has shown in his *Religious Studies: A Global View* (2008), a collective survey work on the state of the academic study of religion around the world, theology's influence on the discipline, even in the most secularized nations, remains pervasive. The idea of the study of religion as a scientific undertaking is often professed but is often entrenched within theological commitments, explicit and implicit, that succeed in blocking establishment of a genuinely scientific study of religion in colleges and universities around the world.

It was not Alles's objective to imagine or spell out a vision for the field. Given his criticisms of the visions for the field developed by such scholars as Mircea Eliade, Wilfred Cantwell Smith, and Ninian Smart, however, it is clear that religiously committed scholarship would have no place in it were he to develop such a vision. But neither would his view of the appropriate study of religion in the global context amount to a strictly scientific study of religious phenomena. Alles acknowledges that "the study of religions aspires to understand and explain human religious thought and behavior in the same manner that we understand all other forms of human thought and behavior" (Alles 2008, 6–7). He also notes that requires scholars in this field to "take the most rigorous, critical stance to what counts as knowledge that human beings are capable of taking" (Alles 2008, 7). However, even though these statements suggest that Alles is concerned with the global extension of scientific studies of religion and religions, he actually opposes it. "To what extent, he asks, "is the study of religion a form of Western science *imposed* on the rest of the world?" (Alle 2008, 314, emphasis added). He suggests that studying religion scientifically is not of great importance in other cultures and that it involves the destruction of other people's beliefs (i.e., engages in "epistemicide") which cannot be justified by simply saying "that science is science, it is what the university does, come what may" (Alles 2008, 316). For Alles, it appears, that science is just another form of knowledge, no better or worse than those it tends to destroy, since, according to Alles, "[n]o one should expect a global vision to escape the limitations of its author's embeddedness in space, time, cultures, politics, economics, and so on" (Alles 2008, 303).

It is true that science (the sciences) emerged and developed in specific cultural contexts and specific periods of history but it is also true that the scientific quest for knowledge of the world in which we live has acquired an uncommon degree of autonomy from the social, moral, and political obligations of the societies from which it emerged and in which it finds itself sedimented today. That is, it has a universal character so that, as Ernest Gellner has remarked in his essay "The Savage and the Modern Mind" (1973) science as the quest for knowledge for its own sake possesses a kind of diplomatic immunity, from all other cultural values, religious and humanistic. It is not, therefore, at all clear as to what Alles considers the essential binding element in a globalized non-confessional "religious studies." The information provided in his global overview of the study of religion provides no evidence for a common methodological commitment that could provide the globalization of the field of "Religious Studies," which is his designation of choice for the enterprise as an integrated epistemic framework of understanding and explanation.

It appears, then, that Alles believes the "academic" (or "scholarly") study of religion must be scientific in a limited way, and that there are indications that some scholars in university departments for the study of religion around the world acknowledge this and function accordingly. Nearly every contributor to the volume, he claims, agrees that the field should keep free from religious and theological concerns; that almost all students in the field argue that there is no special connection between the "academic" study of religion and religion or theology. Yet, even though he is aware that there is no truly global structure for his hoped-for "academic" (but not scientific) study of religion, he thinks it possible that, ultimately, we will be able to create the conditions necessary for a globalized non-confessional study of religions. However, there is no hint of a set of non-scientific methodological tools needed to underwrite it.

Postmodernism and the anti-science phenomenon

To this point in my account of developments in the "academic" study of religions and religion it is generally agreed that the idea that religions could be studied in a strictly scientific fashion was widely acknowledged by the turn of the twentieth century. Indeed, there was considerable interest in the possibility of actually establishing such a study of religion as a scientific discipline in our universities, comparable to the social sciences. Like sociology and anthropology, it was (and still is) argued, that religious thought and practice are purely human phenomena without transcendental reference. Claude Welch, in his *Protestant Theology in the Nineteenth Century, 1870–1914*, for example, writes:

> In the literature we have been examining, the term science of religion…is for all practical purposes interchangeable with the term history of religion and study of religion…What does this term science mean in this context, beyond the free and impartial spirit of inquiry? Plainly, it was intended to suggest the emergence of a discipline comparable to the sciences of anthropology and philology (among the *Geisteswissenschaften*) and even to the natural sciences. It means the thoroughgoing application of a principle of criticism to all religion(s) considered as phenomena of human experience (hence *Religionswissenschaft* rather than *wissenschaftliche theologie*). (Welch 1985, 133)

Even if all of this is true there is still no guarantee, so to speak, that a scientific study of religion will ever be established as an appropriate framework for the study of religion in our modern research universities. The threat to that goal today comes not only from those who champion a hybrid approach that attempts to embrace a variety of sciences, in whatever fashion, within a dominant religio-theological approach to the study of religions, but also from the postmodernist critique of scientific thought as positivist nonsense that ought to be replaced by critical theory and obscure hermeneutical musings on meaning.

The postmodernist challenge to the study of religion in one sense is a far more serious problem than was/is the crisis of identity for the field created by those who sought/seek to harmonize their religious aspirations with their commitment to the academic (scientific) study of religion. For the most part religiously inspired scholars still retained a belief in the possibility of obtaining propositional knowledge of facts and of the possibility of explaining those facts in terms of objectively testable theories. The distinction between sociological theory as an epistemologically grounded account of society and social theory as a philosophical interpretation of society in light of politico-ethical considerations is rejected out of hand. That makes a science of society—and therefore a scientific study of religions—impossible; unless, of course, we are ready to redefine science in non-cognitivist, non-epistemic terms. There are many who are ready to do so, both in the social sciences generally and in religious studies in particular. The impact of such an anti-science movement in anthropology, Gellner notes in his *Postmodernism, Reason, and Religion*, "means in effect the abandonment of any serious attempt to give a reasonably precise, documented, and testable account of anything," including religion (Gellner 1992, 29). The postmodernist project of replacing such scientific knowledge with hermeneutic truth, he argues, provides not liberty but logical permissiveness, relativism, and pluralist obscurity; clarity, he insists, is definitely not one of the attributes of postmodernist thought. The impact of such an anti-science movement in anthropology, he notes, "means in effect the abandonment of any serious attempt to give a reasonably precise, documented, and testable account of anything" (Gellner 1992, 29), and its effect on the study of religion is much the same.

It is difficult to know what would constitute a refutation of decontructivist, postmodernist, and relativist challenges to established notions of rationality, or how the student of religion can, in a positive way, respond to the challenges of such critiques. Can one draw upon the resources of the very rationality which is under critique to ground a refutation of that critique? Would this not be asking the critics of the rationality of science to buy into the very hegemony of reason which they believe themselves to have undermined? On the other hand, if one tries to do this from a postmodernist perspective, we will surely already have given up that which we wish to defend. How then can we respond to the attack on the notion of a natural science of society, of human behavior—and, more specifically, the notion of a scientific study of religion? Ironically, the only possible successful response to the postmodernist challenge is to acknowledge, as spelled out in Chapter 2, that science is a human construct fashioned for the specific purpose of gaining objective—apolitical, areligious, and value-free—knowledge of the world that is universally valid and transcends cultural boundaries. Although establishing institutions in support of gaining such knowledge is a political act, it makes no substantive contribution to the understanding or explanation of religious thought and practice. In this case, the political actions of founding the sciences involves only the commitment to exclude all values from scientific deliberations except the value of achieving objective knowledge of the world for its own sake. The modern research university is one such institution dedicated to the support of that apolitical epistemic objective.

Restating the modern scientific alternative for the academic study of religion

In "On Not Keeping Religious Studies Pure," chapter 8 of his *Casuistry and Modern Ethics: A Poetics of Practical Reasoning* written twenty-five years ago, Richard B. Miller draws on Stephen Toulmin's conception of a scientific discipline (Toulmin 1972) to argue that Religious Studies is "conspicuously unscientific," and is best understood as "a series of overlapping and mutually reinforcing conversations that constitute the fibres of the enterprise" (Miller 1996, 204 and 207). In arguing this claim Miller is critical not only of my position on this matter but also that of scholars like Hans Penner, Edward Yonan, and Samuel Preus, among others. But to see just what force his argument has, it will be helpful to review briefly Toulmin's take on scientific disciplines in his *Human Understanding: The Collective Use and Evolution of Concepts*, even though his account of them is not altogether coherent or perspicuous.

To begin with, Toulmin contrasts fully-disciplined enterprises like physics with what he calls non-disciplinable fields like literary studies, ethics, fine arts, and philosophy. In such "quasi-disciplines," as he calls these non-disciplined (and apparently non-disciplinable) enterprises, intellectual activities cannot be separated from other values; in everyday life, that is, "actions and choices are meshed together" which requires a form of reasoning much broader than that required in the disciplines (Toulmin 1972, 402). The scientist, on the other hand, "pursues the goals of her or his discipline in isolation from extra-professional goals" (Toulmin 1972, 402). Within the disciplinable fields he distinguishes *compact disciplines* (with physics as the best model here) from what he calls *diffuse disciplines* (for which, unfortunately, he provides no examples) and *would-be disciplines* (with the behavioural sciences being his chief exemplars).

A compact discipline for Toulmin is one that, despite showing some striking changes of direction in its historical development, has achieved "agreed goals and strategies around which the cumulative development of a well-structured science can proceed" (Toulmin 1972, 382 and 384). Such disciplines will also have a common set of assumptions and presuppositions, as well as overlapping sets of concepts, methods, and techniques of research. Moreover, they will also have structural and institutional supports including university recognition, professional forums, associations, and societies, formal methods of disseminating the results of their research, and so on.

To all intents and purposes Toulmin lumps the categories of "diffuse" and "would-be" disciplines together. As Miller notes, one problem with these kinds of sciences is that they appear not to have "a sufficiently agreed-upon goal in terms of which common problems can be identified and tackled" (Miller 1996, 204). One reason for that, according to Toulmin, may be that such sciences are "immature," and they may remain immature because they do not have adequate institutional support. But that, according to Toulmin, need have no lasting negative import with respect to the character of such sciences:

> If I have argued here that, at the level of general theory, psychology and sociology remain today "would-be disciplines," I am not claiming any absolute or permanent contrast between the social and the physical sciences. On the contrary: I have merely been trying to diagnose certain special difficulties which face the theoretical sciences of human behaviour at the present time. In earlier centuries, physical theory too had the same inconclusive character; indeed, many of the methodological difficulties afflicting sociology and psychology today had counterparts in earlier physical sciences.
> (Toulmin 1972, 386)

Further on in his discussion he remarks that we "*have discovered that it is both functionally possible and humanly desirable to isolate certain classes of issues, and make them the concern of specialized bodies of enquiries; while with issues of other kinds this turns out to be either impossible or undesirable, or both at once*" (Toulmin 1972, 405, emphasis added).

In my earlier criticism of Miller's critique of those who champion a science of religion, I did not point out clearly enough that the study of religions and religion as carried on (and taught) in many, if not most, of our university departments, in the past and now, is diffuse in character largely because the scholars involved refuse to countenance the possibility of the study of religion as a strictly epistemic pursuit and to distinguish and isolate these intellectual concerns from activities of other kinds. Miller simply fails to see not only that it is possible, but that some scholars have actually been able to separate the search for "knowledge *about*" religion as a human phenomenon from the hope to produce an "understanding of" religion that will transform students into religiously literate persons committed to structuring a meaningful and socially responsible existence in light of a transcendent ultimate reality.

The University of Berlin, established in 1810, was the earliest model for departments of the (academic) study of religions and religion in the modern Western research university. It must be acknowledged, however, that the University of Berlin actually harboured an Emersonian conception of scholarship that involved a great deal more than a search for knowledge or the creation of tools and techniques for obtaining new knowledge. Historian Brad S. Gregory rightly underscores that at its inception, the University of Berlin constituted what he calls "the Romantic research university," in that it was as much concerned with the moral formation of students as it was with producing knowledge; that is, that it was as consciously engaged in *Bildung* as it was with *Wissenschaft*. As Gregory writes in his *The Unintended Reformation: How a Religious Revolution Secularized Society*: "The modern university was originally hatched from a Romantic vision of research as an adjunct to student self-realization" (Gregory 2012, 349). However, Gregory also rightly argues that Protestantism's influence on the sciences over the past two centuries has effected a "secularization of knowledge in research universities" that extends to "the consideration of religious traditions strictly as objects of study rather than as potential sources of knowledge" or avenues of transformation or self-realization (Gregory 2012, 359). What happened to the study of religion in the modern research university of the later nineteenth and early twentieth century then, to use Toulmin's language, is that that enterprise became single-valued in a way that made it possible for scholar-scientists to engage in it in isolation from other everyday and religious activities. In other words, the academic study of religion became a "compact discipline."

A brief description of Religious Studies as a compact scientific discipline here may be helpful in determining "the constant issues in keeping [it] scientific." First and foremost, of course, is that the scientific study of religion operates with the same understanding of the secularization of knowledge that Brad Gregory correctly notes characterizes the modern western research university. This means that the "mission" (i.e., purpose) of the field of the study of religion must be the same as that of any and all other scientific disciplines in the university, namely, that its primary task is to provide a soundly-based knowledge of religion as a human phenomenon. The knowledge sought must not be merely descriptive: that is, providing empirical data, phenomenological portraits, critical comparative analyses of religious traditions, accounts of their historical development, and the like. This, clearly, is an important element of the academic study of religion, but to be fully scientific it must move on to a search for explanations of religious thought, behaviour, institutions, and traditions, and theoretical accounts of human behaviour that give depth to those explanations. To put it bluntly, students of religion must aim at providing intersubjectively testable propositional and theoretical claims about religiously determined states of affairs in the world. This means, contra Miller, that (scientific) purity for the student of religion sets the limits of her/his academic and pedagogical responsibilities. It is especially important here to emphasize the importance of the limits of science for this enterprise given the fact that what one might call "methodological slippage" is more likely to occur in the study of human social and cultural (that is, intentional) phenomena than in, say, the study of physics. The point that needs making is that the "scientific purity," Miller rightly claims is sought by some scholars in the field, is not a search for some comprehensive alternative secular framework within which one might understand one's broader social responsibilities, or within which one might make sense of life in some holistic sense. It is a matter of the utmost importance, therefore, that the scientific student of religion refrain from taking up positions that might be so interpreted because this can only embroil the study of religion in social, political, and metaphysical debates that are outside its mandate. The only social obligation the scientific student *qua* scientist has, that is, is to make the knowledge about religion gained available to the public and to those who have taken on the responsibility for the management of the affairs of society. Those who wish to do more than this, as Stanley Fish advises colleagues in his field of literary studies, should give serious consideration to a change of profession.

Miller, and others, quite correctly claim that departments for the study of religion in most of our research universities do not operate in this fashion; that they do not limit themselves to what can be said about religion within such strict boundaries. He therefore suggests this indicates that the field is, at best, a "diffuse discipline," and more likely a "would-be discipline," and he, consequently, proposes a "poetic" rather than a "theoretical" approach to this field of study (Miller 1996, 200). I suggest, however, that given the significant number of scholars in the field today—both within and without the context of the academy—whose sole purpose is to understand and explain religion in the spirit I have just outlined is a clear indication that, contra Miller, Religious Studies might actually be a compact scientific discipline, even if at the moment it holds only a "minority position" within university and college departments for the study of religions, and may, for all we know, remain so for the foreseeable future. That there are many university-trained scientists and scholars—some even within the academic setting although not likely in departments of biology—who believe in Scientific-Creationism or Intelligent Design Theory and on that basis incorporate socio-political and religious agendas into their work, does not undermine the claim that biology and evolutionary biology are genuine sciences; nor would it do so even if they (the intelligent-design types) were to gain positions within university and college biology departments.

Although the scientific approach to the study of religion will find little, if any, support in today's departments for the study of religion, dominated as they are by a religio-humanistic paradigm for the study of religion, it is nevertheless the case that there is some structural and institutional support for this approach among social scientists in the academy. There are now in many universities today, special institutes, centres, and other units given over to the scientific study of religion. There is, for example, the Institute for Cognition and Culture at Queen's University, Belfast that has for some time been engaged in the scientific study of religion; the more recent establishment of the Centre for Anthropology and Mind at Oxford University and its sponsorship of the Explaining Religion Project; and the Religion, Cognition and Culture research unit in the Department for the Study of Religion at Aarhus University. The Center for Mind, Brain, and Culture at Emory University is another special unit that strongly supports the scientific approach to the study of religious phenomena. In addition to the involvement of such university-based institutions there are also a couple of independent associations, societies, and institutes whose primary objective is to support the scientific study of religion. The International Association for the History of Religions is the oldest of these institutions and its mission statement not only includes its support "for the critical, analytical and cross-cultural study of religion, past and present," but also clearly states that the IAHR "is not a forum for confessional, apologetical, or other similar concerns." More recently those interested in the import of the cognitive and evolutionary approaches for the study of religion formed the International Association for the Cognitive and Evolutionary Science of Religion (IACESR). There are several journals and other publishing ventures that are committed to the support of a science of religion, journals such as *Numen*, the highly regarded journal of the IAHR; *Method and Theory in the Study of Religion*, which accepts articles from a variety of naturalistic/scientific perspectives; the *Journal of Cognition and Culture*, which is a primary venue for research in the cognitive sciences and other evolutionary psychological perspectives; the *Journal for the Cognitive Science of Religion* and, more recently, the *Journal for Cognitive Historiography*. These buttresses to the scientific study of religion lend considerable support to my argument about the possibilities of a scientific study of religion being a compact science.

Conclusion

In his article "Is there a Future for the Scientific Study of Religion?" Luther H. Martin claims that "supportive social conditions for the scientific study of religion have been and still are sporadic" and he speaks of the "aggressive neglect" of the scientific study of religion in the academic world whose history is best described as being "governed by an anti-science trajectory." He writes:

> Both the tenacious pro-religious cognitive and cultural biases and the anti-science historical trajectory of the science of religion argue that any institutionalized study of religion...will continue to be dominated by intuitively credible but epistemologically arid approaches, cloaked in a sophistic jargon of [the] learned practice [of religion]. (Martin forthcoming)

Martin rightly maintains that there are repeated attempts, past and present, of scores of "scholars of religion" with extra-scientific agendas—religious, theological, moral, and political—ready to colonize any institutions that support a scientific approach to religious studies. There are several recent analyses of such colonizing activities that describe the anti-scientific trajectory in the history of the field of religious studies: Leonardo Ambasciano's *An Unnatural History of Religions* (2020); Juraj Franeck's *Naturalism and Protectionism in the Study of Religion* (2020); Martin's and my *Conversations and Controversies in the Scientific Study of Religion: Collaborative and Co-authored Essays* (2016); my *The Learned Practice of Religion in the Modern University* (2020); as well as my earlier *The Politics of Religious Studies: The Continuing Conflict with Theology in the Academy* (1999). Most disturbing in this trajectory of anti-scientific developments in the study of religion is the decision by the Executive Committee of the International Association for the History of Religions (IAHR)—the first organization to provide an institutional framework dedicated to the support of a strictly scientific study of religion—to open its doors to extra-scientific agendas, which I document in my book, *An Argument in Defence of a Strictly Scientific Study of Religion: The Controversy at Delphi* (2021).

Nevertheless, I have not given up the hope that Jastrow expressed regarding the establishment of departments for strictly scientific studies of religion in our colleges and universities, and especially so in our research universities. However, I find myself in agreement with Martin's conclusion that *presently* "any promising future for a strictly scientific study of religion seems to lie... with the initiative of a relatively small cadre of individual scholars, spread across an array of academic departments and programs whose research is pursued in the absence of institutional support or professional patronage" (Martin forthcoming). He is also justified in claiming, however, that "those scholars of religion venturesome enough to explore scientific epistemologies for their study, and to incorporate such approaches into their teaching and research, will be rewarded with expanded intellectual horizons and exciting new questions about and insights into their empirical and historical areas of specialization" (Martin forthcoming). But it seems to me that their influence on other scholars in the field may have a far greater significance than what they achieve for themselves.

— 10 —

Epilogue: A Scientific Revolution in Slow Motion

There is no mandate, law, or revelation that requires a person to espouse the value of knowledge for the sake of knowledge alone in the study of religion, or in any other discipline. However, if one does espouse that value, one is then committed to the special epistemic morality that is linked to the sciences; to a set of intellectual presuppositions and social obligations without which science cannot function, and one is then simultaneously committed to doing what is necessary to keep the study of religions scientific. If one wishes rather to search for the meaning of life and the universe, or to find a way of creating a set of conditions necessary for social harmony, or to discover principles to console the ills and sorrows of one's family, friends, or neighbours, one ought not turn to the research university for support. As Weber pointed out in his lecture on "Science as a Vocation," the university is neither a social agency nor a dispenser of wisdom; its only concern is with objective knowledge, empirical, explanatory, and theoretical, of the world and its contents.

It will be of value here to identify issues that may create obstacles to keeping Religious Studies scientific. The first is a resurgence of religion around the world. On the one hand, governments having to deal with a new set of religious problems are putting pressure on scholars of religion to be "socially relevant" and are beginning to influence, if not politically determine, research agendas in the university. Whereas financial support for basic research is thin, support for research tailored for political agendas seems likely to be approved. On the other hand, this resurgence of religion has encouraged a number of scholars in the field, as well as departments as a whole, to become engaged in the political issues generated. The opportunity to get involved in matters on the national and international stage is just too much for some scholars/researchers to ignore. Some scholars, for example, think we should be very much engaged in public affairs because otherwise we leave the public realm and its concerns with law, justice, social welfare, and the like, open only to the influence of the religious communities studied. Consequently, it is argued, the students of religion should also be public intellectuals. But this, clearly, is to draw students of religion away from their basic responsibilities as scientists—the vocation, as Weber has it—for which we are being paid. Stanley Fish's observation in his *Save the World on Your Own Time* about his colleagues in literary studies who "employ the academy's machinery and resources in the service of those other purposes" also applies to scholars of religion (Fish, 2008, 81). If they wish to save the world, Fish correctly points out, they should do it on their own dime.

The flip side of this problem is what we might call the "New Atheism Problem." Many of our colleagues seem overjoyed with the publicity the New Atheists have brought to the field of Religious Studies. There seems to be some justification for the claim that the interest shown by Richard Dawkins and Daniel Dennett in atheism has brought much-needed public attention to what students of religion accomplish. This needs to be rethought. First, it is clear that the New Atheists have become hopelessly engaged in religio-theological argumentation that can make no positive contribution to our work. Secondly, the New Atheists function not as students of religion but as public intellectuals concerned for the welfare not only of their communities but of the whole world. Neither of these tasks belong to the scientific study of religion. The only atheism that is of interest and benefit to the student of religion is "methodological atheism," and to cosy-up to the New Atheists and their metaphysical and political concerns can only damage the image of Religious Studies as a scientific enterprise. As Joseph Ben-David points out in his *The Scientists' Role in Society: A Comparative Study*, any association with their work and that of other ideologists is problematic for science. As he puts it: "If science is perceived as partial to some social interests, and scientists are seen in an invidious light, then people start doubting the moral value of seeking scientific truth for its own sake and apply it for the purpose of changing the world. This may spell the end of scientific culture" (Ben-David 1971, 180).

Finally, a serious concern for students of religion, especially since the advent of experimental studies and the growth of collaborative research projects in our field, is the lack of sufficient "no-strings-attached-funding." This should not be altogether surprising for a field in which most of the university departments for the study of religion have been largely engaged in programs dedicated to student self-realization and moral and political formation, or to programs of "religious appreciation courses" that are designed to contribute to peaceful relations in pluralistic cultures, or to programs that are designed to show the complementarity of science and religion in order to highlight how the sciences confirm religious truths. The problem, of course, is that since *bona fide* science-funding agencies will be suspicious of such "religious studies projects," funding remains meagre at best. This in turn "pushes" scholars in our field to seek other sources of financial support for their projects and many of these have been religious in character. Whether funding from those sources has actually skewed the writing of research grant proposals in order to ensure favourable attention or not is difficult to tell. Nevertheless, funds from such organizations for research in religious studies will likely only further generate suspicion in many scientific circles about the quality of the "Religious Studies" research being carried out. Serious attention needs to be given to the avenues open to us in gaining access to more reputable sources of financial support for our work.

I trust that the argument in the preceding chapters of this book have shown that the idea and ideal of an empirically testable scientific study of religion is rationally sound. The analyses and commentary on the historical development of this idea show that there were many scholars in Religious Studies in the past who sought and gained a degree of recognition for this field in their universities and beyond. Furthermore, it is an historical fact that there are more such scholars in the field today than there were in the past. The field has seen some very important developments which suggests that a scientific study of religion may actually come to dominate the field in the future including: 1) serious research into the deep history of religious behaviour; 2) taking seriously the fact that the natural and social sciences have set important boundary conditions for the research on religions, and that theories in religion really do need to cohere with theories in other disciplines; and 3) the exponential increase in experimental work that the cognitive science of religion, among other sciences, has brought to the field. These developments may at some point provide the kind of centripetal force that will bring into a coherent pattern what today remains, for the most part, scattered studies of those scholars in the field who are committed to scientific research.

Nearly a decade ago, I co-authored a paper entitled "Religious Studies as a Scientific Discipline: The Persistence of a Delusion" with Luther H. Martin in which we asserted that the "historical record...shows that no undergraduate departments of religious studies have fully implemented a *scientific* program of study and research since such an approach was first advocated in the late nineteenth century—much less any broad establishment of such a disciplinary field of study" (Martin and Wiebe 2012, 587). We did not deny that it is logically possible to establish the science of religion in our modern research universities, nor did we "deny that many in the field have done valuable empirical work, and are increasingly doing so…[only that] it does not follow that "religious studies" *as a field* has been productive, let alone theoretically sound; merely that it has not been entirely sterile" (Martin and Wiebe 2012, 595). However, unlike Martin I have not given up the nineteenth-century hope for the establishment of departments for the strictly scientific study of religions in our modern research universities.

Although Martin sees no hope for a fully established scientific study of religions in research university departments of religion in the future, he does seem to leave some room for advancement of that ideal. It lies implicit in his claim to which I referred in Chapter 8: "[A]ny promising future for a strictly scientific study of religion seems to lie…[only] with the initiative of a relatively small cadre of individual scholars, spread across an array of academic departments and programs whose research is pursued in the absence of institutional support or professional patronage" (Martin forthcoming). Recognizing that, it is not wholly unreasonable to think of this cadre of scholars as the catalyst for the future transformation of religious studies departments into departments for the strictly scientific study of religion. Robert McCauley, for example, presents precisely such a description of the future of the field in his book on *Why Religion is Natural and Science is Not*. McCauley notes that it took more than two hundred years for Antoine van Leeuwenhoek's discovery of micro-organisms to eventually triumph in the germ theory of disease—not to mention the roughly 2000 years for the proto-science of the Milesians to morph into the modern scientific revolution in seventeenth-century Europe—and he goes on to suggest that we might leave open the possibility that a triumph of the scientific study of religion may be a similar, but hopefully shorter, "scientific revolution in slow motion" (McCauley 2011, 108). It is in that light that I will continue with the effort to bring the value of the work of this cadre of scholars to the attention of university administrators and press the case for the establishment of the strictly scientific study of religion as an important element in the curriculum of the modern research university.

— Bibliography —

Alles, Gregory. 2008. *Religious Studies: A Global View*. London: Routledge.
Ambasciano, Leonardo. 2018. *An Unnatural History of Religions, Post-Truth, and the Quest for Scientific Knowledge*. London: Bloomsbury Academic.
Appleby, Joyce. 2013. *Shores of Knowledge: New World Discoveries and the Scientific Imagination*. New York: W. W. Norton and Company.
Barton, Carlin A. and Daniel Boyarin. 2016. *Imagine No Religion: How Modern Abstractions Hide Ancient Realities*. New York: Fordham University Press.
Beckwith, Christopher. 2012. *Warriors of the Cloister: The Central Asian Origins of Science in the Medieval World*. Princeton, NJ: Princeton University Press.
Ben-David, Joseph. 1984 [1971]. *The Scientists' Role in Society: A Comprehensive Study*. Chicago, IL: The University of Chicago Press.
Bloch, Maurice. 2008. "Why religion is nothing special but is central." *Philosophical Transactions of the Royal Society: Biological Sciences* 363: 2055–2061.
Blumenberg, Hans. 1983. *The Legitimation of the Modern Age*. Translated by Robert M. Wallace. Cambridge, MA: MIT Press.
———. 1987. *The Genesis of the Copernican World*. Cambridge, MA: MIT Press.
Bodin, Jean. 1975. *The Colloquium of the Seven about the Secrets of the Sublime*. Princeton, NJ: Princeton University Press. (*Colloquium Heptaplomeres de Rerum Sublimium Arcants Abditis*, 1588).
Bowler, Peter J. and Iwan Rhys Morus. 2005. *Making Modern Science, a Historical Survey: Episodes in the Development of Science*. Chicago, IL: University of Chicago Press.
Bremmer, Jan N. 2007. "Atheism in Antiquity." In *The Cambridge Companion to Atheism*, 11–26. Cambridge: Cambridge University Press.

Bulliett, Richard W. 2005. *Hunters, Herders, and Hamburgers: The Past and Future of Human-Animal Relationships*. New York: Columbia University Press.

Carrier, Richard. 2016. *Science Education in the Early Roman Empire*. Durham, NC: Pitchstone Publishing.

———. 2017. *The Scientist in the Early Roman Empire*. Durham, NC: Pitchstone Publishing.

Chalmers, Alan. 1990. *Science and Its Fabrication*. Minneapolis: University of Minnesota Press.

Chenu, Marie-Dominique. 1968. "The makers of theological 'science.'" In *Nature, Man, and Society in the Twelfth Century: Essays in New Theological Perspective in the Latin West*. Chicago, IL: The Chicago University Press.

Cherry, Conrad. 1995. *Hurrying Toward Zion: Universities, Divinity Schools and American Protestantism*. Bloomington: Indiana University Press.

Chidester, David. 2014. *Empire of Religion: Imperialism and Comparative Religion*. Chicago, IL: The Chicago University Press.

Clark, G. N. 1954. "The Early Modern period: New and old in the fifteenth century." In *The European Inheritance*, edited by Ernest Barker, G. N. Clark and P. Vaucher, 3–18. Oxford: Oxford University Press.

Clarke, James Freeman. 1871. *Ten Great Religions: An Essay in Comparative Theology*. Boston, MA: Houghton, Mifflin.

Cobban, A. B. 1975. *The Medieval Universities: Their Development and Organization*. London: Methuen.

Cohen, H. Floris. 1994. *The Scientific Revolution: A Historiographical Inquiry*. Chicago, IL: The University of Chicago Press.

———. 2015. *The Rise of Modern Science Explained*. Cambridge: Cambridge University Press.

Copleston, Frederick. 2003. *A History of Philosophy, Vol. 1, Part II*. London: Bloomsbury Academic.

Cornford, Francis MacDonald. 1932 [1965]. *Before and After Socrates*. Cambridge: Cambridge University Press.

Cunninggim, Merrimon. 1947. *The University Needs Religion*. New Haven, CT: Yale University Press.

De Deugd, C. 1964. *From Religion to Criticism: Notes on the Growth of the Aesthetic Consciousness in Greece*. Utrecht: Utechtse Publikaties voor Algemene Literaturwetenschap.

Dennett, Daniel. 2017. *From Bacteria to Bach and Back: The Evolution of Minds*. New York: W. W. Norton & Company.

Bibliography

De Santillana, Georgio. 1970. *The Origin of Scientific Thought*. New York: New American Library.

De Vries, Jan. 1967. *The Study of Religion: A Historical Approach*. New York: Harcourt, Brace & World.

Dodds, E. R. 1951. *The Greeks and the Irrational*. Berkeley CA: University of California Press.

Feynman, Richard P. 1998. *The Meaning of it All*. New York: Basic Books.

Donald, Merlin. 1991. *Origins of the Modern Mind: Three Stages in the Evolution of Culture and Cognition*. Cambridge, MA: Harvard University Press.

———. 2001. *A Mind So Rare: The Evolution of Human Consciousness*. New York: W. W. Norton & Company.

Downey, Glanville. 1962. *Aristotle: Dean of Early Science*. New York: Franklin Watts.

Dubuisson, Daniel. 2003. *The Western Construction of Religion: Myths, Knowledge, and Ideology*. Baltimore, MD: The Johns Hopkins University Press.

———. 2019. *The Invention of Religions*. Sheffield: Equinox Publishing.

Dunbar, Robin. 1996. *The Trouble With Science: Science, Magic, and Religion*. London: Faber and Faber.

Durkheim, Emile. 1977. *The Evolution of Educational Thought*. Translated by Peter Collins. London: Routledge and Kegan Paul.

Ede, Andrew and Lesley Cormack. 2012. *A History of Science: Vol. 1 – From the Ancient Greeks to the Scientific Revolution*. Toronto: University of Toronto Press.

Evans, Gillian R. 1980. *Old Arts New Theology: The Beginning of Theology as an Academic Discipline*. Oxford: Oxford University Press.

Farrington, Benjamin. 1936. *Science in Antiquity*. London: Thornton Butterworth Ltd.

———. 1944. *Greek Science (Thales to Aristotle): Its Meaning for Us*. Harmondsworth: Penguin Books.

Finley, M. I. 1959. *The Portable Greek Historians*. New York: Viking Penguin.

Fish, Stanley. 2008. *Save the World on Your Own Time*. Oxford: Oxford University Press.

Fitzgerald, Timothy. 2000. *The Ideology of Religious Studies*. Oxford: Oxford University Press.

Ford, David F., Ben Quash, and Janet Martin Soskice, eds. 2005. *Fields of Faith: Theology and Religious Studies for the Twenty-first Century*. Cambridge: Cambridge University Press.

Franeck, Juraj. 2020. *Naturalism and Protectionism in the Study of Religion*. London: Bloomsbury Academic.

Frede, Michael. 1996. "The Philosopher." In *Greek Thought: A Guide to Classical Knowledge*, edited by Jacques Brunschwig, Geoffrey E. R. Lloyd, 3–19. Cambridge MA: Harvard University Press.

Gay, Peter. 1967. *The Enlightenment: The Rise of Modern Paganism*. New York: Random House.

Gellner, Ernest. 1973. "The savage and the modern mind." In *Modes of Thought*, edited by Robin Horton and Ruth Finnegan, 162–181. London: Faber and Faber.

———. 1974. *Legitimation of Belief*. Cambridge: Cambridge University Press.

———. 1979. "An ethic of cognition." In *Spectacles and Predicaments: Essays in Social Theory*, by Ernest Gellner, 162–181. Cambridge: University of Cambridge Press.

———. 1992. *Postmodernism, Reason and Religion*. London: Routledge.

Gershanson, Daniel. E. and Daniel A. Greenberg. 1964. *Anaxagoras and the Birth of Physics*. New York: Blaisdell Publishing.

Gilson, Étienne. 1938. *Reason and Revelation in the Middle Ages*. New York: Charles Scribner's Sons.

Gombrich, Richard F. 1971. *Buddhist Precept and Practice: Traditional Buddhism in the Rural Highlands of Ceylon*. London: Kegan Paul.

Gopnik, Alison and Andrew N. Meltzoff. 1997. *Words, Thoughts, and Theories*. Cambridge, MA: MIT Press.

Gopnik, Alison and Andrew N. Meltzoff and Patricia K Kuhl. 1999. *The Scientist in the Crib: What Early Learning Tells Us About the Mind*. New York: Harper Collins.

Graham, Daniel. 2010. *The Texts of Early Greek Philosophy: The Complete Fragments and Selected Testimonies of the Major Presocratics*, Vol.1. Cambridge: Cambridge University Press.

Grant, Edward. 1971. *Physical Science in the Middle Ages*. Toronto: John Wiley and Sons.

———. 1996. *Foundations of Modern Science in the Middle Ages*. Cambridge: Cambridge University Press.

———. 2001. *God and Reason in the Middle Ages*. Cambridge: Cambridge University Press.

———. 2007. *A History of Natural Philosophy: From the Ancient World to the Nineteenth Century*. Cambridge: Cambridge University Press.

Bibliography

Gregory, Brad S. 2012. *The Unintended Reformation: How a Religious Revolution Secularized Society*. Cambridge, MA: Harvard University Press.

———. 2017. *Rebel in the Ranks: Martin Luther, the Reformation, and the Conflict that Continues to Shape Our World*. New York: HarperCollins.

Graziosi, Barbara. 2014. *The Gods of Olympus: A History*. New York: Metropolitan Books.

Griffiths, Paul J. 2000. "The very idea of religion." *First Things: A Monthly Journal of Religion and Public Life* 103: 30–35.

———. 1999. *Religious Reading: The Place of Reading in the Practice of Religion*. Oxford: Oxford University Press.

Guthrie, W. K. C. 1950. *The Greeks and Their Gods*. Boston, MA: Beacon Press.

———. 1950. *The Greek Philosophers*. London: Methuen.

Haack, Susan. 1998. "Puzzling out science." In *Manifesto of a Passionate Moderate*, edited by Susan Haack, 90–103. Chicago, IL: Chicago University Press.

———. 2003. *Defending Science Within Reason*. Amherst, NY: Prometheus Press.

———. 2013. *Putting Philosophy to Work: Inquiry and Its Place in Culture*. Amherst, NY: Prometheus Press.

Hahn, Robert. 2010. *Archaeology and the Origins of Philosophy*. Albany, NY: State University of New York Press

Harman, P. M. 1983. *The Scientific Revolution*. London: Taylor and Francis.

Hart, D. G. 1999. *The University Gets Religion: Religious Studies in American Higher Education*. Baltimore, MD: Johns Hopkins University Press.

Haskin, Charles Homer. 1959. *The Rise of the Universities*. Ithaca, NY: Cornell University Press.

Hatch, Edwin. 1890. *The Influence of Greek Ideas and Usages Upon the Christian Church*. London: Williams and Norgate.

Heidel, William Arthur. 1933. *Heroic Age of Science*. New York: AMS Press.

Henry, John. 2010. "Religion in the scientific revolution." In *The Cambridge Companion to Science and Religion*, edited by Peter Harrison, 39–58. Cambridge: Cambridge University Press.

Hermann, Arthur. 2013. *Plato Versus Aristotle and the Struggle for the Soul of Western Civilization*. New York: Random House.

Herodotus. 2003. *The Histories*. Translated by Aubrey De Sélincourt. London: Penguin Books.

Hobart, Michael. 2018. *The Great Rift: Literacy, Numeracy, and the Religion-Science Divide*. Cambridge, MA: Harvard University Press.

Holland, Tom. 2019. *Dominion: How the Christian Revolution Remade the World*. New York: Basic Books.

Howard, Thomas Albert. 2006. *Protestant Theology and the Making of the Modern University*. Oxford: Oxford University Press.

Huff, Toby E. 1993. *The Rise of Early Modern Science: Islam, China, and the West*. Cambridge: Cambridge University Press.

———. 2011. *Intellectual Curiosity and the Scientific Revolution: A Global Perspective*. Cambridge: Cambridge University Press.

Hunt, Lynn, Margaret C. Jacob and Wijnand Mijhardt. 2010. *The Book that Changed Europe: Picart's and Bernard's Religious Ceremonies of the World*. Cambridge, MA: Harvard University Press.

Jaeger, Werner. 1947. *The Theology of the Early Greek Philosophers*. Oxford: The Clarendon Press.

James, William. 1902. *The Varieties of Religious Experience: A Study of Human Behavior*. Cambridge, MA: Harvard University Press.

Jastrow, Jr. Morris. 1899. "The historical study of religion in universities and colleges." *Journal of the American Oriental Society* 20: 317–325.

———. 1900. "The first international congress for the history of religions." *International Journal of Ethics* 10(4): 503–509.

———. 1981. *The Study of Religion*. Chico, CA: Scholars Press.

Jones, Richard Foster. 1965. *Ancients and Moderns: A Study of the Scientific Revolution in Seventeenth-Century England*. Berkeley: University of California Press.

Jordan, Louis Henry. 1905. *Comparative Religion: Its Genesis and Growth*. Edinburgh: T. and T. Clark.

Kemeny, P. C. 1998. *Princeton in the Nation's Service: Religion, Ideals, Educational Practice*. Oxford: Oxford University Press.

King, Ursula, ed. 1990. *Turning Points in Religious Studies: Essays in Honour of Geoffrey Parrinder*. Edinburgh: T & T Clark.

Kirk, G. S., J. E. Raven and M. Schofield. 1983. *The Presocratic Philosophers*. Cambridge: Cambridge University Press.

Kuhn, Thomas. 2012. *The Structure of Scientific Revolutions*. 4th Edition. Chicago, IL: The University of Chicago Press.

Leclerq, Jean. 1962. *The Love of Learning and the Desire for God*. Translated by Catherine Misrahi. New York: New American Library.

Leroi, Armand Marie. 2014. *The Lagoon: How Aristotle Invented Science*. New York: Viking.

Lloyd, G.E.R. 1973. *Greek Science After Aristotle*. London: Chatto and Windus.
———. 1979. *Magic, Reason, and Experience: Studies in the Origins and Development of Greek Science*. Cambridge: Cambridge University Press.
———. 1990. *Demystifying Mentalities*. Cambridge: Cambridge University Press.
———. 2004. *Ancient Worlds, Modern Reflections: Philosophical Perspective on Greek and Chinese Science and Culture*. Oxford: Oxford University Press.
———. 2014. *The Ideals of Inquiry: An Ancient History*. Oxford: Oxford University Press.
Luce, T. J. 1997. *The Greek Historians*. London: Routledge.
Marsden, George. 1994. *The Soul of the American University: From Protestant Establishment to Established Nonbelief*. Oxford: Oxford University Press.
Martin, Luther H. 1987. *Hellenistic Religions: An Introduction*. Oxford: Oxford University Press.
Martin, Luther H. and Donald Wiebe. 2012. "Religious studies as a scientific discipline: The persistence of a delusion." In *Conversations and Controversies in the Scientific Study of Religion*, edited by Luther H. Martin and Donald Wiebe, 221–230. Leiden: E. J. Brill.
———. 2016. *Conversations and Controversies in the Scientific Study of Religion: Collaborative and Co-authored Essays*. Leiden: E. J. Brill.
McCauley, Robert. 2011. *Why Religion is Natural and Science Is Not*. Oxford: Oxford University Press.
McCutcheon, Russell. 1997. *Manufacturing Religion: The Discourse on Sui Generis Religion and the Politics of Nostalgia*. Oxford: Oxford University Press.
McCutcheon, Russell and William F. Arnal. 2013. *The Sacred is the Profane: The Political Nature of "Religion."* Oxford: Oxford University Press.
McKirahan, Richard D. Jr. 1994. *Philosophy Before Socrates: An Introduction with Texts and Commentary*. Indianapolis, IN: Hackett Publishing Co.
Mercier, Hugo and Dan Sperber. 2017. *The Enigma of Reason*. Cambridge, MA: Harvard University Press.
Miller, Richard B. 1996. *Casuistry and Modern Ethics: A Poetics of Modern Reasoning*. Chicago, IL: The University of Chicago Press.
Mithen, Steven. 1999. *The Prehistory of the Mind: The Cognitive Origins of Art and Science*. London: Thames and Hudson.
———. 2002. "Human evolution and the cognitive basis of science." In *The Cognitive Basis of Science*, edited by Peter Carruthers, Stephen Stitch and Michael Segal, 23–40. Cambridge: Cambridge University Press.

Molendijk, Arie. 2005. *The Emergence of the Science of Religion in the Netherlands.* Leiden: Brill.

Müller, Friedrich Max. 1878. *On the Origin and Growth of Religion as Illustrated by the Religions of India.* London: Longmans, Green and Co.

———. 1881 [1867]. *Essays on the Science of Religion.* New York: Charles Scribner's & Sons.

———. 1893 [1873]. *Introduction to the Science of Religion.* London: Longmans, Green, and Co.

———. 1898a. *Natural Religion.* London: Longmans, Green, & Co.

———. 1898b. *Physical Religion.* London: Longmans. Green, & Co.

———. 1898c. *Anthropological Religion.* London: Longmans, Green, & Co.

———. 1898d. *Theosophy or Psychological Religion.* London: Longmans, Green, & Co.

Murray, Gilbert. 1946. "Prolegomena to the study of ancient philosophy." In *Greek Studies,* 65–86. Oxford: Clarendon Press.

———. 1955 [1912]. *Five Stages of Greek Religion.* New York: Doubleday.

Murray, Albert Victor. 1967. *Abelard and St. Bernard: A Study in Twelfth Century "Modernism."* Manchester: Manchester University Press.

Nelson, Benjamin. 1981a. "Civilizational complexes and intercivilizational encounters." In *On the Roads to Modernity: Conscience, Science, and Civilizations, Selected Writings.* Totowa, NJ: Roman and Littlefield.

———. 1981b. "Sciences and civilizations "East" and "West": Joseph Needham and Max Weber." In *On the Roads to Modernity: Conscience, Science, and Civilizations, Selected Writings.* Totowa, NJ: Roman and Littlefield..

Newsome, David. 1972. *Two Classes of Men: Platonism and English Romantic Thought.* London: John Murray.

Nicholson, Ernest, ed. 2003. *A Century of Theological and Religious Studies in Britain.* Oxford: Oxford University Press.

Nongbri, Brent. 2013. *Before Religion: A History of a Modern Concept.* New Haven, CT: Yale University Press.

Passmore, John Arthur. 1978. *Science and Its Critics.* London: Duckworth.

Picart, Bernard and Jean-Frédéric Bernard. 1723–1737. *Religious Ceremonies and Customs of the World (in 7 volumes).* London: Printed for Nicholas Prevost.

Platvoet, Jan G. and Arie L. Molendijk. 1999. *The Pragmatics of Defining Religion: Contexts, Concepts and Contents.* Leiden: E. J. Brill.

Popper, Karl R. 1965. "Back to the Presocratics." In *Conjectures and Refutations: The Growth of Scientific Knowledge,* 136–165. New York: Harper and Row.

———. 1976. *Unended Quest: An Intellectual Autobiography*. London: Fontana/Collins.

Preus, J. Samuel. 1987. *Explaining Religion: Criticism and Theory from Bodin to Freud*. New Haven, CT: Yale University Press.

———. 2001. *Spinoza and the Irrelevance of Biblical Authority*. Cambridge: Cambridge University Press.

Randall John Herman, Jr. 1970. *Hellenistic Ways of Deliverance and the Making of the Christian Synthesis*. New York: Columbia University Press.

Reuben, Julie. 1996. *The Making of the Modern University: Intellectual Transformation and the Marginalization of Morality*. Chicago, IL: The University of Chicago Press.

Réville, Albert. 1884a. *Prolegomena on the History of Religions*. Translated by A. S. Squire, with an introduction by Max Müller. London: Williams and Norgate.

———. 1884b. *Lectures on the Origin and Growth of Religions as Illustrated by the Native Religions of Mexico and Peru*. London: Williams and Norgate.

———. 1900. "The International Congress of the History of Religions." *The Open Court: A Monthly Magazine*, May, 271–275.

Rubenstein, Richard. 2003. *Aristotle's Children: How Christians, Muslims, and Jews Rediscovered Ancient Wisdom and Illuminated the Dark Ages*. Orlando: Harcourt Books.

Russo, Lucio. 2004. *The Forgotten Revolution: How Science Was Born in 300 BC and why It had to be Born Again*. Translated by Silvio Levy. Berlin: Springer.

Saler, Benson. 1993. *Conceptualizing Religion: Immanent Anthropologists, Transcendent Natives, and Unbounded Categories*. Leiden: E. J. Brill.

Saliba, George. 2011. *Islamic Science and the Making of the European Renaissance*. Cambridge, MA: Harvard University Press.

Sedley, David. 2007. *Creationism and Its Critics in Antiquity*. Los Angeles, CA: University of California Press.

Sharpe, Eric. 1986. *Comparative Religion: A History*. 2nd edition. London: Duckworth.

Shepard, Robert S. 1991. *God's People in the Ivory Tower: Religion in the Early American Universities*. New York: Carlson Publishing.

Slingerland, Edward. 2018. "Who's afraid of reductionism? Methodological naturalism and the academic study of religion." In *The Question of Methodological Naturalism* edited by Jason N. Blum, 167–205. Leiden: E. J. Brill.

Smart, Ninian. 1973. *The Phenomenon of Religion*. London: Macmillan.

———. 1990. "Concluding reflections: Religious studies in global perspective." In *Turning Points in Religious Studies: Essays in Honour of Geoffrey Parrinder*, edited by Ursula King, 299–306. Edinburgh: T & T Clark.

Smith, Christian. 2019. *Religion: What Is It, How It works, and Why it Matters*. Princeton, NJ: Princeton University Press.

Smith, Jonathan Z. 1999. "Religion, religions, religious." In *Critical Terms for Religious Studies*, edited by Mark C. Taylor, 269–284. Chicago: The University of Chicago Press.

Smith, Wilfred Cantwell. 1962. *The Meaning and End of Religion*. New York: The MacMillan Company.

Spiro, Melford. 1966. "Religion: Problems of definition and explanation." In *Anthropological Approaches to Religion*, edited by M. Banton, 85–126. London: Tavistock.

Stroumsa, Guy. 2010. *A New Science: The Discovery of Religion in the Age of Reason*. Charlottesville: University of Virginia Press.

Sutcliffe, Steve J., ed. 2004. *Religion: Empirical Studies*. Aldershot: Ashgate Publishing.

Thrower, James. 2000. *Western Atheism: A Short History*. Amherst, NY: Prometheus Books.

Tiele, Cornelis Petrus. 1897. *Elements of the Science of Religion, Vol. I: Morphological, Vol. II Ontological*. Edinburgh: William Blackwood and Sons.

Tomasello, Michael. 1999. *The Cultural Origins of Human Cognition*. Cambridge, MA: Harvard University Press.

———. 2008. *Origins of Human Communication*. Cambridge, MA: MIT Press.

———. 2009. *Why We Cooperate*. Cambridge, MA: MIT Press.

———. 2014. *A Natural History of Human Thinking*. Cambridge, MA: Harvard University Press.

———. 2019. *Becoming Human: A History of Ontogeny*. Cambridge, MA: Harvard University Press.

Toulmin, Stephen. 1972. *Human Understanding: The Collective Use and Evolution of Concepts*. Princeton, NJ: Princeton University Press.

———. 1990. *Cosmopolis: The Hidden Agenda of Modernity*. New York: The Free Press.

Turner, James. 2011. *Religion Enters the Academy: The Origins of the Study of Religion in America*. Athens: University of Georgia Press.

———. 2014. *Philology: The Forgotten Origins of the Modern Humanities*. Princeton, NJ: Princeton University Press.

Bibliography

Van der Leeuw, Gerardus. 1938. *Religion in Essence and Manifestation*. Translated by J. E. Turner. London: George Allen and Unwin.

Vernant, Jean-Pierre. 1983. "The formation of positivist thought in archaic Greece." In *Myth and Thought Among the Greeks*, 343–374 London: Routledge & Kegan Paul.

Versnel, Henk S. 2011. "Did the Greeks believe in their gods?" In *Coping with the Gods: Wayward Readings in Greek Theology*, 539–559. Leiden: E. J. Brill.

Veyne, Paul. 1988. *Did the Greeks Believe in Their Myths? An Essay on the Constitutive Imagination*, Translated by Paula Wissing. Chicago, IL: The University of Chicago Press.

Weber, Max. 1919. "Science as a Vocation." In *From Max Weber: Essays in Sociology*, edited by H. H. Gerth and C. Wright Mills, 129–156. Oxford: Oxford University Press.

Weisheipl, James A. 1971 [1959]. *The Development of Physical Theory in the Middle Ages*. Ann Arbor: University of Michigan Press.

Welch, Claude. 1985. *Protestant Theology in the Nineteenth Century 1970–1914*. New Haven, CT: Yale University Press.

Wellmon, Chad. 2015. *Organizing Enlightenment: Information Overload and the Invention of the Modern Research University*. Baltimore, MD: Johns Hopkins University Press.

Wheeler-Barclay, Marjorie. 2010. *The Science of Religion in Britain, 1860–1905*. Charlottesville: University of Virginia Press.

Whitmarsh, Tim. 2015. *Battling the Gods: Atheism in the Ancient World*. New York: Alfred A. Knopf.

Wiebe, Donald. 1981. *Religion and Truth: Towards an Alternative Paradigm for the Study of Religion*. The Hague: Mouton.

———. 1999. *The Politics of Religious Studies: The Continuing Conflict with Theology in the Academy*. New York: St. Martin's Press.

———. 2020. *The Learned Practice of Religion in the Modern University*. London: Bloomsbury Academic.

———. 2021. *An Argument in Defence of a Strictly Scientific Study of Religion: The Controversy at Delphi*. Toronto: Institute for the Advanced Study of Religion.

Wolpert, Lewis. 1992. *The Unnatural Nature of Science*. London: Faber and Faber.

———. 1993. *The Unnatural Nature of Science: Why Science Does Not Make (Common) Sense*. Cambridge, MA: Harvard University Press.

Wooton, David. 2015. *The Invention of Science: A New History of the Scientific Revolution*. New York: Harper.

Yinger, Milton. 1970. *The Scientific Study of Religion*. Cambridge, MA: Harvard University Press.

Ziman, John. 1967. *Public Knowledge: The Social Dimensions of Science*. Cambridge: Cambridge University Press.

———. 1978. *Reliable Knowledge: An Exploration of the Grounds for Belief in Science*. Cambridge: Cambridge University Press.

———. 2000. *Reliable Science: What It Is, and What It Means*. Cambridge: Cambridge University Press.

— INDEX —

A

Abelard, Peter 81
  conflict with Bernard of Clairvaux 93, 95–97, 99, 102, 103
Abington School District vs Schempp (U.S. Supreme Court judgment) 176–177
Adams, Hanna 133–134
Age of Discovery 133, 144
  introduces Europe to world's diverse religions 125, 136
Alexander the Great 65, 71
Alles, Gregory 178–179
Ambasciano, Leonardo 148–149, 150, 187
American Academy of Religion (AAR) 136, 177
Anaxagoras 50, 58–59, 66
Anaximander 49, 53–54, 55
Anaximenes 49, 53
Anselm of Canterbury 95, 102
Appleby, Joyce
  Age of Discovery and diversity of religions 126–127
Aristotle 65, 68–71, 98, 102
Aristotelianism 92, 98, 99, 115
  and framework of Milesian revolution 69, 81
  introduced into medieval universities 91–92
  natural philosophy of 65, 68–70, 73, 80, 81, 85, 91, 99
  rediscovered by Islamic scholars 76–78

astronomy 113–114
atheism
  methodological 55, 190
  new 190
Atomism, Atomists 47, 49, 59, 66
Augustine, Saint 16, 76, 78, 79, 81, 100, 168
Augustinians 99
Averroes 100

B

Bacon, Francis 107, 131, 138–139
Barton, Carlin A. and Daniel Boyarin
  "religion" derived from Latin *religio* and Greek *thrēskia* 13, 15
Beckwith, Christopher
  Aristotle and science in medieval Latin civilization 91–92
Ben-David, Joseph 190
Bloch, Maurice 12
Blumenberg, Hans
  modern age 120–123
Bodin, Jean 127–128, 137
Bowler, Peter J. and Ivan Rhys Morus 111–112
Bremmer, Jan 58
British Association for the Advancement of Science (now British Science Association) 156–157
British Association for the Study of Religions (BASR) 171–172
Bulliet, Richard W. 40–41

C

Carolingian Renaissance 85, 86
Carrier, Richard 72–74, 79
  early Christians hostile to scientific thought 75
Casaubon, Isaac 106–107
  cathedral schools 88–89
Chalmers, Alan 20, 113
Chantepie de la Saussaye, Pierre Daniel 154–155
Charlemagne (king) 85
  reviving classical learning 86
Chenu, Marie-Dominique 98
Cherry, Conrad 173, 175, 177
Chidester, David 13
Clark, G.N. 105–106, 126
Clarke, James Freeman 134
Cobban, A.B.
  first European universities as "guild organizations" 89
  medieval university as wholly new institution 90–91
cognitive capacity in human evolution 25–33, 36, 39–41, 47, 66, 68
  see also Donald, Merlin; Mithen, Steven; Wolpert, Lewis
Cohen, H. Floris 26, 43, 55–56
  scientific revolution 82–83
Coleridge, Samuel Taylor 69
comparative religion 149, 158, 161
  see also religion, scientific study of
Constantine (emperor) 15–16, 82
Copleston, Frederick 72
Cornford, Francis M. 49, 50–51, 66, 78, 79
Cunninggim, Merrimon 175

D

Dawkins, Richard 190
Democritus of Abdera 47, 48, 50, 53, 66
Dennett, Daniel 27, 190
Descartes, René 109–110, 111
Dewey, John 109
disciplinable fields
  "compact" discipline 182
  "diffuse" and "would-be" disciplines 182–183
  Religious Studies as "compact," "diffuse," or "would-be" discipline 184–185
Dodds, E.R. 54
  "age of anxiety" in ancient world 71–72
Donald, Merlin 44
  evolution from minds of apes to modern humans 30–32
  transition from mimetic to mythological thinking 32–33, 43
Downey, Glanville 68
Dubuisson, Daniel 14
  "religion" as fundamentally Christian term 13
Dunbar, Robin 26, 27, 35
Durkheim, Émile 88–89, 93, 96, 102–103
  Greek mode of thought counter to church's nature 88, 93

E

Ede, Andrew and Lesley Cormack 98, 99, 103
  knowledge 88
  Renaissance 106, 107
Eliade, Mircea 176, 178
Empedocles 50, 59
Enlightenment 111, 118–121
Euhemerus 167
Evans, Gillian 93, 94, 96–97
  Anselm of Canterbury 95, 102

F

Farnell, Lewis 148
Farrington, Benjamin 49–50
Feynman, Richard 59
Fingarette, Herbert 176
Finley, M.I. 63
First Enlightenment 168
First International Congress of the History of Religions (1900) 154, 155–156, 164–166, 169, 170, 172
Fish, Stanley 185, 190
Fitzgerald, Timothy 4–5, 7–8, 13
Fontenelle, Bernard 137
Franeck, Juraj 187
Frede, Michael 48
  Thales of Miletus 48–49
Freud, Sigmund 176

206

Index

G
Galileo 83, 109, 111, 115–117
Gay, Peter 105
   Enlightenment 119–120
   modernity 117–120
   Newton, Sir Isaac 119
   "pagan Christianity" 119
   Renaissance 107, 117–120
Gellner, Ernest 56, 179, 181
   gap between primitive and modern mind 41–43
   Western epistemic tradition 123, 167
Gershanson, Daniel E. and Daniel A. Greenberg 66
Gilson, Étienne 99, 100
   Augustinians 99
   Tertullianists 99, 100
   Thomists 99, 100, 103
Gombrich, Richard F.
   search to define "religion" trivial and futile 7
Gopnick, Alison 33
Gopnick, Alison and Andrew Meltzoff
   cognitive development in childhood and adulthood 27–28
Gopnick, Alison, Andrew Meltzoff and Patricia Kuhl 26–27, 28
Graham, Daniel 48
Grant, Edward 76, 80, 85
   concept of the corporation 87–88
   medieval university as wholly new institution 90–91
Gregory, Brad S. 143–144
   "unintended consequences" of Protestant Reformation 141–142
   University of Berlin as "Romantic research university" 183–184
Griffiths, Paul J. 17
   impossibility of scientific study of religion 4, 8–9
   religion and "mystifying ideologies" 5
   Wiebe, Donald 5–7
Guthrie, W.K.C. 47, 54

H
Haack, Susan
   definition of science 21–22
Hahn, Robert 55
Harman, P.M.
   scientific revolution 112
Harrison, Jane Ellen 148
Hart, D.G.
   study of religion in the university 175–177
Haskins, Charles Homer 89
Hatch, Edwin 78–79
   Milesian thinking absorbed by Christian thinkers 92–93
Heidel, William Arthur 65–66
Heilsgeschichte (salvation story) 140
Hellenistic period 70, 72, 75, 76, 168, 174
   and science 65, 71, 73, 77, 79, 85–86, 168
Henry, John 112
Heracles 63
Heraclitus 53
Herbert of Cherbury 128, 137
Herman, Arthur
   Aristotle as father of science and the scientific method 69
   Renaissance 106
Herodotus 46
   proto-historian of religions 63, 167
Hesiod 47, 57, 58, 62
   Theogony 55
Hobart, Michael 4, 83, 115, 116–117
Hobbes, Thomas 128
Holland, Tom
   religio 15–16
Homer 57, 58, 62, 63
Howard, Thomas Albert 150–151, 153–154
Huff, Toby 92
   autonomous medieval universities 89–92
   Investiture Controversy and first modern system of law 87–88
   scientific revolution 87
Hume, David 119, 137–138
Hunt, Lynn, Margaret C. Jacob and Wijnand Mijnhardt 128–132
Huxley, Aldous 148, 154
Hypatia 73

I

International Association for the History of Religions (IAHR) 170, 171, 172, 186, 187
invention of the printing press 126
Investiture Controversy 86–87
Ionians 46–47, 49, 50–51, 54–55, 57, 61–62, 63, 68, 87, 92, 101, 122
  see also Milesians
Israel, Jonathan 105

J

Jaeger, Werner 58
James, William
  and religious studies in America 135–136
Jastrow, Morris
  science of religion as university discipline 172–173, 174, 187
Jesuits
  civil religion 139–140
Jones, Richard Foster 107, 138
Jordan, Lewis Henry 133, 149
Justinian (emperor) 168

K

Kemeny, P.C. 177
Kirk, G.S., J.E. Raven and M. Schofield 47, 50
Knight, David 150
knowledge 19–20, 59, 71, 79
  as divinely revealed truth 3, 81, 102
  folk knowledge 32
  knowledge claims 42, 55
  knowledge about religion 177, 183, 185
  and naturalism 7
  for its own sake 20, 22, 40–41, 43, 47, 56–57, 61–62, 67–68, 73, 123
  as rationally justifiable beliefs 45–46
  religion and knowledge 82, 138, 157, 168
  religious knowledge compared with knowledge about religion 174
  scientific knowledge 25, 74, 112–113, 173, 179, 181
  secularization of knowledge 143–144, 157, 184
  uncensored knowledge 129–130
  and universities 151
  and wisdom 69
  see also Blumenberg, Hans; Cohen, H. Floris; Durkheim, Émile; Ede, Andrew and Lesley Cormack; Evans, Gillian; Gay, Peter; Gilson, Étienne; Hobart, Michael; Howard, Thomas Albert; Jones, Richard Foster; Leclerq, Jean; Milesians; Mithen, Steven; Müller, Friedrich Max; Popper, Karl R.; Stroumsa, Guy; Tiele, Cornelis Petrus; Toulmin, Stephen; Wellmon, Chad; Wooton, David
Kuhn, Thomas 137, 140

L

Lagard, Paul de 153
Lang, Andrew 148
Lash, Nicholas 172
Leclerq, Jean 93–94, 97, 98
Leertouwer, Lammert 169–170
Leroi, Armand Marie
  Aristotelean mode of thought as "scientific enterprise" 69
Leuba, James H. 135
Leucippus of Miletus 47, 50, 53, 66
Lévi-Strauss, Claude 27, 39–40
Lévy-Bruhl, Lucien 67
Lloyd, G.E.R. 19–20, 48, 51–52, 66–68, 72, 85
  analogous ambitions to science in ancient civilizations 69–70
Luce, T.J. 62–63
Luther, Martin 16

M

Machiavelli, Niccolo 128
Marduk (Babylonian god) 50
Marsden, George 177
Martin, Luther H. 65, 186–188, 192
Martin, Luther H. and Donald Wiebe 187, 191–192
McCauley, Robert 192
McCutcheon, Russell 13
McCutcheon, Russell and William F. Arnal 13
McKirahan, Richard 54, 58
Melissus 50
Mercier, Hugo and Dan Sperber 36

Index

reason as evolutionary trait 37–39
Milesians 52–56, 57, 58, 59, 60, 62, 68, 102, 103
  and birth of modern science 66, 67
  and Christian thinkers 92–93
  and knowledge 45, 46, 78, 92, 167–168
  methodological atheism 55, 190
  new transitional mode of thought 44, 45, 47, 48–51
  philosophy transcends "inherited conglomerate" 52
  proto-science 192
  revolution (Ionian Enlightenment) 61
  see also Ionians
Miller, Richard B. 182, 184
  disciplinable fields 183, 185
Mithen, Steven 35–36, 37, 40
  evolution of brain and mind in early man 26, 28–30
  "folk knowledge" hardwired into brain 32
  requirements for emergence of science 44
  three phases in emergence of modern mind 29
  modernity 102, 105, 107, 108–109, 110, 111
Molendijk, Arie 154–155, 162, 164, 170
  monastic and scholastic theology 93–95, 96, 97, 101
Montaigne, Michel de 108, 109, 110
More, Thomas 128
Müller, Friedrich Max 148, 149, 154, 156, 157–161, 162, 164, 165
  Comparative Theology 149, 158, 161
  father of modern scientific study of religion 149, 155
Murray, Albert Victor 95–96
Murray, Gilbert 51
  "inherited conglomerate" of Greek culture 49, 52, 58
  shift from knowledge to solace 72

N

National Association of Biblical Instructors (NABI) 136, 177
Neo-Platonism 76, 168
Nelson, Benjamin
three basic types of consciousness 100–102

Newsome, David 69
Nicholson, Ernest 172
Nongbri, Brent 15
  and modern concept of religion 12–13

O

Overbeck, Franz 153

P

Parmenides 49, 53
Passmore, John 20–21
Peace of Westphalia (1648) 142–143
Penner, Hans 182
  phenomenology see religion, scientific study of
Picart, Bernard and Jean-Frédéric Bernard 126–127
  role in emerging study of comparative religion 128–132
Plato 47, 58, 69, 76, 79, 80, 81, 85
  hybrid mode of thought 92
  Phaedo 59, 68, 78
Platonism 79, 98, 102
Platvoet, Jan G. and Arie L. Molendijk
  universal "true definition of religion" not needed 14
Popper, Karl R. 10, 22, 44, 52–54, 167
  arguing about definitions "specious and insignificant" 7
  conjectural-refutational thinking 39
postmodernism
  challenge to study of religion 180–181
pre-Socratics 55–56, 61–63, 167
  advancement of science-like thinking 65
  emergence and development of science 49–60
  study of religion 47–48
Preus, Sam 127–128
  study of religions 137–139, 182
Protestant Reformation
  Gregory, Brad S. 141–143
  separation of church and state 141, 143, 144
  sola scriptura 142
Ptolemy
  Almagest 77
Pusey, Nathan 176
Pythagoras 49

Q

Quadrivium (arithmetic, geometry, astronomy, music) 89, 95, 106

R

Radical Enlightenment 105–106, 117
Randall, John Herman Jr. 75, 76, 79
reason 19, 21–22, 37–39, 46, 51–52, 55, 57, 62, 68, 78, 81
  abstract reason 66
  emancipation from religious constraint 82
  and faith 81
  and myth 59
  and revelation 86
religio 13, 15–16
religion
  as "abstract English noun" 10, 21
  attempts to define 1–17
  fundamentally Christian term 13
  steeped in Western ideology 13
  as translation of Latin *religio* and Greek *thrēskia* 13
religion, academic study of 1–11, 13, 25, 133, 135–136, 147–148, 175–177
  in Britain 170–171
  as "crypto-Christian" intellectual enterprise 8
  ecclesiastical control of 1, 2, 25, 90, 123, 148
  in Holland 170
  knowledge about and understanding of 183
  and naturalism 6–7, 9, 17, 68, 98, 137, 143
  in the U.S. 135–136, 172–178
  see also theology
religion, scientific study of (science of religion) 5, 46, 57, 135, 148, 153–155, 156–163, 164, 166, 167, 169, 172–173, 174, 180, 185–186, 187
  emerges in 16th-century Europe 3
  funding 190–191
  obstacles to 189–190
  as scientific enterprise 2–6, 8–11, 13, 17, 22–23, 69, 189–190
  special espistemic morality of 189
  see also theology; "Victorian 'science of religion' "
religiones 15
Religionswissenschaft (religious studies) 174–175, 176, 180
Renaissance 73–74, 77, 83, 103, 105, 106, 107–111, 117, 118, 122, 141, 144
Renaissance and Romanticism, period between 105, 166
Reuben, Julie 173, 174–175
Réville, Albert and Jean Réville 154, 155–156, 164–166, 169
Robertson, David 170
Rorty, Richard 109
Rubinstein, Richard 81
Russo, Lucio 77, 85
  appearance of "exact science" after Aristotle 70–71
  rise of religion and magic over science in 2nd century BCE 73–74
  three "beacons" of scientific revolution 71

S

Saler, Benson 14
Saliba, George
  Islamic scholars rediscover Aristotle 76–78
Sambursky, Samuel 66
de Santillana, Georgio 66
Sassi, Maria Michela 57
Scaliger, Joseph Justus 140
science
  as "abstract English noun" 21
  attempts to define 19–22
  decline during rise of Christianity 85–86
  emergence of 26–27, 45, 62, 67, 179
  proto-science 65, 168
  scientific method 20–21
  see also cognitive capacity; Mithen, Steven; religion; Wiebe, Donald; Wolpert, Lewis; Ziman, John
science of religion *see* religion, scientific study of
scientific revolution 71, 82–83, 87, 106, 111–112, 113–116, 117, 133, 144

new model for study of religions and
religion 136–137
Sedley, David 58–59
Sharpe, Eric 148, 149–150, 154, 155, 161, 164, 165
    Müller as father of modern scientific study of religion 149
    Tiele as co-founder of science of religion 149
    comparative religion 156, 171
Shepard, Robert S. 174
Simon, Richard 140, 144
Slingerland, Edward 18–19
Smart, Ninian 11, 12, 171, 178
Smith, Christian 10
Smith, Jonathan Z. 10–11, 13–15
Smith, Wilfred Cantwell 178
    replacing "religion" with "faith" and "tradition" 11–12
Smith, William Robertson 148
Socrates 59, 68, 78, 79, 85, 92
    philosophy shifts from study of nature to study of human life 49, 50–51
Spinoza, Baruch 138–139
Spiro, Melford 10
    on defining religion 6
Starbuck, E.D. 135
Stroumsa, Guy 82, 106–107
modern study of religion 105, 137, 139–141, 144–145, 147, 166, 169
    see also religion, academic study of; religion, scientific study of
Sutcliffe, Steven 171–172

T

Taylor, Charles 18
Tertullianists 99, 100
Thales of Miletus 48–49, 50, 51, 53
    see also Milesians
Theodosius, Flavius 65, 85
theology 2, 3, 4–5, 8, 81, 93, 95, 101–102, 143–144, 149–150, 153–154, 169, 170, 172, 177
    see also religion; religion, academic study of; religion, scientific study of
Thomas Aquinas, Saint 102
Thomists 99, 100, 103

Thrower, James 58
Tiele, Cornelis Petrus 11–12, 154, 156, 161–163, 165
    as co-founder of science of religion 149, 155, 161, 170
Tomasello, Michael 40, 43
    collective intentionality 33–34
    human modes of thought 32–37
Toulmin, Stephen 105, 182, 184
    disciplinable fields 182–183
    Renaissance 107–111, 112, 114, 117
Trismegistus, Hermes 112
Trivium (grammar, rhetoric, logic) 89, 95, 106
Turner, James
    scholarly study of religion 132–137

U

universities
    Bildung (building moral character in students) 151, 152, 153, 184
    as corporations 89–90
    departments of comparative religion 149–150
    early 89
    Enlightenment universities derived authority from state 152
    medieval universities derived authority from church 152
    modern research university 152–153
    theological faculties 2, 8, 90, 95, 96, 101, 134, 143–144
    Wissenschaft (modern specialized science) 151, 153, 180, 184
University of Berlin
    earliest model for departments of academic study of religion 183–184
    founding as modern research university 150–151, 153
University of Chicago
    first study-of-religion program without ministerial training 134

V

van der Leeuw, Gerardus 12, 170
van Leeuwenhoeck, Antoine 192
Vernant, J.-P. 48
Versnel, Henk S. 62

Veyne, Paul 59
   belief of ancient Greeks in gods 60–62
   "scientific" and "imaginative" truths of myth and religion 61–62
"Victorian 'science of religion'" 147–148, 149, 150, 166, 171
   see also religion, scientific study of
de Vries, Jan
   pre-Socratics and the "germ of a science of religion" 46, 57

W

Watson, Peter 113
Weber, Max 151, 189, 190
Weisheipl, James A. 69
Welch, Claude 180
Wellmon, Chad 151–153
Wheeler-Barclay, Marjorie 154
   "Victorian 'science of religion'" 147–148, 149, 150, 166
Wiebe, Donald 8
   science of religion 5–7
   see also Griffiths, Paul J.
Wittgenstein, Ludwig 109
Wolpert, Lewis 44
   on scientific method 21
   technology of ancient cultures not science-based 39–40
Wooton, David
   Age of Discovery 125–126
   astronomy as "first true science" 113–114
   "extended patchy revolution" from Milesians to Atomists 49
   scientific revolution 113–116, 117
World Parliament of Religions (1893) 155, 156, 166

X

Xenophanes 57–58, 167

Y

Yinger, Milton 10
Yonan, Edward 182

Z

Zeno 50
Ziman, John 20

www.ingramcontent.com/pod-product-compliance
Lightning Source LLC
Chambersburg PA
CBHW061245230426
43662CB00020B/2427